IT'S A FREE COUNTRY

PERSONAL FREEDOM IN AMERICA
AFTER SEPTEMBER 11

Edited by Danny Goldberg,
Victor Goldberg, and Robert Greenwald

RDV BOOKS
NEW YORK

Published by RDV Books/Akashic Books
©2002 RDV Books

Design and layout by Sohrab Habibion
Front cover cartoon ©The New Yorker Collection 2002 Robert Mankoff from cartoonbank.com.
All rights reserved.

ISBN: 0-9719206-0-5
Library of Congress Card Number: 2002092041
All rights reserved
First printing
Printed in Canada

RDV Books
130 Fifth Avenue, 7th Floor
New York, NY 10011

Akashic Books
PO Box 1456
New York, NY 10009
Akashic7@aol.com
www.akashicbooks.com

*Thanks to contributing editor David Silver
and special advisor Alys Shanti.*

*Special thanks to Nadine Strossen, Robin Klein, MaShana Hobbs,
Jennifer Au, Jessie Hutcheson, Amira Pierce, Johanna Ingalls,
and Johnny Temple at Akashic Books.*

TABLE OF CONTENTS

PART 7: PERSONAL TESTIMONY

FOREWORD: LIFT EVERY VOICE
by Cornel West

This historic book bears witness to a precious truth of American life after the ugly catastrophe of September 11, 2001: The spirit of freedom is still alive in the face of panic-driven government policies. And since dissent and criticism are the life-blood of freedom in a democratic society, this book is in the best of the American grain. It is no accident that the voices in this volume are those of progressives, liberals, and conservatives: No ideology has a monopoly on the rich tradition of freedom and the fragile heritage of protecting rights and liberties. Yet at this moment of crisis the major threats to this tradition and heritage come from a myopic Bush administration, a deferential Congress, and a dogmatic attorney general. Although the first utterances of President Bush were encouraging—such as his refusal to demonize Islam or stigmatize Arab-Americans—his subsequent policies have been disheartening. In short, he has succumbed to a dangerous pattern in American history first articulated in the wise warning of Alexander Hamilton: Americans have to be willing to be less free in order to be more safe. The fundamental fear expressed in this book is that the present American obsession with safety may undermine freedom, that security could trump liberty, that democracy might be lost in the name of declaring war on terrorism. In the brave words of Congressman Dennis J. Kucinich (D-OH), we unequivocally oppose "risking democracy itself with the militarization of thought which follows the militarization of the budget."

We are mindful of the relative waning of freedom and civil liberties during periods of war in American history. The Alien and Sedition Acts of 1798 (in the face of a war with France), Lincoln's suspension of habeas corpus and strict censorship of wire-service news (during the Civil War), the Espionage Act of 1917 (in the face of a war against Germany), Roosevelt's executive order that was used exclusively against Japanese-Americans (during World War II), and

1

Congressional McCarthyism (during the Cold War) are low points in American legal history. The U.S.A.-Patriot Act of 2001—the pillar of the Bush administration's war against terrorism—stands in this authoritarian lineage. Despite noble intentions, the consequences of this hasty piece of legislation are frightening. It elevates executive action beyond accountability to the judiciary. Police powers—from detaining and wiretapping, to monitoring us—are expanded with little or no protection for citizens. Military tribunals replace civil courts—with weak due process. And government actions are shrouded more and more with a veil of secrecy. The five thousand American residents interviewed and 1200 people arrested or detained—disproportionately Arab-Americans and Muslim-Americans—are but the visible peak of this invisible and illegitimate set of policies that threaten the rights and liberties of all American residents or citizens.

In this monumental text we simply declare that "It's a Free Country," precisely because past and present citizens of all colors, cultures, and religions have fought to make it free and safe—even against those well-intended citizens who would curtail our basic liberties in the name of security. The complex balance of freedom and safety is always a fragile one. Our precious yet precarious democracy requires we proceed carefully, not hysterically—based on cautious constitutional defensibility, not raucous governmental frenzy. The best way to pay homage to those innocent fellow human beings who were viciously killed on September 11, 2001, and those courageous fellow citizens who sacrificed their lives to rescue the innocent ones, is to insure that their loved ones—as well as ourselves—live in an American democracy forever vigilant in its quest for freedom, and forever vigorous in its efforts to secure our precious liberties alongside our safety.

Cornel West is a professor in the African-American Studies Department at Princeton University. His book Race Matters *(Vintage Books, 1994) is widely recognized as a seminal work in the field.*

INTRODUCTION
by Danny Goldberg

Compared to those directly affected by the thousands of deaths on September 11, my family is lucky. We are lucky that although for weeks after the World Trade Center attack our Greenwich Village neighborhood smelled of acrid smoke when the wind blew north, we never had to abandon our home like our friends who lived further downtown in neighborhoods like TriBeCa. We are lucky that members of our family did not work in the World Trade Center—unlike the several people we know who died there.

We are lucky, but as I write this in June 2002, my kids still draw pictures of planes crashing into the World Trade Center, we still have the cheap plastic smoke masks that were suddenly on sale from street-corner vendors last fall, and from time to time my wife and I still wonder if New York City, the place in which we feel most at home, is really the right place to live.

I do not begrudge anyone their concerns about personal security.

But it's one thing to have passing emotions, fears, anger, and frustration, and entirely another to act on them without the filters of logic and history. Even more dangerous are government policies based on those emotions. Irrational emotions in the immediate aftermath of September 11 led a few misguided Americans to harass and in some instances brutalize non-Muslim brown-skinned immigrants such as Hindus and Sikhs, and to ostracize foreign-born Muslims who have no connection to or sympathy for terrorism, simply because of their religious beliefs. Acting on unfiltered emotions rather than balancing them with rationality has led to many of history's worst evils. This book is an attempt to create a rational and moral context in a difficult time.

The term "civil liberties" seems lacking in emotional reality, yet it represents civilization as Americans have come to cherish it, the balance that adds up to freedom as we know it.

3

Civil liberties transcend traditional left/right divisions. Because we wanted to get this collection out in time for the first anniversary of September 11, and because Victor Goldberg, Robert Greenwald, and I have spent our political lives most often on the left, there are a disproportionate number of lefties in this collection. We have tried to be vigilant in limiting their focus to civil liberties issues, but the after-effects of September 11 are so profound that some of our authors, especially those with an artistic bent such as Ani DiFranco and Michael Moore, took the civil liberties theme and migrated to a wider range of opinions that may offend some conservatives and pure civil libertarians. On the other hand, many of our friends on the left may be appalled that we included a conservative like Bill Clinton's nemesis, Representative Bob Barr, a Republican from Georgia.

Readers will also note that this volume includes a fair amount of repetition of key historical and legislative information pertaining to civil liberties in America; given that much of this information has not been widely reported in our history books or by today's news media, this repetition was unavoidable.

There are a thousand gradations of the trade-offs between security and freedom, and it is a big lie to pretend that there are two, and only two, choices. There are very few people who would consent to a law requiring everyone to walk through airport security devices in the nude, and there is almost no one who objects to walking through those same devices with their clothes on.

Even people who say they believe in torture to get information do not necessarily believe in the psychotic torture practiced by the worst governments. And even the most militant civil libertarian advocate of the broadest interpretation of the Bill of Rights believes that murderers should be arrested and prosecuted, and, if convicted, punished.

The issues discussed in this book are not bumper-sticker issues. But neither are they obscure. There is nothing obscure about being detained for weeks unable to talk to your family, or being fired from your job because of your political opinions. Meanwhile, there is no evidence that civil liberties protections helped cause the September 11 attack, nor any evidence that legislation, such as the more draconian aspects of the Patriot Act, would have helped prevent it.

The following are some security-enhancing measures that do not infringe upon civil liberties:

—Prosecute people suspected of crimes under pre–Patriot Act law,
  which allows search warrants, surveillance (including wiretaps as

long as a judge sees probable cause), arrests, limitations on bail (if the suspect can be proved dangerous), jail time up to life imprisonment, etc. These very tools have already created a prison population greater than any democratic nation in history.

—Hire more police officers and give them special training to deal with terrorism.

—Institute higher pay for security workers of all kinds. Since private business cannot generally afford this, such a plan would require government spending funded through—yes—taxes. The same polls that show people will give up "some" rights for security also show they will give up "some" taxes. More and better-paid security personnel, not only at airports but at train stations, on buses, in movie theaters, etc., would make us more safe.

—Guard our borders with more soldiers, especially our porous northern border. Again, this is an economic issue, not a civil liberties issue, but surely it is better to know who is coming into the country.

The fact is, there are people in our body politic, and I think John Ashcroft is among them, who have always wanted more government authority and less personal freedom for ideological reasons having nothing to do with September 11. Such people have long advocated greater government and police powers and less personal freedom for Americans.

There has been no answer to Congressman Jerrold Nadler's haunting question on the floor of Congress during the debate on the Patriot Act: "If the sole purpose of the new powers granted to the FBI and other police agencies is to protect against terrorism . . . why weren't these powers limited to investigation of terrorism?"

I found a metaphor that spoke loudly to me in an article in the *New York Times* on February 27, 2002, about the official response in New Jersey to the 1999 murder of several high school students in Columbine, Colorado. Like the events of September 11, the school shooting and several others that preceded it created an understandable anxiety among parents and school officials, and government policies were changed to reduce the likelihood of such awful attacks occurring again. As a parent of school-age kids, I can easily relate to such concerns.

In this climate, many government and school officials who had long advocated clamp-downs on "difficult" kids were able to implement excessive policies that went far beyond protecting schools from violence. Instead of focusing solely on violent kids, such officials broadened their mandate to target all sorts of nonconformists, based on the kids' clothes, unorthodox political or religious views, or just smart-ass attitudes. The problem with clamping down on all smart-asses is that many of history's greatest figures were, as we know, at one time labeled "difficult."

One story that attracted my attention was about a fifteen-year-old boy named Michael Mallner from Livingston, New Jersey. In 1998, Michael and another boy were caught on a Saturday with a supposedly explosive device. The bomb squad was summoned. TV crews surrounded his house. Cops removed a computer from his room.

Prosecutors themselves later acknowledged that the boys weren't out to hurt anyone. The so-called bomb was a collection of relatively harmless objects, including M&Ms.

Instead of typical punishment—suspension, community service, probation—Michael was subject to onerous post-Columbine "zero tolerance" regulations. He spent six weeks at a juvenile center in Newark where he was attacked by other kids. He was expelled from school and a year later is still under house arrest, unable to go out except with permission from a parole agent, and then only with a parent. Michael wasn't able to attend his sister's bat mitzvah because he couldn't get approval in time—family outings are often denied. Michael is not allowed to use the Internet.

"If this had occurred ten years ago, none of this would have happened. The authorities can't see the difference between showing off, testing the boundaries—and killing people," Michael's dad Anton Mallner told the *New York Times*. As I read the story I reflected on my own teenage years during which I and many of my friends did things just as bad. What would our lives be like today if we'd been subjected to such draconian punishment?

What does any of this have to do with September 11? It demonstrates how genuine tragedy and danger can sometimes bring out unfair and irrational behavior from authorities. The threat of future terrorism is a thousand times scarier than that of future Columbines, and so is the possibility of overreaction—or idiotic reaction—in place of, or alongside genuinely needed enhanced security measures.

One of the encouraging aspects of American society in 2002 is the degree to which public opinion has internalized many civil liberties principals that only a few decades ago were considered esoteric. We want criminals arrested and punished but we believe that those accused of crimes have the right to remain silent, and have the right to an attorney. So far the public, and thus the government, have been much more cautious in infringing on individuals than during previous conflicts. This is cold comfort if you're a family member of the two thousand detainees. To sit in a jail cell without knowing what you're charged with, cut off from your family, unable to work, unsure of your future, is a Kafkaesque nightmare.

But government reaction has been nowhere near as bad as the Palmer Raids or Japanese internment or blacklisting/McCarthyism. Unfortunately, in this regard, Ashcroft's recent directive to "register" (i.e., fingerprint and photograph) 100,000 Middle Eastern men threatens to bring about a major historical setback. Ideas can seem flimsy and insubstantial when confronted with the pragmatic deadline of elections, or the power of armies or police, but ideas drive politics both in our country and around the world. The decades of steady, lonely work by civil libertarians, especially since the blacklisting years, has paid off in the currency of today's debate. Questions are asked about how we treat unpopular residents and citizens and those suspected of crimes that were not asked of those in authority in epochs past. Let us do our part to further strengthen this vision of democracy that includes the rights for our worst enemies that we wish for ourselves.

Danny Goldberg is Chairman of Artemis Records, an independent company with an artist roster that includes Steve Earle, Rickie Lee Jones, Warren Zevon, Boston, Kittie, and Khia. A longtime political activist, Goldberg is on the Board and Executive Committee of the NYCLU, and is President of the ACLU Foundation of Southern California. He has written for The Nation, The American Prospect, Los Angeles Times, *and* Tikkun, *for which he served as co-Publisher along with his father Victor.*

PART 1

THE CRISIS IN CIVIL LIBERTIES, PAST AND PRESENT

MORE SAFE, LESS FREE: A SHORT HISTORY OF WARTIME CIVIL LIBERTIES
by Ira Glasser

In 1787, during one of the debates over the new Constitution, Alexander Hamilton worried that the loss of liberty would always be a consequence of war and the fear of war, regardless of constitutional guarantees. He predicted that the new Constitution would be ignored under such circumstances and that America would "resort for repose and security to institutions which have a tendency to destroy their civil and political rights. To be more safe, they, at length, become willing to run the risk of being less free."

Today, 215 years later, Hamilton's warning, and the question it posed, seems startlingly contemporary. After September 11, that question is on everyone's lips and in everyone's mind: In order to be more safe, do we need to be less free?

When we evaluate that question, we naturally tend to focus on current details: Do we need military tribunals, which even in their amended form, everyone concedes are procedurally less fair than civilian trials and even less fair than military courts-martial; do we need to give the government expanded wiretapping and email surveillance powers; do we need to put video cameras in public places and transform George Orwell's nightmare vision into a practical necessity; do we need to target people of Arab descent or Muslim beliefs for special surveillance, special questioning, special detention; do we need to detain people for indefinite periods of time, without revealing their names or the charges against them; do we need to restrict immigration and deport aliens already here, especially those of Arab origins; do we need to restrict the right of appeal from such deportation orders; and do we need to expand the legal jurisdiction of the CIA to watch American citizens? These sorts of questions, and others like them, are now on the table. How should they be answered?

Before considering these questions and getting into specific details and their pros and cons, it is useful, perhaps critically so, to step back and put these current questions and our current feelings, fears, and anxieties into the context of history. We need to look at other periods in our history when war and the fear of war produced similar questions. And we need to look at how those questions were answered, and how those answers turned out.

When we do look at history, we learn a number of lessons:

1. During periods of war, or the fear of war, all governments, including democratic governments and including governments apparently devoted and committed to liberty and individual rights, use the fear that is abroad in the land as an opportunity to expand government power at the expense of rights and to suppress dissent from whatever policies they want to pursue. The government answers the crucial question clearly and without ambivalence: Everything is now changed; we do indeed need to be less free in order to be more safe, for unless we are safe from the evil that threatens us, we shall lose all our freedoms. Every government, to one extent or another, makes that claim during wartime.

2. Most people, because they are afraid, go along. This includes most people who have always believed themselves to be supporters of individual rights. They hope that the reductions in freedom will be minimal and that they will not endure beyond the perceived emergency. But they go along. Traditional freedoms seem "too extravagant to endure" when evil threatens. And most people, when they are afraid, will not take a chance on freedom.

3. The question at times like this is not whether the underlying fear is legitimate. Sometimes it isn't, and often it may be exaggerated. But on many occasions the fear is legitimate. It was certainly legitimate on December 8, 1941, the day after Pearl Harbor. It was certainly legitimate during periods of the Cold War, when we were locked in an adversarial relationship with another aggressive nuclear power. And it was certainly legitimate on September 12, 2001, a day after the World Trade Center bombing. And those fears remain legitimate today. So the difficult question isn't whether the fear is legitimate; it's whether the remedies proposed to deal with those fears are necessary, whether they will work, and whether the government has selected the right targets. This last question is especially important in light of our history.

A key question today is whether the targets of government action are in fact sources of danger or whether our fears have been displaced from those we cannot easily identify, find, or control—Bin Laden, wherever he is, or unknown terrorists lurking (where?)—to those we can easily identify and find, e.g., Americans and legal immigrants of Arab descent. Our history shows that at times like this, our fears, and measures adopted by the government to address those fears, often find the wrong targets. By attacking those targets, we are made to feel safe without being safe.

The history of this phenomenon is important to explore because the argument for giving up some of our freedoms rests upon the assumption that we need to do so in order to be safe. But if that assumption is false, or highly unlikely to be true, if in fact measures that reduce our freedoms do not make us safe, then there is no trade-off.

So before evaluating the current answers to the questions raised at the outset, let's take a brief look at our history.

We begin shortly after Alexander Hamilton's warning, delivered in 1787, during the debate about the new Constitution. Scarcely more than a decade later, when virtually all of the principals in that debate were still alive, most of them in positions of influence, and only seven years after the Bill of Rights was ratified and added to the Constitution to help insure rights against the tendency Hamilton identified, the fear of war hung over the new republic like an ominous cloud.

War with France seemed imminent. And there were many French refugees in the United States. Very quickly, they became feared as a potentially subversive and traitorous element. John Adams, who before the Revolution had been a rock of libertarian thought, was then president. He encouraged this fear and even opposed the visit of a group of French scientists, calling them "incompatible with the social order." Encouraged by the government, war hysteria mounted, national origin became a proxy for real evidence of criminality or espionage, and the French became targets of fear and hate. Undeterred by the Bill of Rights, Congress quickly passed four laws which collectively came to be known as the Alien and Sedition Acts.

Three of the four new laws targeted aliens: one increased the residence requirement from five to fourteen years before an alien could be considered for citizenship; another authorized the president to deport aliens thought to be dangerous; the third authorized incarceration and banishment of aliens during wartime. (Is this beginning to sound familiar?)

There was, of course, significant dissent over these policies, which swiftly became characterized by the administration and its allies as treasonous and unpatriotic. And thus came the fourth law: the first federal sedition act ever passed by Congress. It was aimed at "domestic traitors," by which was meant anyone who criticized the government. The Sedition Act made it a crime, punishable by both a fine and imprisonment, to publish "false, scandalous, and malicious" criticism of the government, Congress, or the president with the intent to heap contempt upon them or damage their reputations. All this within seven years of the passage of the First Amendment.

The Alien and Sedition Acts were justified primarily by the need to assure the fledgling republic's safety against a foreign threat and its ethnic agents in the United States. The threat seemed real enough, the fear was widely shared, and the trade-off between rights and safety seemed persuasive even to a generation that had fought a revolution and established the new nation "to secure the blessings of liberty."

But as it turned out, the Alien and Sedition Acts identified no traitors and made no Americans safer. To the contrary, American citizens and their rights were the only casualties. The war with France never came, and the fear of the French subsided. No alien was ever deported or incarcerated, and a few years later the expanded durational residence requirement for citizenship reverted to five years. But the Sedition Act was widely enforced against American citizens, all of them Republicans (members of Thomas Jefferson's party) and political opponents of President Adams and his administration's policies. The trade-off between safety and freedom had been struck, but the targets consisted entirely of loyal Americans who had criticized Adams and his policies. Editors (including the grandson of Benjamin Franklin), scientists, pamphleteers, and even one member of Congress were arrested, tried, and convicted; all were fined and imprisoned; one, Franklin's grandson Benjamin Bache, died in jail. No one was made safer by these prosecutions, because the targets posed no danger to public safety.

* * * *

Nearly 120 years later, history repeated itself. World War I was fast approaching, and America seemed headed into it. When the United States did enter the war, opposition, while not as broad as the opposition to the Vietnam War during the 1960s, was nonetheless intense, and led to a substantial amount of political protest and unrest. And just as the fear of war with France had in 1798 led to the nation's first federal sedition act, so now, for the first time since 1798, Congress passed another sedition law, aimed at suppressing dissent and protest. Congress had already passed the Espionage Act in 1917, only nine weeks after declaring war against Germany. And just as fear of French agents had served as the pretext in 1798 for the prosecution and imprisonment of domestic critics, so in 1917, fear of German agents led to the same result.

As the war went on, popular support for it grew, and tolerance for dissent diminished. President Woodrow Wilson had requested Congress give him the explicit power to censor the press, and had been rejected. But the Espionage Act was worded broadly enough to permit the government to prosecute people for nothing more than critical opinions strongly expressed. Over two thousand prosecutions were brought under the Espionage Act, and more than a thousand resulted in convictions, almost all of them for expressing criticism of the war. State laws mimicked the federal intolerance for dissent, and additional prosecutions were brought under state laws. One man was sentenced to prison for reading the Declaration of Independence in public. A minister was sentenced to fifteen years for saying that the war was unChristian. A newspaper editor was convicted for questioning the constitutionality of the draft and charging that Wall Street interests had dragged us into the war. And the labor leader Eugene V. Debs was imprisoned for denouncing the war as a capitalist plot. Although these criticisms and opinions were harshly expressed, often with invective, they were no different in that respect from the rhetoric of American colonists or from Republican editors in 1798 or from Democratic critics of Lincoln's policies during the Civil War.

A year after the Espionage Act was passed, the Sedition Act became law. This new law left nothing to chance, and did not require the interpretation of critical words as espionage. Under the 1918 Sedition Act, it became a crime to print, speak, write, or publish any words that heaped contempt or scorn upon government or used scurrilous or abusive language to damage the reputation of the government or to disparage its military uniforms. The penalties for violating this law were not trivial: twenty years in prison and a $10,000 fine for each separate offense.

The Sedition Act was harshly enforced and thus almost completely suffocated criticism of the war. But not a single traitor was found. No spies were convicted, or even indicted. The targets of the Espionage and Sedition Acts were critics, political dissenters, pacifists, labor radicals, and immigrants, often of Italian or German or Russian descent. Although the government claimed that those indicted were dangerous, and much of the public felt safer as a result, no one was made safer by their prosecution and imprisonment. There was no trade-off between safety and liberty. Only liberty suffered.

On December 7, 1941, Japan attacked Pearl Harbor, provoking the United States' entrance into World War II and stoking fear throughout the country and especially on its West Coast, which many felt was vulnerable to Japanese attack and even invasion. In fact, according to army estimates at the time, "there was no real threat of a Japanese invasion." But there were a large number of people of Japanese ancestry living in California, Oregon, and Washington. And although they never exceeded more than one percent of the West Coast population, prejudice against Americans of Japanese descent was widespread, especially in California. Fear for domestic security soon led to pressure to "relocate" these Americans. Certainly, the fear of Japan was legitimate. But whether any Americans were made safer by targeting Japanese-Americans was, at best, doubtful. Yet before the hysteria was spent, American public officials, including liberals like then-governor of California Earl Warren and, of course, President Roosevelt, initiated, endorsed, and implemented what in retrospect was the single worst governmental act of racism in our history with the exception of slavery itself.

In the beginning, no one in the national government seriously suggested that anyone be moved. In Hawaii, which actually had been attacked and was much closer to the Pacific war zone, one-third of the population was of Japanese ancestry, yet no one ever proposed evacuating them. On the West Coast, however, the tiny Japanese-American community came to be seen as a threat. On February 19, 1942, President Roosevelt signed an executive order authorizing the military to exclude anyone they wanted from any area in the United States if, in the military's judgment, it was necessary to protect against espionage and sabotage.

In a country gripped by fear, it sounded like a reasonable measure to almost all Americans. But the order allowed the military to proceed without any actual evidence of espionage or sabotage against anyone. One month later, Congress passed a law—without a single dissenting vote—making it a federal crime for anyone subject to the order to refuse to "relocate." And although the executive order on its face applied to any American, in practice it was used exclusively against American citizens of Japanese origin.

The new law first subjected everyone of Japanese descent to a curfew: people were not allowed to leave their homes between 8:00 p.m. and 6:00 a.m., and even in non-curfew hours they were barred from moving outside a five-mile radius of their homes or places of work. Ultimately, they were forced into camps, and the idea of "resettlement" yielded to the reality of detention, under a harsh regime of barbed wire and armed guards that made no adequate provisions for family or personal privacy. By October 30, 1942, 112,000 people, mostly American citizens, were confined in ten camps scattered from the California desert to the swamps of Arkansas. Not one of the 112,000 was ever charged with any crime, nor individually accused of espionage or sabotage. No evidence was ever alleged; no hearings held. People were rounded up and detained, their homes and businesses stolen for the duration of the war solely on the basis of their skin color and their national origin. Everything was justified on the basis of safety and security, but no evidence was presented to support those claims. And nearly all Americans accepted this, looked the other way, and felt safer because they were afraid. What the government was doing seemed reasonable to them under the circumstances.

Forty years later, government documents were revealed that showed the government had knowingly lied to the Supreme Court in claiming that the evacuations were militarily necessary. Even President Reagan in 1988 called the detention an act of "war hysteria and racism." But that was forty-six years too late. Liberty matters when liberty is denied. And when liberty was denied in 1942, no American was made safer, because the targets of the detention posed no threat to public safety.

Seven years later, in 1949, fear of the Soviet Union was rampant in America. Only a year before, the Soviet Union had blockaded Berlin and overthrown the parliamentary government of Czechoslovakia. The United States was locked in a growing struggle with its former World War II ally, and the Cold War was underway. The fear of the Soviet Union may have been legitimate, but that fear swept over the land too broadly and resulted in the persecution and in some cases imprisonment of people who had committed no crime and posed no danger to public safety.

Eugene Dennis was an early victim. Dennis was an official of the American Communist Party, and in the America of the late '40s that was enough. He was indicted and convicted under the Smith Act, which had been passed in 1940 and which made it a crime to belong to any organization that taught the desirability of revolution. Just as the fear of war with France led to the suppression of dissent at home in 1798 and just as the fear of espionage led to the suppression of dissent in 1917—as if dissent and criticism of the government were the equivalent of espionage—so now mere membership in the Communist Party was equated with a conspiracy to overthrow the government by force and violence. No specific conspiracy was ever alleged. No plan to commit any crime was ever uncovered.

The U.S. Supreme Court, which only a few years earlier had upheld the detention of Japanese-Americans, upheld Dennis's conviction with only two dissenting Justices: Hugo Black and William O. Douglas. Black pointed out in his dissent that Dennis had never been charged with an attempt to overthrow the government, nor with any overt acts designed to overthrow the government, nor even with saying or writing anything specifically advocating the overthrow of the government.

Douglas picked up Black's theme. If Dennis had been teaching techniques of sabotage, planning the assassination of government officials, or plotting to sabotage or to plant bombs, that would be one thing. But all Dennis did, Douglas pointed out, was organize people to teach Marxist-Leninist doctrine as set forth in four books that were not outlawed and could be freely published, bought, and read. If such books are not outlawed, and can remain on library shelves, Douglas asked, "by what reasoning does their use in a classroom become a crime?" There was no good answer to this question. Fear overcame both logic and liberty, and people were once again sent to prison for their political beliefs. No one was made safer by the imprisonment of Eugene Dennis. Only liberty was lost.

After the Supreme Court upheld Dennis's conviction, many more such conspiracy prosecutions were brought between 1951 and 1956, and convictions were obtained in every case. Senator Joe McCarthy and the House Un-American Activities Committee, together with J. Edgar Hoover's FBI, launched a reign of terror against political beliefs and associations that was justified by claims of national security and the need to protect Americans against the Communist threat. Loyalty oaths proliferated, blacklists were circulated, and many people lost their jobs. Although there may have been a need to protect ourselves against the Soviet Union, no one was made safer by targeting people on the basis of their political beliefs and associations, and against whom no evidence of actual criminality was ever produced or even alleged. Once again, rights were lost in a claimed trade-off for enhanced safety, but there was no such trade-off, because the targets presented no danger. Most Americans went along, some enthusiastically, and felt safer because of it. But safety was not gained; only liberty was lost.

In 1957, after most of the damage had been done, the Supreme Court in effect conceded its mistake and reversed fourteen Dennis-type convictions in a single decision. By that time, the Cold War hysteria had substantially subsided and its leaders like Senator McCarthy had been discredited. The 1957 decision effectively ended the use of the Smith Act to suppress unpopular political beliefs and associations. But by then 141 people had been indicted, and 29 went to prison. Not one was ever charged with a crime other than their association with Communist ideas.

When people are afraid, particularly when the fear is legitimate and based on actual dangers, they are especially vulnerable to government measures that appear to provide safety and protection at the cost of rights. This is markedly true when the measures are aimed at targets, which for political, religious, or racial reasons, describe populations that we already fear, or against whom we harbor prejudice. The more different they are from us, the easier it is to project our fears upon them and justify what the government proposes to do. Years later, the mistake is recognized, and everyone regrets the violation of rights that occurred. We look back upon that time and wonder how it could have happened. And then, when there are fresh reasons to be afraid, we do it again.

Often, in looking back upon these incidents, we focus on the rights of innocent people that were violated. We look back at 1942 and focus on the Japanese-Americans who lost so much. But what happened to our Japanese-American citizens was also a fraud perpetuated on all Americans. It was a fraud because we were told we were being made safe when we were not. It was a fraud because at a time of genuine national peril, the government spent a huge amount of time, energy, and money on going after the wrong people. When government targets people based on skin color or national origin or religion or political beliefs and associations instead of evidence, it inevitably ends up neglecting actual criminal behavior. And that makes us less safe, as well as less free.

Consider this example from the field of ordinary criminal law. In the mid-1960s, there was an especially gruesome murder that took place in New York City. Two young women—Emily Hoffert and Janice Wylie—were found murdered, nude, and bound together in their apartment. The double homicide rightly terrorized the entire city, and especially those people who lived in the neighborhood. People were afraid, and they had good reason to be afraid. The police were under pressure to find the killer, and in a very short time they did. They announced that they had arrested a young black man named George

Whitmore and obtained an exceptionally detailed and lengthy confession. The papers printed these claims, and everyone breathed a sigh of relief and felt safe: The monster had been apprehended and no longer posed a danger to us.

But many months later—perhaps a year and a half, if memory serves—another individual arrested for a different crime was found to have been the one who murdered the two women. Whitmore was innocent. He had been subjected to oppressive and relentless "questioning" in the back room of a police station without benefit of a lawyer for a very long time, and his confession had been coerced; in fact, it had been written by police officers and, finally, signed by a weary and frightened Whitmore. This was before the Supreme Court's *Miranda* decision and the *Miranda* warning requirement that millions of viewers of television police dramas now know by heart. In fact, the Whitmore case was one of the predecessor cases to *Miranda*, ultimately forcing review of the inquisitorial "questioning" that in those years was routine.

Whenever the Whitmore case is discussed, the emphasis is always on what happened to George Whitmore: how his rights were violated, how skin-color prejudice drove the police to believe in his guilt and coerce his confession, how unfair it was for him to have had to undergo that ordeal, and the time in jail he unjustly spent. All of that is true. But it has always seemed to me that what happened to George Whitmore was not only an offense against him; it was also an offense against us. Because while we were told that the murderer was in custody, and that we were safe, the real murderer was still out there—still posed a danger—and no one was looking for him. No one is made safer when innocent people are arrested; when innocent people are targeted and arrested and imprisoned, guilty people remain free. When irrelevant considerations like race or religion or national origin or political beliefs become proxies for evidence, we are all less safe. When the police practice that led to George Whitmore's confession was criticized by civil rights advocates, the police defended what they did by citing the need to protect citizens from homicidal criminals. The rights of the accused were thus balanced against and traded for the safety of the rest of us. But in fact, there was no such trade, no such balance. We were made less safe, not more safe, because of what happened to George Whitmore, and that is why the trade-off posed by the government was fraudulent: In the Whitmore case, rights were lost *and* safety was compromised. We allowed the violation of his rights because it made us feel safer, but we were actually made less safe by what was done to George Whitmore.

I am reminded in these instances of the old joke about the man arriving home very late one night who comes across another man crawling around on his hands and knees under a lamppost. The man under the lamppost is drunk, and appears to be looking for something. The first man stops and offers help. "What are you doing?" he asks. "I'm looking for my keys," says the drunk. "I'll help," says the man, "where did you lose them?" "Six or seven blocks from here," answers the drunk. "Then why are you looking here?" says the first man. "Because the light is better here," responds the drunk.

And that's what the police did in the Whitmore case. They didn't look where the murderer was, they looked where the light was better, and it is always easier to see a black man when a crime is committed and there is no easily available evidence. "Round up the usual suspects" means looking under the lamppost when the real criminal is somewhere else. No one is made safer by that sort of police work.

They were looking under the lamppost in 1798, when they went after people of French descent and those who criticized government policies, as if they represented a real danger, when they did not.

They were looking under the lamppost in 1917, when they arrested and imprisoned people like Eugene Debs for criticizing the government's war policies, as if they were treasonous, when they were not.

They were looking under the lamppost in 1942, when they sent 112,000 innocent Japanese-Americans to detention camps, as if they were saboteurs, when they were not.

They were looking under the lamppost in 1949, when they sent Eugene Dennis to prison for encouraging people to read certain books, as if that were the equivalent of plotting crimes, when it was not.

Today we are being told that we need video surveillance on public streets, and that the loss of privacy will be more than balanced by the gain in national security. But in London, where a comprehensive system of such cameras was installed a few years ago explicitly to protect against terrorists, no terrorists have been apprehended. In some boroughs, the cameras haven't resulted in a single arrest in three years; in others, the arrests are for petty crimes that would never have justified such a massive surveillance system in the first place. What has happened is that ordinary citizens, innocent of any wrongdoing, are now watched all the time.

Today we are told we need to give the government expanded authority to wiretap our phones and our email. But the problem prior to September 11 was not the lack of legal authority to wiretap, but the fact that the government had no idea whom to tap. Like the cameras in London, expanded wiretap powers are justified by the need to apprehend terrorists, but there is no good reason to believe that apprehension would occur if such powers were granted; more likely other people, including many innocent people, would be spied upon instead. Most new authority to eavesdrop will be used against American citizens, not foreign terrorists. Moreover, it is likely to be used, as in the past, against the wrong people, based on their politics or their religion or their ethnicity. To the extent that it is used to uncover crime, they are likely to be petty crimes, not serious ones. That is the documented history of wiretapping in America.

In addition, expanding the authority of the government to collect more and more information with less and less relevance to actual criminal evidence inhibits the government's ability to find the criminal evidence. When the haystack gets too large, the needles become harder to find. As every recent official study of American intelligence-gathering has concluded, for years intelligence agencies have collected far more information than they can analyze in depth. That may be one reason the terrorists were able to achieve what they did on September 11. Thomas Powers, whose studies of American intelligence are well-respected, even by veterans of the CIA, says that current proposals to add email to telephone and cable taps are problematic. "They are now proposing," he says, "to add email communications in God knows how many difficult languages to the [already existing] cubic acres of untranslated, unread, unanalyzed, unabsorbed information . . . The request for broader powers is the excuse of first resort of anyone who's failed at national security or law-enforcement tasks. This notion—that if we could only read every email message in the universe, that no one could cause us trouble—is a big mistake." In other words, the government's claim that violating our privacy and intercepting all our communications is worth it because it will make us safe is a fraudulent claim. It will make us less safe. Too much of the wrong information makes it easier for the information we need to remain hidden and obscured by irrelevant volume; we begin to want to look under all lampposts, when the keys are not under any lamppost. Focusing on race or politics or national origin instead of evidence means not only that rights will be violated, but that real evidence will go undiscovered. We will be less free, *and* less safe.

That is also what is wrong with the government's program to interview—and in some cases detain—Americans of Arab descent and Muslims, as if those characteristics were proxies for criminal evidence. Interviewing five thousand people based on national origin is like imprisoning the Japanese-Americans: The time and energy spent on innocent people not only violates their rights, it diverts the FBI from investigations based on evidence. The rationale, which appeals to many Americans, is that since the WTC bombers were Muslims of Arab origins, the investigation of terrorism ought logically to begin with American Muslims of Arab origins. That is the very same logic that led to the Japanese-American internment. It is the same logic that leads the Drug Enforcement Agency and countless state troopers trained by them to pull over cars driven by black drivers to search for drugs. As one state trooper said in defending that practice, most drug dealers are black or Latino, so it makes sense to pull cars over driven by blacks or Latinos. But even assuming he was right that most drug dealers are black and Latino, it does not follow that most blacks and Latinos are drug dealers. Most NBA basketball players are black, but most blacks are not NBA basketball players. Most American jazz musicians are black, but most blacks are not jazz musicians. And if you wanted to find a good jazz band, you wouldn't begin by rounding up random blacks. Nor would you draft an NBA team that way. Yet that is exactly what the government is doing when it targets Arab-Americans for questioning: Being Arab-American is not a likely link to evidence of information about terrorist crimes any more than being opposed to abortion is evidence of bombing abortion clinics. And the racist nature of what Attorney General John Ashcroft is doing is revealed by the fact that he never suggested pursuing abortion-clinic terrorists by questioning everyone opposed to abortion.

The dangers we face from people who are willing to kill themselves in order to terrorize us are clear after September 11. Those dangers are real. But the targets of many of the government's actions and proposals are not connected to those dangers by any evidence. Rather, our fears are being manipulated, as they have been in past crises, to gain support for measures that violate rights without providing safety; indeed, in some cases, safety is compromised. We are looking under lampposts again, but the keys we seek aren't there. We may be led to feel safe, and therefore be willing, as Alexander Hamilton predicted 215 years ago, to relinquish our rights, but feeling safe is not the same as being safe, as our history repeatedly teaches us.

No one is made safer when we arrest, detain, or spy on the wrong people. When the innocent are arrested, the guilty remain free. When the innocent are investigated, the guilty remain hidden. And when rights are violated in the name of safety, most often we lose both our rights and our safety. We need only to look to our own history to read this cautionary tale.

Ira Glasser served for almost a quarter-century as Executive Director of the ACLU. He is the author of Visions of Liberty: The Bill of Rights for All Americans *(Arcade Publishing, 1991).*

A PRIMER: WARTIME EROSION OF CIVIL LIBERTIES
by Howard Zinn

Americans are proud of the Bill of Rights, and especially of the First Amendment to the Constitution, which declares that Congress may make no new law "abridging the freedom of speech, or of the press." Not many of them know that the First Amendment, while it looks good in print, becomes inoperable when the nation is at war, or when there is some tense international situation short of war (a "cold war").

It is ironic that exactly when a free marketplace of ideas is necessary, when matters of life and death are the issues, when Americans may be killed in war, or may kill others, our freedom of speech disappears. Yet that is exactly what the Supreme Court decided at the time of the First World War, when the venerable Oliver Wendell Holmes, speaking for a unanimous court, said that freedom of speech cannot be allowed if it creates "a clear and present danger" to the nation.

In fact, the case before the Supreme Court at that time was that of a man named Schenck, who had been imprisoned under the Espionage Act of 1917, which made it a crime to say or write things that would "discourage recruitment in the armed forces of the United States." That was interpreted by the courts to mean that any statement made in criticism of the United States' entry into World War I would constitute such discouragement, and was therefore punishable by up to ten years in prison.

But long before that "clear and present danger" criterion was enunciated by Holmes, it was, in effect, operating to negate the First Amendment. Indeed, barely seven years after that amendment became part of the Constitution, Congress did exactly what the amendment said it could not: "Congress shall make no law abridging the freedom of speech." That was 1798, when, oddly enough, both the new revolutionary government in France and the new one in the United States were in a tense situation of "cold war." Congress passed the

Alien and Sedition Acts which made it a crime to say anything "false, scandalous and malicious" about government officials "with intent to bring them into disrepute." A number of people who criticized the administration of John Adams were arrested and sent to prison under this Act.

But it was in the twentieth century, and especially during World War I, that suppression of free speech made the constitutional guarantee meaningless. Two thousand people were prosecuted, and a thousand imprisoned, for speaking against the conscription law, or against the war. An atmosphere was created in which it became very difficult to speak one's mind, either because of fear of government prosecution, or because zealous citizens, catching the war fever, harassed and persecuted fellow citizens who opposed the war.

As an example of the absurdities that accompany wartime hysteria, the World War I period saw the prosecution of a filmmaker who made a movie about the American Revolution. Since the "enemy" in that movie was Britain, and since the U.S. was now allied with Britain, the court ruled that the film violated the Espionage Act. The title of the film was "The Spirit of '76," and the name of the court case was *U.S. vs. Spirit of '76*.

At the end of World War I came the notorious "Palmer Raids," named after Attorney General A. Mitchell Palmer. Thousands of non-citizens were arrested, detained, and deported without hearings or any of the due process guarantees of the Constitution.

World War II brought more repressive legislation in the form of the Smith Act, which made it a crime to "teach and advocate" the overthrow of the government by force and violence. During World War II, eighteen members of the Socialist Workers Party in Minneapolis were given prison terms, not for specifically advocating such ideas, but for distributing literature like the *Communist Manifesto*. And over 100,000 Japanese-Americans were put in detention camps simply because of their national origin, a cruel act of wartime excitement.

The Cold War period that followed the Second World War created an atmosphere in which a hysterical fear of Communism led to loyalty oaths for government employees, imprisonment for Communists, and jail terms for anyone refusing to answer questions put to them by the House Committee on Un-American Activities about their political affiliations. It was a time when the FBI was compiling lists of hundreds of thousands of Americans who had in some way registered their dissent from government policies. Congress passed legislation allowing the deportation of non-citizens who were members of organizations listed by the attorney general as subversive. Although the United States was by far the most heavily armed nation in the world, there was an induced fear of the Soviet Union, and then of Communist China, which enabled the government to ignore the Bill of Rights. The fear was far out of proportion to the actual danger, to the point where children were told to hide under their schoolroom desks as protection against nuclear bombs.

Thus, there is a long history of loss of liberty in wartime which forms a precedent for what is happening in the United States since September 11: the intimidating proliferation of American flags, the harassment of people from the Middle East or indeed anyone looking like a Middle-Easterner, the mass detention of non-citizens without trial or due process.

The question is whether Americans will at some point begin to understand that the "war on terrorism" has also become a war against the liberties of Americans, and will demand that these liberties be restored. Without the right to speak freely, to dissent, we cannot evaluate what the government is doing, and so we may be swept into foreign policy adventures with no oppositional voices, and later lament our silence.

Howard Zinn was a bombardier during World War II. As a professor at Atlanta's African-American universities in the 1950s, he took part in civil rights picket lines. He wrote the controversial and influential A People's History of the United States *(Harper Perennial, 1980) and was one of the first academics to strongly oppose the war in Vietnam.*

AMERICAN PRESIDENTS AND CIVIL LIBERTIES
by Paul Starr

Wartime generates violations of civil liberties. Wartime justifies restrictions of civil liberties. So we have heard since September 11 from people variously trying to explain or to defend departures from standing protections of individual rights. A historical perspective suggests, however, that we have reason for vigilance but not for resignation about liberty's fate—and at this point no grounds for believing doom is at hand.

America's wartime history is actually mixed. Four presidents—Adams during the undeclared war with France in 1798, Lincoln during the Civil War, Wilson during World War I, and Roosevelt during World War II—were responsible for egregious violations of the Bill of Rights.

The Adams administration tried to shut down the opposition press and succeeded in closing major Jeffersonian papers. Lincoln suspended habeas corpus and used military control of telegraph lines to impose a strict censorship on wire-service news. Roosevelt, of course, approved the Japanese internment camps.

The Wilson administration had the worst record. It denied the use of the mails to publications that might "embarrass" the government, and sent more than a thousand critics of the war to jail. The socialist leader Eugene V. Debs received a ten-year prison sentence for a speech in which he told a crowd: "You need to know that you are fit for something better than slavery and cannon fodder." Another socialist, Mrs. Rose Stokes, received a ten-year sentence after writing a letter to the editor of the *Kansas City Star* in which she said: "No government which is for the profiteers can also be for the people." Not satisfied, President Wilson sent a note to the attorney general asking whether the government might also prosecute the editor who allowed the letter to be published.

Even more insidiously, the Wilson administration organized an American

Protective League made up of a quarter of a million civilians who opened letters, wiretapped phones, and conducted such vigilante actions as raids on German language newspapers. General anti-German hysteria, encouraged by some public officials, resulted in mob violence, including lynchings.

Not all wars have occasioned repression and hysteria, however. Neither Madison during the War of 1812 nor Polk during the Mexican War tried to suppress dissent. And despite the FBI harassment of protest groups, the response of the Johnson and Nixon administrations to the anti–Vietnam War movement was comparatively mild. After the Supreme Court's 1964 decision in *New York Times Co. vs. Sullivan,* the right to criticize public officials was more firmly established than it had been ever before.

Recent decades, moreover, have seen a widespread public repudiation of earlier wartime measures. The Sedition Acts of 1798 and 1918 are now generally agreed to have been unconstitutional. The anti-German and anti-Japanese measures of the world wars are now recognized as having been two of the most shameful chapters in our history.

September 11 has not changed this understanding of how America ought to conduct itself in wartime. Notwithstanding occasional remarks by the president's press secretary or attorney general, there has been no repression of dissent comparable to the measures adopted by Adams, Lincoln, and Wilson. The First Amendment survives.

The detentions primarily of people of Arab descent following September 11 raise genuine due-process issues. But in terms of scale and harms, the detentions scarcely bear comparison with the two closest historical parallels: the anti-German and anti-Japanese measures during the world wars. We have neither mass hysteria nor mass internments, and public officials have been quick to condemn discrimination against Muslims and Arab-Americans.

The military tribunals for trying "unlawful combatants" who are not American citizens raise troubling questions. It seems doubtful that the president has authority to suspend the jurisdiction of federal courts. But Congress could provide authority for the tribunals and might do so in a more narrowly drawn statute. It is clear that "unlawful combatants" come under a well-recognized exception to international legal protections of captured soldiers; the legitimate question, however, is who comes under the rubric of "unlawful combatant." Much depends on the actual use of the tribunals.

For the moment, Bush does not yet rank with Adams, Lincoln, Wilson, and

Roosevelt among the great wartime trespassers of the Bill of Rights. But, then, he doesn't rank with them in other respects as well—though he still has time (and John Ashcroft) to claim a portion of notoriety.

Paul Starr co-founded The American Prospect *in 1990 and has been co-editor with Robert Kuttner of the magazine ever since. He has been a Professor of Sociology at Princeton University since 1985. This article originally appeared in* The American Prospect, *vol. 13, no. 2, January 28, 2002. It may not be resold, reprinted, or redistributed for compensation of any kind without prior written permission from the author. Direct questions about permissions to permissions@prospect.org.*

WE CAN LEARN FROM HISTORY
by Paul Simon

I grew up in the state of Oregon where my parents were active in what we then called race relations, efforts that would receive the civil rights label today. My father was a Lutheran minister. In February 1942, two months after the Japanese attack on Pearl Harbor, President Franklin D. Roosevelt ordered 115,000 Japanese-Americans living in California, Oregon, and Washington to sell everything they owned in one to three days, put everything they needed into one suitcase, and be sent to camps. Some were not technically citizens, even though they had lived here many years, because our immigration laws discriminated against Asian immigrants becoming citizens.

My father spoke out against the president's action. I was thirteen at the time and I remember him explaining to my brother and me why the president's actions were wrong. Our family received some hate mail and phone calls, but mostly I remember my friends giving me a rough time, not physically, but in ways that embarrassed me. I wished my father had not done it. Now I look back at what he did with pride.

I also reflect on all the people who should have stood up for the civil liberties of these Japanese-Americans. Where was the Bar Association? Where were other members of the clergy? Where were the academic leaders? Where was the media? Roger Baldwin, then head of the American Civil Liberties Union, denounced the president's action, but a hastily called national board meeting of the ACLU by a 2-1 margin backed the president and not Roger Baldwin. Patriotic fervor overcame our sense of right and wrong.

The cause took strange twists. Fred Korematsu, a young shipyard worker in California, legally contested the president's actions. The case went to the U.S. Supreme Court. One of those who agreed with Korematsu—hold your breath— was J. Edgar Hoover, head of the FBI. The Supreme Court upheld the president's atrocious action, the majority opinion written by—hold your breath again—Justice Hugo Black, with Justice William Douglas concurring.

The nation has since belatedly apologized to these people or their children, and made a monetary gesture which makes the apology more meaningful.

What can we learn from this?

In moments of passion, administrations can grossly violate our basic civil liberties—and when those actions are taken in times of tension, the American public will back the president. (Patriotic fervor that backs the leader happens in other nations as well. When we apply economic and military sanctions against Iraq, it apparently strengthens Saddam Hussein's hold in that nation rather than weakening it. Economic sanctions worked in the case of South Africa because virtually the entire community of nations cooperated. That is not the case in Iraq, nor in Cuba, where the only nation to apply economic sanctions is the United States. Our aim there is to topple Fidel Castro. He has been in power forty-three years, during which time we have had nine presidents. That is an important digression, but a digression.)

Former Senator Thomas Eagleton writes, "Attorney General John Ashcroft looks upon the Bill of Rights as an inconvenience and an impediment to vigorous law enforcement." In times of tension it is easy to give up civil liberties, and in subsequent years they then become harder to protect.

During World War II, Nazi saboteurs landed by submarine on our shores. They were caught and tried in a military tribunal, without the normal protections of the constitution and the law. They easily could have been convicted in the normal prosecution and judgment process. But because that bad precedent was set, now another president, under less trying circumstances, wants to use military tribunals.

The excuses for violating civil liberties "to protect the nation" are easy to find. But history views those excuses unkindly. It is better to have the unpopular awkwardness of following the Constitution and the law than the popular crudeness of violating our important heritage of freedom.

Paul Simon, former U.S. Senator from Illinois, is Professor of Political Science and Journalism at Southern Illinois University, where he also directs the Public Policy Institute.

EXPERT PERSPECTIVE ON CIVIL LIBERTIES CURTAILMENT:
AN INTERVIEW WITH NAT HENTOFF
conducted by David Silver

March 29, 2002

DAVID SILVER: Supreme Court Justice Robert Jackson's majority opinion in *West Virginia Board of Education vs. Barnett* said: "The test of its substance is the right to differ as to things that touch the heart of the existing order." In this existing order being a so-called "state of war" . . .

NAT HENTOFF: Well, it's not a state of war. That's the first question. He wanted Congress. I think there were initial moves to get a congressional declaration of war but he did not get it. So we are not in a state of war. The Supreme Court in the Civil War, after Lincoln suspended and in effect abolished habeas corpus, arrested all kinds of people including Maryland legislators because they didn't agree with his policies, and set up military tribunals. After that in 1868, the Supreme Court said, "Hey, even in a time of war,"—that was certainly a state of war—"the courts are still open. The civilian courts are still open. He had no right to do any of that."

DS: Are the Bill of Rights a bulwark against bullying by the majority?

NH: Well, that was the whole point of it. Alexander Hamilton and some of the other Federalists thought, "You don't need it. You don't need a Bill of Rights. The Constitution doesn't say that you can't have a free press," and all that sort of stuff. But Madison said, and I'm paraphrasing, "Now that we've conquered George III or at least we've gotten rid of him, our main problem, our main threat, is the majority over the minority."

And the key reason for the Bill of Rights is that it protects the individual, however dissenting he is, against the majority as manifested in legislatures or high school principals in public schools. The First Congress introduced a bill that would have the Bill of Rights, including the First Amendment, apply to each of the states and therefore for municipalities and all that sort of thing. That didn't pass. But in the Fourteenth Amendment, which said "equal protection of the laws," and all that sort of thing, as a result of that—although it took Justice Hugo Black many years to convince his brethren of that—almost all of the Bill of Rights now apply to the individual states as well as to the federal jurisdiction, and that means to municipalities and towns and all—wherever there is government.

DS: How significant is the will of the majority of the people?

NH: No matter who does the legislating, whether it's Congress or the individual states, the administration very accurately judges the approbation, the support, of the great majority of the people, because the great majority of the people don't know very much about the Constitution. It's taught so badly in the schools. As a result, they're indifferent to their own liberties and rights under the Constitution. Therefore, they're indifferent to other people's rights. And when you say "security," and the very accurate point that there are invisible enemies among us, that's all they have to hear!

Now there's been some resistance over time. And there'll be more because there is a coalition of all kinds of civil liberties groups. This is just beginning to surface, all the press has been very remiss in this: under the U.S.A.-Patriot Act, the FBI can go to the Foreign Intelligence Surveillance Court, the FISA Court, which is a secret court that the chief justice appoints rotating federal judges to. And you go to them, if you're in the FBI, and you get the power to go to a library or a bookstore and find out which books people under suspicion of domestic terrorism, let us say, are reading. And one of the definitions of "domestic terrorism" is if what they're doing appears to be intended to influence the policy of a government by intimidation or coercion—that's the definition for domestic terrorism. The other ones are things like "acts dangerous to human life that are a violation of the criminal laws." This is what makes this unprecedented in First Amendment history. And you think the press would wake up to this, once the FBI agent gets the list, the librarian or the bookstore owner is forbidden by law to tell anyone that the visit has been made. They can't call the press.

The gag order is on the press as well. And the American Library Association and the Booksellers Freedom of Expression Foundation have told their constituents, "When that visit comes, call us! Don't tell us the FBI has come because then you're going to get into trouble. You'll break the gag rule. Just tell us, we want to talk to your counsel." So far as I know, there have at least been three of those visits so far. And that is about as anti-Constitutional, anti-Bill of Rights, anti-American as anything I can think of.

DS: What's wrong with the Patriot Act?

NH: Under the U.S.A.-Patriot Act Act, the government can now find out what emails you're sending, can find out what websites you go to on your web. In terms of telephone taps, they have rolling wiretaps now, which means that once they get a wiretap on one phone, they can use any phone you use. And they also have a one-step provision so that previously you'd have to get a wiretap within the jurisdiction of that judge. Now, if you get it from any judge it applies to the entire country. They're all very vague. Because they're operating under FISA, they really need nothing more than to say to a judge, "We have information that so and so may be engaging in terrorist activity." To get a wiretap, it used to be Fourth Amendment criteria—probable cause that a crime is underway, or has been underway, or is about to get underway. Then it became much less—reasonable suspicion. It's at a lower level than reasonable suspicion now, in terms of most of that act.

DS: And Clinton's 1996 act? Was that the beginning of this erosion?

NH: It wasn't the beginning but it was a big step forward. Some of what Ashcroft has been doing is based on that. The Anti-Terrorism and Effective Death Penalty Act, for example, allowed secret evidence to be used in immigration proceedings. And that meant that neither the defendant nor his or her lawyer could see what the evidence was! And it also allowed for very arbitrary ways to deport people.

Let's say some years before you had given a check to the African National Congress, which was engaged at the time in some kind of terrorist activity as defined but also who's doing a lot of other things—that alone could give you reason for deportation. But Clinton was as bad as Bush.

DS: Are John Ashcroft's actions cynical?

NH: He's not a cynic. That's why he's dangerous. He believes all this stuff.

DS: How come he has never even begun to take the position of the libertarian right, given how right-wing he's always been?

NH: He is a right-wing, God-driven conservative. The evangelicals are not necessarily civil libertarians. There are people on the right who are. For example, Bob Barr is one of the best civil libertarians in Congress. He's certainly a conservative. But Ashcroft is convinced he's on a God—I mean, literally, he's been appointed by God to do this. And he thoroughly believes that whatever liberties, civil liberties, there are in the Bill of Rights, etc., have to be suspended— you know, they point to Lincoln suspending habeas corpus. They point to FDR doing it during the Second World War. They don't know the fact that the reason the Supreme Court permitted those military tribunals and said they were legal was that FDR said to his attorney general who later told a couple of members of the Court, "I don't care what the Court does. I'm going to execute them anyway." So they were under threat.

But anyway, if Ashcroft was cynical, you might be able to reach him. But he's a total believer. And Bush is just . . . ignorant of all of this stuff. I mean, as he demonstrated when he was the governor of Texas.

DS: Which makes it even more dangerous that he's actually the final arbiter in the military tribunal.

NH: Yeah, even with the new rules, which by the way allow for no independent review in the courts, in our courts. You can't go to the Supreme Court so, as a matter of fact, that means the end of habeas corpus for those defendants. But he's the one himself who decides who gets into these tribunals, who gets to be a defendant.

The appeal procedure, with the military tribunals, now has a review board. They have a couple of people that can appoint other civilian judges temporarily as military judges. You know, like a sheriff used to do in Dodge City.

But when it comes to the final verdict, whether it's capital punishment or anything else, the only person who can decide is Bush, unless he designates that power to Donald Rumsfeld as secretary of defense. So he starts the process. He ends the process. And that's supposed to be justice.

DS: You said in one of your pieces that Bush's deputy secretary of defense, Paul Wolfowitz, admitted that there was a definite presumption of guilt and that there had to be.

NH: Yeah. But the phrase was something like: "We only put these people in military tribunals whom we know have committed some of the most dastardly crimes in history." Talk about presumption of innocence!

DS: How come there hasn't been more outrage from the media?

NH: Well, it's interesting, there's been selective indignation. The military tribunals were so sloppily drafted and so obviously unconstitutional that you did get some pressure. I think probably the most effective reason that the White House, which was surprised to see this indignation, did change the rules was William Safire in the *Times*. He's a conservative. He's also a civil libertarian. And he really let them have it. And more to the point, he has contacts in Washington over the years with the establishment, including some of the lawyers, and they put pressure on too. But to me, the library and bookstore thing, I told you, would be an obvious thing. But part of the problem is, first of all, the U.S.A.-Patriot Act is over three hundred pages. A lot of journalists are lazy. And okay, we've got a twenty-four-hour news cycle. We got synergy where some of the guys have to be on television at the same time they write their stories. But they're lazy. You have to read this stuff. It takes time. If you're on a daily beat, which I've tried to avoid most of my life, I can understand the problem. But somebody in the papers should read this stuff. I remember when Ted Kennedy joined with McClellan, the very right-wing senator, to revise the entire code of criminal justice. And it was incredibly awful! I mean, Kennedy was no more civil libertarian than Clinton or Bush. And a friend of mine was doing a column for the *New York Times*, and he was a lawyer. And I said, "Hey, I'm writing about it for the *Voice*, but that won't have any kind of clout compared to what you can do." He said, "Well, it's a very long bill!" And the other part of it is—and that's more fundamental—if you look at who the journalists and the editors are, they've gone to the same schools as most of the rest of us, even the so-called "better" schools. But again, this stuff is not taught. People do not know their constitutional rights and that includes journalists.

DS: Given that the response to 9/11 was really a viscerally fear-filled response, how do you counter a very understandable concern by people that they want to be secure? They want to be safe. "Please, let's look where we weren't looking before." Racial profiling. How do you counter that? How do you educate people?

NH: The only way you can do it, it seems to me, is try to show how these violations—you know you can call them "violations"—of basic privacy and basic rights will affect them. Let me go back to the U.S.A.-Patriot Act. Do you know about the black bag jobs? The fact that the FBI now can go into your home or office when you're not there, with a warrant. They can first case the joint, read the hard drive, insert into your computer what they call a "magic lantern" which registers every stroke you take—all that sort of stuff. Then they come back, download the magic lantern, and take more stuff. They don't have to tell you they've been there for up to ninety days. And that can be extended indefinitely by a judge. Now this does not apply only to so-called terrorism investigations. This now allows them to do this in any kind of criminal investigation. Now, some people ought to get worried by that. They could've had the wrong address, the wrong lead, or those people may not want to know—have the FBI know— what they're doing with their computers. Or they can go into their drawers and get manuscripts and stuff. There was an interesting *New York Times*/CBS poll, I think in November, when some of the people (although the overall majority by far were saying, "Yes, we'll trade security for civil liberties") were beginning to worry, "Hey, maybe this stuff isn't only for non-citizens. Maybe this could affect us."

DS: I read that Patrick Leahy, for all his original outrage, was eventually almost threatened with treason if he fought the original Patriot Act.

NH: No, but after the Patriot Act was over—even though the changes that Leahy had wanted to get in, and thought he had gotten in too as chairman of the Judiciary Committee, were taken out in a late-night meeting at the White House—even then he said, "Oh well, we did a reasonably good job."

DS: So he, in fact, capitulated.

NH: He caved in. Yes.

DS: Do you think that the so-called left in Congress really do not believe in the slippery slope in the future?

NH: Oh, look, the fact that Russ Feingold was the only senator to vote against it doesn't mean that Paul Wellstone doesn't know the difference, for God's sake, and some of the others. Wellstone tried to get himself out of it by saying, "In four years we're going to look at it again." He knows better than that! They're scared.

DS: Do you think that the fact that there's no real progress in the finding of any associates of the 9/11 terrorists via these massive internments is going to eventually work against Ashcroft and his whole philosophy?

NH: It will work only if some of these lawsuits that are being brought against what's happening for the detainees—the unlawful keeping them in detention, not letting their lawyers get to them and all that stuff, brutalizing them—get through the courts and if the lawsuits are covered by the press. Then some of the people will have some kind of empathy with or concern with injustice.

But a lot depends on the media. And most Americans, according to all those polls, get most of their information from television. Broadcast television, except for Ted Koppel and a few others, are useless. And cable is mostly people shouting at each other. And increasingly, the problem with the Internet is—and I've seen all kind of surveys about this—people go to those sites with which they know they're going to agree. So what kinds of diversity of information are you going to get out of the Internet? Very little, I think.

DS: Like so many things, doesn't it boil down to how the children at a very early stage are educated about the whole matter?

NH: Well, that's why my obsession for I don't know how many years now has been student rights, getting students passionately involved with challenging things that happen to them that are violations of their own rights under the

Constitution. And I found over time that, so far as I can track some of these people after I get to know them in middle schools and high schools, they're usually the ones who grow up and get involved in protesting this sort of stuff.

DS: Your feelings about the ACLU's position on all of this?

NH: They really rose to the occasion, although the press missed much of this, when during the alleged debate on the U.S.A.-Patriot Act, the ACLU put together the most extraordinary and extensive coalition I've ever seen all through the right, left, middle, etc.

DS: God forbid there's another really terrible attack upon America. But if there were, wouldn't this mean even more threat to basic civil liberties?

NH: Of course. I don't know how much more profiling Ashcroft could do, but I'm sure he would think of some way. And one of the things going on now, and you'd think there'd be some kind of concern about this among more than a few people, this kind of camera surveillance on public streets in New York. What was the last number—must have a couple hundred cameras in various places. And they have them in Washington. And these, as the technology evolves, they got zoom lenses. They can even see what you're reading on the street, if you stop and read something. But you'd think people would care about that stuff. Oh no! And obviously the worst of that is what they take down gets into a database. What's my alternative? You just keep writing and working in getting into coalitions with people. On the one hand, you get some of the people, even law professors, who say, "Oh, don't worry about it. It's cyclical and all this will come back." It doesn't come back unless you fight it then.

William O. Douglas once told a group of young lawyers, "We're not going to have a coup d'état here. But you're going to have incremental deprivations of liberties." He called it "the twilight." And the signs won't be very evident. Well, the signs happen to be quite evident now. But after a while, if this goes on and you have a generation coming up who are now, let's say, in high school, middle school, elementary school—oh, and, "This is the ordinary way of life"—that's going to be harder to slice in the years to come because they'll be conditioned to accept this as the normal definition.

DS: Is it any kind of just criticism that there could have been a preemptive action that could have prevented 9/11?

NH: Well, there's been very obvious criticism of our alleged intelligence services but this is all so speculative that I don't pay it any attention. If you get people who are willing to kill themselves, they're likely to find a way to do it. The question is, once they have, what can you find out about what organization they're with? They didn't have the resources to do this all by themselves. But in terms of prevention, who the hell knows? You're supposed to have a decent intelligence service. But now you find out that the flight school—they got the visas—all that sort of stuff. Sure, you always get bureaucrats that don't know what the hell they're doing.

Nat Hentoff has authored numerous publications, articles, biographies, and novels, specializing in civil liberties, free speech, and the history of jazz. He pens a weekly column for the Village Voice *and writes about music for the* Wall Street Journal.

IT'S EMPIRE VERSUS DEMOCRACY
by Tom Hayden

In the aftermath of September 11, American conservatives launched a political and intellectual offensive to discredit any public questioning of the Bush administration's open-ended, blank-check, undefined war against terrorism. The conservative message, delivered through multiple media outlets, was that dissenters from the Bush administration's war were those who allegedly "blamed America first," that is, dared to explore whether Bin Laden's terrorism was possibly rooted in Western policies toward the Islamic world, the Palestinians, and the oil monarchies of the Middle East.

The strike against domestic dissent was a preemptive one, since most progressives were too stunned, traumatized, and confused by the September 11 attacks to dissent anyway. But Susan Sontag was targeted for a right-wing stoning for an article in the *New Yorker,* and Bill Maher for not being politically correct. Vice President Cheney's wife helped monitor college classrooms for dissenting voices. Rapid articles appeared in the *New Republic.* Intimidating full-page ads by William Bennett announced plans to expose anyone who "blamed America first." White House spokesman Ari Fleischer added an official warning when he crafted an "offhand" remark that Americans should "watch what they say." Chief Republican political strategist Karl Rove proposed that his party's candidates make the war on terrorism an election issue. Senate Republican leader Trent Lott accused Democratic Senator Tom Daschle of being soft on Saddam Hussein (because Daschle opposed Arctic oil drilling). The chairman of the Republican House Campaign Committee declared that all questioners were "giving aid and comfort to the enemy."

Civil liberties were rapidly becoming the domestic collateral damage of the war on terrorism. It almost could be said they died without a fight, except for a brave but ineffective handful of stragglers in their progressive enclaves.

Some will ask, so what? Isn't the right to dissent a secondary concern when thousands of innocent Americans have been killed in terrorist attacks? A fair question. The truth is that Osama Bin Laden set the stage for this political shift to the right by his strategy of targeting civilians. And Bin Laden is no aberration. Radical Islamic fundamentalism has risen in the vacuum created by the failures of political Arab nationalism (and the end of the Soviet Union, which, whatever else may be said, supported non-religious revolutionary movements). The radical religious-based movements are here to stay.

So it is understandable that the vast majority of Americans responded to September 11 with existential cries for public safety and a military response. And if Bin Laden or his successor carry out further attacks against American civilians, the politics of repression will deepen. The problem is that conservatives inside and outside the Bush administration are seeking to take advantage of America's understandable fears to push a right-wing agenda that would not otherwise be palatable. In short, they are playing patriot games with the nation's future.

The *Wall Street Journal* gave the secret away in an October 2001 editorial declaring that September 11 created a unique political opportunity to advance the whole Republican-conservative platform. Worse, the real conservative agenda is to create an American empire, not simply rout out the al-Qaida organization. No sooner had the September 11 attacks occurred than the *Wall Street Journal*'s editorial writer, Max Boot, published "The Case for American Empire" in the conservative organ, the *Weekly Standard*. Boot endorsed a return to nineteenth century British imperialism, this time under American hegemony. "Afghanistan and other troubled lands today cry out for the sort of enlightened foreign administration once provided by self-confident Englishmen in jodhpurs and pith helmets" (see *NYT*, Mar. 31, 2002). The orchestrated call for empire was "out of the closet," according to conservative columnist Charles Krautheimer, and was echoed in the works of historians Paul Kennedy and Robert D. Kaplan (who found nice things to say about Emperor Tiberius, namely that he used force to "preserve a peace that was favorable to Rome").

The skilled but immoral and deceitful machinations of these would-be Romans have been described by David Brock in his confessional bestseller, *Blinded by the Right, the Conscience of an Ex-Conservative*. Brock should know the game. He consciously distorted the facts to gun down Anita Hill and protect Clarence Thomas's nomination to the Supreme Court. Not satisfied, he invented the "Troopergate" allegations against the Clintons. He admits that the conservative agenda was to impeach Clinton even before there was a Monica Lewinsky scandal. He describes in detail the "vast right-wing conspiracy" of investigators, muckrakers, pundits, talk show hosts, and hard-line Republican Congressmen who made Newt Gingrich Speaker for two years, instigated the Iran-Contra scandal, nearly brought down Clinton, and eventually mobilized the ground troops which shut down the Florida recount for George Bush.

With the Cold War ended, these conservatives asked what the new enemy threat was that would justify the continuation of a growing military budget and an authoritarian emphasis on national security. The answer, brewing long before September 11, was the threat of "international terror"—sometimes described as Islamic fundamentalism, sometimes as the drug cartels—but in any event suitably nebulous and scary to justify the resurrection of priorities not seen since the Cold War.

Let us review those Cold War priorities for those who didn't live through the era of the '50s and '60s, the era that shaped—indeed, finalized—the consciousness of the Bush family, Dick Cheney, Donald Rumsfeld, and many others fingering the military trigger today. The fundamental paradigm of the Cold War era was that an innocent democratic America was threatened by a shadowy Communist conspiracy representing two billion people in countries with nuclear capabilities and an amoral disregard for human life. This fearful paradigm justified America's first permanent military establishment, alliances with despotic right-wing dictators around the world, and a domestic politics that smeared dissenters who were charged with being soft on communism."

Those are exactly the dynamics in play again today. The difference is that, with the fall of the Soviet Union, the U.S. government and our multinational corporations are bidding for global preeminence. According to interviews with White House officials by Nicholas Lemann in the *New Yorker*, the new American strategy is to transcend traditional balance-of-power politics by an assertion of American military dominance, which incidentally would lay the foundation of empire. One example of this imperial thinking is the leaked Pentagon strategy paper of January 2002 which called for a new reliance on usable nuclear weapons targeted for possible use against China, Russia, and several other countries. The previous nuclear strategy of "mutual assured destruction" was dangerous enough, but this radical new U.S. doctrine—never publicly debated—introduces the ambition of nuclear dominance.

What can be done about this journey from Afghanistan to empire? For now, counting on an electoral alternative seems like wishful thinking. The Democratic Party, whatever doubts it may harbor, will remain devoted to the war on terrorism, including spending for a new generation of weapons and reinvigorated intelligence programs, as long as it is popular. The framework of the war on terrorism will be accepted as the litmus test of political legitimacy, and partisan differences will be limited to social security, unemployment benefits, Enron-inspired regulatory reform, and the like. Those differences are not unimportant, but the truth is that spending alone on the war on terrorism will cause permanent underfunding of important social programs for many years to come. For the Democrats to offer themselves as simply a liberal version of the war on terrorism will not address the root causes nor protect programs for which earlier generations of liberals, unionists, and Democrats have struggled.

The same bipartisan lockstep politics dominated the Cold War era of the '50s. Democrats stood for civil rights and progressive domestic issues, but blindly accepted the doctrine that "politics ends at the water's edge" until the anti-Vietnam movement finally shattered the consensus. It will take the same popular discontent in the years ahead to shake the Democrats and challenge the framework of the war on terrorism. At first, that discontent will arise from a prophetic minority.

How to make it a mainstream issue? Conservative crusades have a way of backfiring when, unchecked by effective dissent, they go too far. McCarthyism began to unravel when the Wisconsin senator started searching for Communists in the army. The Nixon Administration, teethed on McCarthyism, repeated the same extremist folly with Watergate. Inevitably, the same fate awaits the unchecked war on terrorism. A combination of military quagmire abroad and neglect of priorities at home will sooner or later shape an opposition.

The U.S. military is involved in more multiplying fronts of the war on terrorism (the Middle East, Afghanistan, the southern Philippines, Colombia, Georgia, Indonesia, not to mention threats of future action against Iraq, Iran, and North Korea) than it can sustain without eventually causing domestic repercussions. These interventions are being carried out—thus far—with little or no congressional oversight or fiscal accountability. The Bush defense budget augmentation request of $50 billion—which itself is larger than the military budget of any other country—when combined with massive tax breaks for the wealthy will steadily erode funding for Social Security, health care, education, and the environment.

At the same time, a new human rights movement is sweeping the planet, with protests against corporate globalization and militarism. Before September 11, these American protests, especially those in Seattle in December 1999, were more forceful than any I can recall since the 1960s. While that American protest energy has been drained or divided since September 11, the battle continues to explode globally in places like Quebec City, Genoa, and Porto Allegre. Corporate globalization, led by the U.S. government, has spawned a new globalization of conscience. For a valid comparison of the historic impact, one would have to revisit the global confrontations of 1968 and, before the '60s, the period of the 1840s in Europe, when the world order was last threatened and rearranged by revolts from below.

The war on terrorism is simply incompatible with serious efforts to alleviate world poverty, just as it was impossible for President Lyndon Johnson to afford both "guns and butter" in the '60s. There are two billion people on the planet working for daily wages of less than two U.S. dollars. At ten hours a day in degrading workplace conditions, without health benefits, without union protections. A recent appeal by workers in Bangladesh, a Muslim country that supplies most of America's apparel, pleaded for thirty-four cents in wages from every seventeen-dollar U.S. baseball cap, up from twenty-four cents. Global sweatshops are among the petri dishes in which anti-Western violence is grown.

The conservatives strain to deny any connection between world poverty and terrorism. That is what their bullying tirades against "blaming America first" are all about. They fear the blame. But they cannot deny that humiliation fostered by poverty and arrogance is a long fuse leading to the suicide bomber.

Take the story of Laura Blumenfeld as an example. A young reporter for the *Washington Post,* her father, a rabbi, was shot and wounded by a Palestinian militant in Jerusalem in 1986. The assailant simply wanted to kill a Jew, and Laura Blumenfeld's father was available. At first seeking revenge, Laura Blumenfeld concealed her identity and began a correspondence with the imprisoned Palestinian gunman, finally revealing herself and confronting him in a courtroom. She then came to know his family, ventured into a complicated reconciliation, and wrote a book on her experience. Reflecting on the Israeli-Palestinian conflict, she told the *New York Times* on April 6, 2002:

> I think for them [the Palestinians], humiliation is sometimes more
> important than the actual offense. Humiliation drives revenge more
> than anything . . .They feel honor and pride are very important in

> their culture, and they feel utterly humiliated, whether it's by road-blocks or just by the sheer wealth and success of society that's set up right next to them . . . I found that feelings of humiliation and shame fuel revenge more than anything else.

Blumenfeld's thoughtful analysis distinguishes mere poverty from shame and degradation. Poverty is sometimes bearable if the poor feel respected or hopeful; for example, the Aristide government in Haiti has campaigned on a slogan of "poverty with dignity." But usually the policies that allow poverty to grow as if it were a natural condition of market economics are accompanied by a rationale that transfers blame from the rich and powerful to the poor and powerless. That shaming inherent in globalization is the triggering source of violence, as shown in numerous studies such as those of James Gilligan at Harvard. The syndrome we can call the *will to empire* (like Nietzche's famous *will to power*) is wrapped into a need to shame others.

Instead of recognizing the reality of global interdependence, the will to empire seeks American independence by plunging other nations, cultures, and classes into dependence, which in turn triggers a spiral of resentment and resistance. Actually, the conservatives who condemn thinking about "root causes" as "blaming America" have a root cause in mind themselves—the belief that all terrorists and the cultures that spawn them are incorrigible enemies because they are "evil." American conservatives substitute theology for sociology, psychology, and history. Since the evil they seek to purge is defined as innate to human nature, and satanic, it arises from no causes that can be addressed politically or economically. The only option for Pentagon planners when confronted with evil is war, which is the secular equivalent of exorcism, or conversion to the American Way of Life.

That this is actually a logical crutch, a rhetorical device, is shown by the ease with which the stamp of evil is applied and removed. Mujahideen, including Osama Bin Laden, were not "evil" when the U.S. government supplied them with weapons and funding in the 1980s, because then the Islamic fundamentalists were battling true "evil" in the form of the Soviet Union. But the label of evil has its uses. It serves to shut off rational debate, for example. It stimulates public fear. It justifies the killing of people whose annihilation might be problematic if they were classified as simply desperate. Fighting evil is good politics.

A domestic analogy might be useful in understanding how this process works. In 1988, George Bush (senior) was battling for the presidency against

Michael Dukakis. Bush's media consultant then was Roger Ailes, now the top executive at Rupert Murdoch's Fox television news. The Bush campaign concocted the famous "Willie Horton" ads, depicting a shadowy and menacing black figure, and blamed Dukakis for being soft on crime. The attack, which manipulated fears of black violence, served the purpose of the Bush campaign. Taking advantage of the formula, the Republican conservatives ushered in a law-and-order politics that justified the drug wars, disproportionate sentences for powder versus crack cocaine, and the largest prison build-up per capita in the world. In the process, job training and numerous social programs were slashed, private investment was drawn toward speculative mergers instead of the inner cities, and the oppression of the underclass became so severe that fully one-third of all African-American males between the ages of eighteen and twenty-five were ensnared in the criminal justice system. As politics, the law-and-order campaign was successful, while the long-term consequences of worsening the racial divide in America were left for a future generation to sort out.

The current war on terrorism is the internationalization of the Willie Horton campaign. Instead of going along with the conservative agenda out of fear or expediency, it is time to outline an alternative.

The litmus test for political bravery at present is whether one questions the framework of the war on terrorism. Progressives might still disagree about whether a U.S. military response against al-Qaida was justified, but all can agree that while seeking to demobilize al-Qaida is one thing, using September 11 as a pretext for an open-ended war leading to a new empire is, to say the least, a policy worthy of debate. Even if one supports the right of U.S. self-defense against al-Qaida, there should be broad consensus on the need for congressional hearings and oversight. Patriotism should not mean the restoration of the imperial presidency.

Were there flaws or biases in U.S. intelligence gathering that made September 11 more likely? Have the Taliban actually been defeated, or simply faded into the mainstream population? Are Afghan women better off under warlords? Will a global glut of heroin result from greater opium reduction "expected to enrich tribal leaders whose support is vital to the American-backed government" (*NYT*, April 1, 2002)? Is Texas-based Unocal's oil pipeline across Afghanistan now "feasible once again" (*NYT*, April 1, 2002)? Should Bush have appointed a former Unocal consultant the new American ambassador to Afghanistan? The nearly one year of silence in Washington on these reasonable questions is a measure of the fear that has eroded the democratic process already.

Beyond Afghanistan, the political questions are whether this war should be conducted unilaterally by the executive branch, whether its budget should be unlimited, whether congressional oversight should be waived, and whether the battle should be conducted wherever undefined terrorists are alleged to be based, whatever their threat to the American people.

Is the Bush administration, intoxicated with gladiator fantasies, trying to build a new Roman Empire by neutralizing the checks and balance intended by having a vigorous legislative branch? (It should be remembered that the Russell Crowe character in *Gladiator* was committed to defending the Roman Senate and the Republic against the imperial designs of the emperor—this is one case where Washington should definitely mimic Hollywood.)

How to challenge this imperial framework cloaked, with apparent legitimacy, as the war on terror? My advice is: carefully, thoughtfully, but deliberately and for the long haul. For demonstrators interested in mass outreach in a time of manipulated patriotism, it may mean calling for a process of greater oversight, greater attention to priorities, and greater tolerance of dissent, instead of, for example, calls for military withdrawal from Afghanistan. For Democrats in the mainstream, it will mean provoking debate in the party over how to challenge the Bush framework, then nurturing and promoting a new generation of Democrats for peace.

In either scenario, here are some fruitful issues to raise that will resonate with a majority of voters: First, progressives and Democrats should take the position that those in power have failed over the years to make America safer from terrorist attack. There should be full public disclosure of what Condoleeza Rice has called the increased "chatter" of intelligence cables concerning a possible al-Qaida attack before it happened. Questions should be asked. For example: Why did the Federal Aeronautics Administration (FAA) make a finding that Bin Laden was "a significant threat to civil aviation" in late July 2001, but do nothing about airline security regulations which were so lax that knives with four-inch blades could be carried on planes? These questions go to the heart of the bipartisan special-interest nature of the state that has strangled accountability and democracy for a very long time.

Public questioning is urgently needed about the unprecedented U.S. strategy of making nuclear warfare feasible in the future. This classified military strategy represents the return of Dr. Strangelove to the Pentagon, and is certain to make Americans less safe from an uncontrolled nuclear arms race.

Another key question that needs to be addressed concerns budget priorities. In concrete, easy-to-understand terms, the costs of the war on terrorism need to be conveyed to a public now shielded from the facts. For the Bush administration and the military-industrial complex, the moment has come for a massive increase in Pentagon spending. Non-governmental organizations and Democrats must make clear to the public that the daily spending on terrorism means less funding for everything from family farms to inner city schools.

Next, progressives and Democrats should question whether the massive intelligence failure surrounding September 11 really justifies returning to the Cold War policies of hiring as operatives or allies the same unsavory elements that brought us the Bay of Pigs and the Central American "dirty wars" of the '70s and '80s.

The war on terrorism should not become pretext for undermining the Freedom of Information Act and preventing disclosure of presidential files from the first Bush era. Bush's solicitor general is arguing in court that government has a right to misinform and disinform the American people.

Nor should the war be a further excuse to advance the agenda of the oil industry, whether drilling in Alaska, protecting Occidental pipelines in Columbia, enmeshing ourselves with the Saudi royal family, or launching joint ventures for Unocal on the old Silk Road through southern Asia.

Before any further subsidies are granted to the Bush-Cheney friends in the oil industry, the government should take the lead in charting a transition to energy conservation and renewable resources. A modest fuel-efficiency increase of 2.7 miles per gallon would eliminate the need for any Persian Gulf oil. In the Middle East, the U.S. should promote a settlement that results in a viable Palestinian state, the end of Israeli occupation, and a military guarantee of secure Israeli borders. Instead, the war on terrorism is being used as the new rationale for the use of U.S. weapons in assisting an Israeli occupation.

Finally, the "new world order" should be based on living wages, not starvation sweatshops, and the United States should lead the G-7 powers to meet the aspirations of the United Nations to double foreign aid by 2015. So-called "free trade" and "fast track" agreements now blatantly being justified by the war on terrorism will reinforce divisions between the rich minority and the poor majority. Demanding peace is not enough. What is at stake is a conflict in the American soul between empire and democracy that will shadow our lifetimes.

Tom Hayden was elected to the California State Senate in 1992. He was a leader of the student, civil rights, and anti-war movements in the 1960s and the environmental and anti-nuclear movements in the 1970s. He is the author of nine books.

CONSERVATIVES AND LIBERALS UNITE TO CONSERVE LIBERTY AND SECURITY
by Nadine Strossen

INTRODUCTION

The American Civil Liberties Union has always been staunchly non-partisan, reflecting the fact that support for civil liberties—as well as opposition to them—cuts across ideological lines. That general pattern is certainly true concerning our current defense of the many civil liberties that have been jeopardized in the wake of the horrendous September 11 attacks. In the ACLU's efforts to ensure that the U.S. remains both safe and free, our allies—inside and outside government—have included individuals and organizations of every ideological stripe, from the most liberal to the most conservative. In a related vein, since we are championing our government's dual responsibilities to maintain both personal liberty and national security, our allies include not only civil libertarians, but also national security experts.

Our government can and should protect both human life and human rights. As the Preamble of the U.S. Constitution proclaims, "We the People" formed our government "in Order to . . . provide for the common defense . . . and secure the Blessings of Liberty to ourselves and our Posterity." The monstrous terrorist attacks on September 11 not only destroyed thousands of innocent lives. These savage attacks also sought to destroy the intangible values symbolized by the targets: democracy, the rule of law, liberty, and equal opportunity. As President Bush said on that dreadful date, we must bring the perpetrators of these atrocities "to justice,"[1] and we must prevent future such atrocities. Precisely because we seek justice, our counterterrorism campaign must itself comply with standards of justice consistent with U.S. and international law. We must fight terrorism without undermining the very ideals that the terrorists themselves attacked.

We do not have to choose between national security and personal liberty. To the contrary, we all value both, and we cannot enjoy either one without the other. This is not a zero-sum game. Cutbacks on our freedom do not necessarily guarantee gains to our safety. Conversely, there are measures that can enhance our safety without cutting back on our freedom.

Since September 11, I have repeatedly been asked, "Aren't you willing to give up some freedom to increase your safety?" Of course, like any rational person, my answer is "Yes!" Unlike our attackers, I certainly do not seek martyrdom. And I do not share the sentiment expressed in Patrick Henry's famous statement, "Give me liberty or give me death!"

Conversely, though, no rational person would choose to give up freedom *without* gaining safety. Unfortunately, though, too many measures that are now touted as countering terrorism are the worst of both worlds: they demonstrably violate cherished rights, with no demonstrable security benefits. Worse yet, some of these measures may well be counterproductive in terms of national security. They therefore have been critiqued not only by civil libertarians, but also by national security and law enforcement experts.

CRITIQUES OF POST–9/11 LIBERTY-INFRINGING MEASURES FROM A NATIONAL SECURITY PERSPECTIVE

Many prominent present and past officials of the Federal Bureau of Investigation and the Central Intelligence Agency have criticized a number of post–9/11 measures specifically from a national security perspective. One such critic is especially noteworthy, since he was the director of both the FBI and the CIA under Presidents Reagan and Bush—William Webster. In November 2001, he said:

> From 1981–2000, the FBI prevented more than 130 terrorist attacks. We used good investigative techniques and lawful techniques. We did it without all the suggestions that we are going to jump all over . . . people's private lives . . . I don't think we need to go in that direction.[2]

William Webster and I recently shared a platform at the University of California at Santa Barbara, for what was billed as a "dialogue about national security and personal liberty."[3] It was appropriately called a dialogue rather than a debate, since we agreed with each other far more than we disagreed.

Significantly, Webster went out of his way to praise the ACLU and to stress that our role is especially important in times of crisis, including the present.

Let me cite just a few of the post–9/11 measures that have been condemned from the perspectives of both national security and personal liberty. One is the president's Military Order authorizing military tribunals to try, and potentially execute, any non-citizen that the president deems a suspected terrorist, without the most basic due-process protections. These tribunals have been denounced by no less staunch a conservative than *New York Times* columnist William Safire, who served as President Nixon's speechwriter. In Safire's words, this "infamous . . . order replaces . . . the American rule of law with military kangaroo courts."[4]

In issuing regulations to implement the order, the Defense Department chose to provide significantly more fair-trial protections than the order requires, but the resulting procedures still fall far short of fundamental due-process norms under U.S. and international law. Of gravest concern, the only appeal is to military judges, so there is no review by independent civilian judges. Accordingly, Safire continued to criticize these military tribunals and to urge that any prosecutions take place only in our civil courts.[5]

As Safire and other critics have recognized, there is another serious downside to the unilateral military tribunal order: It has caused U.S. allies to refuse to extradite suspected terrorists to the U.S. Our government therefore loses the opportunity not only to prosecute these suspects, but also to interrogate them. We thus forfeit invaluable information that we could obtain from them to help thwart future attacks.

Another widely criticized aspect of the government's post–9/11 policies, from the perspectives of both safety and freedom, is its use of mass dragnet interrogations, arrests, and incarcerations, sweeping in large groups of people based on who they are, rather than what they have done. The targets of these dragnet devices apparently have been selected based largely on national origin and religion, and not on evidence that they have any pertinent information about terrorism, let alone any involvement in terrorism.

A remarkable article in the *Washington Post* in November 2001 quoted eight former top FBI officials, on the record, criticizing these dragnet law enforcement tactics as undermining effective counterintelligence. These former FBI officials, including William Webster, concurred that this approach "will inevitably force the bureau to close terrorism investigations prematurely, before agents can identify all members of a terrorist cell."[6]

These dragnet techniques have also been criticized because they are based on ethnic or religious profiling. They therefore violate individual rights by substituting discriminatory stereotypes and guilt-by-association for individualized suspicion. Thus, it is not surprising that civil libertarians have criticized this profiling approach on principled grounds. But many people are surprised to learn that this profiling approach also has been criticized by counterterrorism experts on pragmatic grounds, noting that it is ineffective at best, counterproductive at worst. That point was made, for example, by a group of senior U.S. intelligence specialists in a memo sent to law enforcement agencies worldwide shortly after September 11, 2001. The memo warned that looking for someone who fits a profile is just not as useful as looking for someone who behaves in a suspicious manner. Indeed, the memo even suggested that overreliance on profiles might be one of the reasons for our government's tragic failure to prevent the September 11 attacks. According to these officials, "Any profile based on personal characteristics . . . draws an investigator's attention toward too many innocent people, and away from too many dangerous ones."[7]

More recently, U.S. intelligence agencies have expressed increasing concern that future terrorist attacks may involve al-Qaida members from Asia or Africa, expressly to elude the ethnic profiles that U.S. security personnel are apparently now using. As one senior official said: "The next face . . . is not going to be an Arab face, but possibly Indonesian, Filipino . . . Malaysian . . . or even African. They understand the security profile we're operating on."[8]

"SOLUTIONS" THAT DO NOT ADDRESS THE ACTUAL PROBLEM ONLY MAKE US LESS FREE, NOT MORE SAFE

I would now like to take a step back from specific post–9/11 measures to outline general principles and analyses that we should use to assess any particular measure. The overarching principle at stake was eloquently stated by President Bush himself in his first statement to the American people after the horrific attacks. The president hailed the U.S. as "the brightest beacon for freedom and opportunity in the world," and vowed that "no one will keep that light from shining."[9] Ever since then, the ACLU has been working very hard to help the president keep that vow! In short, we can and should be both "safe and free," the unifying theme for all of the ACLU's post–9/11 actions, summarized in the "safe and free" section of our website. We must not let the terrorists terrify us into abandoning the very ideals that they attacked.

This point was powerfully made by Wisconsin Senator Russell Feingold, who courageously resisted the administration's unprecedented pressure on Congress to enact the massive so-called "anti-terrorism" legislation immediately after the attacks, with almost no deliberation or debate. In Senator Feingold's words:

> It is very important that we give the Department of Justice and the intelligence agencies the tools they need to combat and prevent terrorism. But it is also crucial that civil liberties in this country be preserved, otherwise . . . terror will win this battle without firing a shot.[10]

Consistent with these wise cautionary words of Senator Feingold, the ACLU and our diverse allies are simply asking government officials to base any action on some reasoned analysis, rather than acting—or reacting—in a panicked rush. Of course, our government had to act swiftly to bolster its counterterrorism campaign in response to the September 11 catastrophe, but it could not do that effectively without understanding what went so tragically wrong on that dreadful date. This was forcefully argued immediately following September 11 by Congressman Bob Barr, the conservative Georgia Republican who has special expertise on these issues given his background as a U.S. attorney and CIA official:

> Our immediate reaction must not be to blindly expand law enforcement's investigative authority, or the government's prosecutorial authority, without at least first engaging in a serious deliberative effort to examine how and why execution of current authority was not successful.[11]

To date, there has been no showing that the government's colossal failure to protect our personal safety or national security on September 11 had anything to do with lack of law enforcement powers. Rather, many top law enforcement and national security experts have said that the problem was, instead, a failure to deploy effectively the ample powers that already existed.

Just as I was completing this piece, we saw yet another graphic illustration of the government's shocking mishandling of the most basic information about terrorism. We learned that the Immigration and Naturalization Service (INS) had wrongly issued visa waivers for four Pakistanis who arrived in the U.S. on a

Russian merchant ship and quickly disappeared. This incident prompted Attorney General John Ashcroft to criticize the INS's chronic mismanagement of intelligence information in the strongest possible language, especially considering his strict religious beliefs: "[W]hat's happened in the INS is enough to drive a man to drink."[12] And this is only the latest in a series of similar slip-ups, going beyond the INS, including the fact that two of the September 11 hijackers were on FBI watch lists of suspected terrorists, yet they were still allowed to board the planes that day.

These gaffes underscore the fact that the U.S. government's failure to forestall the September 11 attacks does not appear to be due to the lack of power to obtain information through surveillance and searches, so much as the failure to effectively process and act on the information it already has. A similar point was made by Ashcroft himself, even while he was spearheading the Bush administration's push for what he called "sweeping powers"[13] to engage in even more intrusive, pervasive surveillance and searches under the new post–9/11 antiterrorism law. Ashcroft expressly admitted that none of those "sweeping powers" would have prevented the September 11 atrocities,[14] nor can they protect us against another terrorist attack.

CONSERVATIVE CONGRESSIONAL ALLIES

Many members of Congress from both political parties have joined with the ACLU and other citizen groups in resisting the rush to increase the already expansive power of the executive branch of our federal government, including the broadscale power to spy on the communications and transactions of countless innocent individuals, with only minimal judicial oversight. Not surprisingly, many respected conservatives are in our camp, since they also seek to limit government power, especially at the federal level.[15] Accordingly, our allies in preserving safety *and* freedom have included such prominent conservative Republicans as Congressman Barr and House Majority Leader Dick Armey, from Texas.

The ACLU has worked closely with Congressmen Barr and Armey throughout their congressional careers on issues of common concern—in particular, the effort to protect personal privacy from unwarranted government surveillance. The resulting mutual respect and effective collaboration on these issues—regardless of strong differences on other issues—was stressed by Bob Barr just a month after the terrorist attacks, when he and I happened to make back-to-back appearances on Fox News TV's "Hannity & Colmes" show. We had been expressing similar criticisms of the administration's unjustified intrusions on individual privacy and freedom in its domestic anti-terrorism campaign. I was on air first, and when Barr subsequently came on camera, the liberal co-host, Alan Colmes, kiddingly said to him, "Nadine Strossen on the way out said she'd be happy to give you a card so you could be a card-carrying member of the ACLU." Barr responded: "Well, I tell you, they have done tremendous work over the last several years. We don't agree on everything, but they are a very powerful ally."[16]

Dick Armey has collaborated with the ACLU on important privacy issues, both before and after September 11. For example, during the summer of 2001 the ACLU and Armey held a joint press conference to announce our request that the General Accounting Office study the increasingly pervasive hi-tech surveillance devices that local governments are deploying against all of us when we drive or walk in public places.[17] In February 2002 the District of Columbia activated a pervasive video surveillance network, citing—no surprise—concerns about terrorism. Unfortunately, this is all too typical of many post–9/11 measures. The government raises the spectre of terrorism as a purported justification for repressive laws and policies, and rather than stimulating debate, that mantra shuts it down.

The anti-terrorist label should not scare politicians or the public into uncritical acquiescence. This point was stressed by Congressman Barr when John Ashcroft first tried to stampede the House Judiciary Committee into rushing through his new so-called anti-terrorism law right after September 11. Questioning the reason for the hurry, Barr asked:

> Does it have anything to do with the fact that the Department [of Justice] has sought many of these authorities on numerous other occasions, has been unsuccessful in obtaining them, and now seeks to take advantage of what is obviously an emergency situation?[18]

I regularly refer to the new law that Ashcroft pressured Congress to pass, with the most minimal consideration, as the "so-called anti-terrorism law" for precisely the reason Congressman Barr's pointed question underscores: the law expands government's powers generally, far beyond the scope of its anti-terrorism efforts. The law's intrusive new surveillance powers can be used to investigate all crimes, not only terrorist or violent crimes. In fact, based on longstanding past experience, we can confidently predict that the government's new surveillance will largely be used not against violent terrorist crimes, but instead against the consensual, nonviolent crimes of drug possession, gambling, and prostitution. That has already been the case with the government's greatly increased surveillance powers under the 1996 anti-terrorism law, passed in the wake of the 1995 Oklahoma City bombing. Another reason why the "anti-terrorism" label is a misnomer for the new law is that it empowers the government to spy on the communications and transactions of completely innocent citizens who are not suspected of any wrongdoing at all.

CONSERVATIVE ORGANIZATIONAL ALLIES

Just as the members of Congress who have criticized civil liberties violations in the current crisis span the ideological spectrum, the same is true for citizens' groups. Holding our government accountable to constitutional standards is a core traditional American value cutting across all spectrums. That is why the ACLU always has been staunchly non-partisan.

Immediately following the terrorist attacks, the ACLU spearheaded an extraordinarily broad, diverse coalition of about 180 concerned citizens' groups. In a September 20 press conference at the National Press Club in Washington, D.C., we released a joint statement called, "In Defense of Freedom at a Time of Crisis."[19] The unprecedented breadth and diversity of the participants included prominent and influential organizations ranging from the left end of the political spectrum—the Alliance for Justice, Americans for Democratic Action, Common Cause, the Leadership Conference on Civil Rights, and People for the American Way—to the right end—the American Conservative Union, Grover Norquist's Americans For Tax Reform, Phyllis Schlafly's Eagle Forum, Paul Weyrich's Free Congress Foundation, and major gun-owners' rights associations.

The overall thrust of the principles that this broad coalition endorsed can be summed up as follows: We should not adopt measures just because they are labeled as anti-terrorist; we should instead carefully evaluate each proposed measure to ensure that it actually maximizes national security with minimal intrusion on liberty. To this end, we urge a three-prong analysis before the government implements any new measure that is touted as counterterrorist or pro-security. First, any such measure must be genuinely effective, rather than just create a false sense of security. Second, any such measure should be implemented in a non-discriminatory manner; government should not target any individuals based on their actual or perceived race, ethnic origin, or religion. Finally, if a security measure is found to be genuinely effective, the government should implement it in a way that minimizes its adverse impact on fundamental freedoms, including due process, privacy, and equality. As a constitutional law professor I should note that this basic analytical framework closely mirrors the general approach that the U.S. Supreme Court has mandated for assessing the constitutionality of measures that infringe on constitutional rights.

Many measures that the government has adopted since September 11 do meet these basic tests. This is true, for instance, of many aviation-security measures, such as fortifying cockpit doors, using sky marshals on flights, and matching luggage to passengers to ensure that no luggage is carried unless the person who checked it is also a passenger on the same flight. These kinds of measures demonstrably advance safety with no significant cost to freedom.

In contrast, too many other measures that have been adopted, or are being considered, turn this equation upside down. They significantly invade freedom with no demonstrable gain to safety. That is true for many of the provisions in the massive anti-terrorism legislation signed into law on October 26. The ACLU's staff experts have written a series of briefing papers about various liberty-restricting aspects of the new law.[20] Each one has a title that starts with the phrase, "How the Law . . ." and I will list the remainder of each title, in alphabetical order:

—Allows for Detention and Deportation of People Engaging in Innocent Associational Activity

—Enables Law Enforcement to Circumvent the Privacy Protections Afforded in Criminal Cases

—Expands Law Enforcement Sneak and Peak Warrants

—Limits Judicial Oversight of Telephone and Internet Surveillance

—Permits Indefinite Detention of Immigrants Who Are Not Terrorists

—Puts the CIA Back in the Business of Spying on Americans

—Puts Financial Privacy at Risk

—Puts the Privacy of Student Records at Risk

—Would Convert Dissent into Broadly Defined "Terrorism"

THE NEW GOVERNMENT SURVEILLANCE POWERS CLEARLY MAKE US LESS FREE BUT DO NOT CLEARLY MAKE US MORE SAFE

This new law vastly expands the government's power to monitor the communications and transactions of countless innocent individuals who are not suspected of any wrongdoing, let alone any involvement with terrorism. The government merely has to allege that it is investigating international terrorism to then conduct massive fishing expeditions through the records of banks, credit bureaus, hospitals, hotels and motels, libraries, telephone companies, and universities, with minimal judicial oversight. Similarly, the new law also allows the government to intercept all online communications that pass through any computer, or any service-provider, that the target of an investigation "might" use.

Congress came up with a tortured name for the law to generate its acronym, the "U.S.A.-Patriot[21] Act." This acronym was part of the juggernaut toward the law's enactment with minimal debate, since it suggests that anyone who would dare to vote against it is not patriotic. However, as one commentator quipped, when it comes to privacy and freedom, the law is not a Patriot *Act*, it's a Patriot *Missile!*[22]

All of the stepped-up surveillance unleashed by the new law obviously has a dramatic adverse impact on personal privacy. But as discussed earlier, there is also no basis for believing that it will actually advance national security. Experts report that law enforcement and security officials are already collecting so much data—given their extensive monitoring powers even before the new law—that they cannot possibly process or analyze it all. In addition, no matter how carefully all the data might be combed, it will not yield any clues about the many potential terrorists who do not communicate electronically, or who do not communicate much at all.

A recent issue of the newsletter of the National Defense Industrial Association quoted national security experts who strongly condemned the U.S. government's overreliance on high-tech surveillance pre–9/11 as a colossal failure. Accordingly, these experts condemned the increased surveillance powers, post–9/11, as exactly the wrong way to go—again, strictly from a security perspective.[23]

THE "DETAINEES" OR THE "DISAPPEARED"?

I would like to stress just one more post–9/11 U.S. policy that violates core rights without advancing national security: the government's shroud of secrecy over the hundreds of individuals who, by its own admission, have been "detained"—a euphemism for incarcerated—even though the vast majority of them apparently are not thought to have any information about terrorism, let alone any involvement with it. Even beyond the very serious concerns about whether these prisoners are being treated fairly or humanely, there is the overarching public concern about the total lack of information. The Bush administration has stonewalled repeated requests from Congress, journalists, and citizens' groups for the most basic information about these secret prisoners, including who they are, where they are being held, whether they have been charged with any crimes or immigration violations, and whether they have access to lawyers or family members.

All we get from the attorney general are bland assurances that the legal rights of these "detainees" are being respected. Alas, the actual information that has come to light—from some former detainees who have managed to get lawyers and win release—has been far from reassuring. Some individuals have been held for weeks, even months, without being charged. Systematic obstacles have thwarted their access to counsel, and some even have been held incommunicado from family members. Moreover, there are credible allegations of physical mistreatment at the hands of guards and other inmates.

I am glad that there has been so much attention paid to the situation of the three hundred captives from the U.S. military operations in Afghanistan being held at Guantanamo Bay, Cuba. Under international law, anyone captured in combat is at least entitled to fair and humane treatment, as the Bush administration finally recognized in response to domestic and international pressure. Many outside observers—including members of Congress and delegates from the International Committee of the Red Cross—have inspected the conditions of confinement at Guantanamo to confirm that this humane standard is being honored.

I wish, though, that there was even a fraction of this amount of attention paid to, or information gained about, the far greater number of individuals who have been secretly imprisoned all over the U.S. as part of the post–9/11 roundup. According to the Bush administration, approximately 1200 such people had been imprisoned as of November 2001, which was the last time it gave out numbers. From all the information we have gleaned from various sources, we think the total number of individuals who have been imprisoned since September 11 (many of whom have been released after detentions of various lengths, ranging to up to more than two months) is about two thousand. And, in contrast to the three hundred military captives in Guantanamo, these two thousand U.S. prisoners were hardly armed enemy soldiers captured in combat. To the contrary, they were apparently law-abiding civilians living peacefully in our midst. Surely they too are entitled at the very least to fair and humane treatment. And surely all of us are entitled at the very least to basic information about them so that we can assure this fair and humane treatment.

Significantly, the administration's secret detention policy has been criticized by one of the most archconservative newspapers in the U.S., the *Washington Times,* even though it has strongly supported other aspects of the administration's post–9/11 anti-terrorism program.[24] Likewise, strong criticism of these mass secret detentions has been voiced by a respected commentator who has supported many of the administration's measures, the legal journalist Stuart Taylor. He writes:

> Not since the World War II internment of Japanese-Americans have we locked up so many people for so long with so little explanation. [We must] ensure that these people are treated with consideration and respect, that they have every opportunity to establish their innocence and win release, and that they do not disappear for weeks or months into our vast prison-jail complex without explanation.[25]

These critiques, by Stuart Taylor and the *Washington Times,* were issued back in November 2001. Yet as of the time this piece is being completed, five months later, we still know almost nothing about these secret prisoners, hundreds of whom are still incarcerated. In February 2002 the *Independent* newspaper in London featured an article about the plight of the so-called detainees, which had a shocking but all-too-accurate title: "The Disappeared."[26]

THE NEW SHROUD OF SECRECY OVER GOVERNMENT POLICIES

The Bush administration's stubborn refusal to reveal basic information about the detainees is part of a larger shroud of secrecy that it is pulling over an increasing range of government policies and actions post–9/11, all contrary to core principles of free speech and democratic governance.

Among many other instances of such secrecy, the attorney general issued a directive to all government agencies reversing the previous stance regarding requests under the Freedom of Information Act (FOIA). The previous stance had been a presumption of openness, leading to disclosure of any requested information unless there were some specific legal obstacle or concern for resulting harm. Under the new directive, the presumption is exactly the opposite—against disclosure, and in favor of secrecy. Post–9/11, the government has also imposed a new policy of automatically closing any immigration hearings to the press, the public, and even family members, whenever the Justice Department so directs. There is not even an explanation of the grounds for closure, let alone an opportunity to challenge it.

The ACLU, along with diverse allies, has initiated a number of lawsuits to challenge the government's unprecedented new secrecy policies. These lawsuits are based on common-law principles, constitutional guarantees of free speech and due process, and federal and state freedom-of-information statutes. As of this writing, two such lawsuits have resulted in court rulings and both were resounding victories for the ACLU and all advocates of open government.

First, a New Jersey trial court ordered officials of that state—where most of the post–9/11 detainees are apparently being incarcerated—to disclose certain basic identifying information about all such individuals in their custody. New Jersey Superior Court Judge Arthur D'Italia strongly condemned the administration's "secret arrest" policy as "odious to a democracy."[27]

Second, a federal trial court struck down the government's new closure policy for immigration hearings. In holding that this policy violates core First Amendment principles and precedents, Judge Nancy G. Edmunds of the federal district court in Detroit stated: "Openness is necessary for the public to maintain confidence in the value and soundness of the government's actions, as secrecy only breeds suspicion."[28]

These rulings are welcome indications that the courts will appropriately scrutinize government measures that infringe on constitutional freedoms and not simply defer to executive branch assertions that such measures are warranted in the compelling cause of countering terrorism. In short, these judges are looking behind the anti-terrorist label and insisting on actual evidence that each measure really is justified.

RELYING ON THE COURTS AS THE ULTIMATE SAFETY-NET FOR INDIVIDUAL RIGHTS

In addition to the ACLU's lawsuits challenging various post–9/11 government secrecy policies, we have also brought a number of lawsuits challenging a range of other civil liberties violations in the wake of the terrorist attacks—everything from suppression of dissent, to wholesale discrimination against completely law-abiding non-citizens, to airport strip-searches based on religious profiling without any individualized suspicion.

I am optimistic that we can count on the judges in these cases, and others that will arise in the context of the new counterterrorism campaign, to fulfill their intended constitutional role as the ultimate safety-net for the rights of individuals and minority groups. Under the U.S. Constitution, the federal courts are intentionally insulated from majoritarian political processes, so that they are better situated to resist pressures to invade relatively unpopular rights of relatively disempowered individuals and groups.

To be sure, there are shameful episodes in American history when the courts did not fulfill their intended role and simply rubber-stamped rights violations that government officials asserted in the name of national security. One dramatic example is the U.S. Supreme Court's sanctioning of the internment of approximately 120,000 Japanese-Americans during World War II, based on the executive branch's unsubstantiated assertions that these individuals posed threats of espionage or sabotage.[29] However, this decision and others in the same vein have been universally repudiated, so I am hopeful that current judges will have learned from their predecessors' mistakes.

So far, the ACLU's post–9/11 court record bears out this optimism. As I just noted, we have won two lower court victories in challenges to government secrecy policies. We also won a resounding victory in the only one of our many pending lawsuits that has come to a conclusion with a final judicial ruling. We represented a group called School of the Americas Watch, which monitors the School of the Americas (SOA) at Fort Benning in Columbus, Georgia. The school (which in January 2001 was renamed the Western Hemisphere Institute for Security Cooperation) trains military personnel from Latin America, and SOA Watch (along with other critics, including Amnesty International) maintains that many SOA graduates have committed egregious human rights abuses throughout Latin America. Since its founding in 1990, SOA Watch has held an annual demonstration at the school. It has always been peaceful, with no damage to any person or property. This year, though, the city government sought a court order to prevent the planned demonstration, invoking generalized national security concerns. The government stressed that Fort Benning has been on a state of "high alert" since September 11 and it relied on a purported "war exception" to the First Amendment's free-expression guarantee.

U.S. Magistrate-Judge Mallon Faircloth issued an excellent oral opinion from the bench, strongly upholding free speech rights and rejecting the government's asserted "war exception." Even more important, the judge's rationale applies to all cherished freedoms. First, Judge Faircloth noted an important general point that is too often overlooked, given the wartime rhetoric we are constantly hearing—we are not actually at war! In his words: "Only Congress has the constitutional power to declare war. That has not happened." Judge Faircloth further noted:

> War does not, in and of itself, add anything to the constitutional powers. At the same time, it does not remove any constitutional limitations safeguarding basic liberties of the people. Wartime or not, we learned through the Japanese experience in World War II, when we made some awful mistakes, [a national emergency] is not a time to blanketly abridge constitutionally guaranteed rights.[30]

I am hopeful that Judge Faircloth's wise words foreshadow other judicial rulings—and, for that matter, other decisions by government officials—in our ongoing fight to remain both safe *and* free. We look forward to continuing to collaborate with our ideologically diverse allies, inside and outside government, to promote these dual, interrelated goals.

Nadine Strossen is the President of the American Civil Liberties Union and a professor at New York Law School. She gratefully acknowledges her chief aide, Amy Fallon (NYLS '03), and her research assistants, Mara Levy (NYLS '02) and Robert Georges (NYLS '04), for assistance with the research and notes. This essay reflects events as of its completion date, April 5, 2002.

ENDNOTES:

1. George W. Bush, "Address to the Nation in the Wake of Terrorist Attacks," *New York Times*, September 12, 2002, A-4.

2. Jim McGee, "Ex-FBI Officials Criticize Tactics on Terrorism; Detention of Suspects Not Effective, They Say," *Washington Post*, November 28, 2001, A-1.

3. The Arthur N. Rupe Distinguished Dialogue Series, Interdisciplinary Humanity Center, University of California at Santa Barbara, March 3, 2002.

4. William Safire, "Seizing Dictatorial Power," *New York Times*, November 15, 2001, A-31.

5. William Safire, "Military Tribunals Modified," *New York Times*, March 1, 2002, A-37.

6. *Supra* note 2.

7. Bill Dedman, "Fighting Terror/Words of Caution/Airport Security; Memo Warns Against Use of Profiling as Defense," *Boston Globe*, Oct. 12, 2001, A-27.

8. Eric Pianin and Bob Woodward, "Terror Concerns of U.S. Extend to Asia; Arrests in Singapore and Malaysia Cited," *Washington Post*, Jan. 18, 2002, A-18.

9. *Supra* note 1.

10. Robin Toner, "A Nation Challenged: The Legislation; Not So Fast, Senator Says, as Others Smooth Way for Terror Bill," *New York Times*, Oct. 10, 2001, B-10.

11. Jill Zuckman, "Privacy Rule Changes Face of Skepticism," *Chicago Tribune*, Sept. 19, 2001, 4.

12. Fox News Sunday, Transcript # 032404cb.250, Mar. 24, 2002.

13. Jerry Seper, "Ashcroft to Immediately Enforce New Measures to Fight Terrorism," *Washington Times*, Oct. 26, 2001, A-14.

14. "Hearing of the Senate Judiciary Committee on Homeland Defense in the Wake of September 11, 2001, 107th Congress" (Statement of John Ashcroft, Attorney General of the United States).

15. See "In Bed with Bob Barr; How Conservatives Became the ACLU's Best Friends," *The American Prospect*, Nov. 5, 2001, 19.

16. Fox News, "Hannity & Colmes," Oct. 5, 2001, Transcript #100504cb.253.

17. "Proliferation of Surveillance Devices Threatens Privacy," Joint Statement of House Majority Leader Dick Armey, R-TX, and the American Civil Liberties Union, July 11, 2001, at: http://www.aclu.org/news/2001/n070601a.html.

18. *Supra* note 12.

19. At: http://www.aclu.org/news/2001/n092001a.html.

20. At: http://www.aclu.org/safeandfree/index.html.

21. The full name of the law is: United and Strengthening America by Providing Appropriate Tools Required to Intercept and Obstruct Terrorism.

22. Christopher Dreher, "He Knows What You've Been Checking Out," *Salon*, March 6, 2002 (quoting Mary Minow, a Librarylaw.com consultant working on a book about library law for the ALA).

23. John J. Stanton, "U.S. Intelligence Community Reaches Crossroads: CIA Official Says Agency is Implementing Reforms to Address New Threats," *National Defense 86:12*, Dec. 1, 2001.

24. "Victory Abroad . . . Constitutional Concerns at Home," *Washington Times*, Dec. 7, 2001, A-22. ("[I]n response to questions about the administration's unwillingness to make

public the names of . . . non-citizens jailed on immigration violations and other criminal charges, Mr. Ashcroft did little to clarify the confusing and seemingly contradictory explanations coming from the administration . . . [T]he administration has failed . . . to make the case for . . . keeping detainees' names secret.")

25. Stuart Taylor, "Bad Answer, Mr. Ashcroft," *The Legal Times,* November 19, 2001, 60.

26. Andrew Gumbel, "The Disappeared," *The Independent (London),* Feb. 26, 2002, Features 1, 7.

27. *American Civil Liberties Union vs. County of Hudson,* No. HUD-L-463-02 (NJ Sup. Ct. Hudson Cty), Mar. 26, 2002. The court granted the government's request for a forty-five-day stay, so this information will not be released until all appeals are exhausted.

28. *Detroit Free Press vs. Ashcroft,* No. 02-70339 (consolidated with 02-70340) (E.D. MI Apr. 3, 2002).

29. See *Korematsu vs. United States,* 323 U.S. 214 (1944).

30. *Consolidated Government of Columbus, Georgia vs. Roy Bourgeois and Jeff Winder* (M.D. Ga.) (Unpublished opinion of Magistrate Judge Mallon Faircloth on November 16, 2001).

THE SORROW AND THE PITY OF RACIAL PROFILING
by Ralph Temple

If Jewish extremists, like Yigal Amir who assassinated Israeli Prime Minister Yitzakh Rabin in 1995, ever engaged in acts of terrorism in the United States, a roundup of foreign Jews would be likely to follow. There is an echo of lynchings and pogroms in the indiscriminate arrests of over eleven hundred Middle Eastern men following the September 11 terrorist attacks. Such raids are an atavistic yet time-honored response. The dragnet of Arabs and Muslims has not yielded results, any more than did the 1920 Palmer raids, the 1940s internment of Japanese-Americans, or the 1979 crackdown on Iranians during the hostage crisis. But the roundups reassure the public.

For Muhammad Rafiq Butt, a fifty-five-year-old working-class Pakistani free of any links to terrorism whose only offense was an expired visa, the experience meant death. The first fatality of the racial profiling of Arabs and Muslims following the September 11 attacks, Butt, arrested by the FBI, died of a heart attack after languishing for thirty-three days in a New Jersey county jail. In *The Gulag Archipelago*, Aleksandr Solzhenitsyn characterizes that experience: "Arrest! Need it be said that it is a breaking point in your life, a bolt of lightning which has scored a direct hit on you? That it is an unassimilable spiritual earthquake not every person can cope with . . ."

Many other accounts of broken lives have emerged from the sweep arrests, and, as of this writing nine months later, hundreds are still being held. The arrests were followed by the Justice Department's program to interrogate another five thousand Arabs and Muslims, and in March 2002 several thousand more were added to the interrogation list. In June 2002 the department announced that it planned to fingerprint and photograph an additional 100,000. Middle Eastern people boarding airliners are being specially screened, and harassed.

The public, identifying with the three thousand murdered in the September 11 attacks, has not concerned itself much with the implications of this broadscale targeting of an ethnic minority. Bombarded on our own soil for the first time in two centuries, Americans are desperately afraid that one of us may be next—on an airliner, in a building, on the street. The traumatized political atmosphere has encouraged a vast expansion of government powers at the expense of traditional rights, and is reflected most dramatically in the public's embrace of racial profiling of Muslims.

Some liberals have joined the stampede. Journalist Michael Kinsley, in a September 30, 2001, article in the *Washington Post*, argues, "[T]oday we're at war with a terror network that just killed six thousand innocents and has anonymous agents in our country planning more slaughter. Are we really supposed to ignore the one identifiable fact we know about them? That may be asking too much."

Kinsley reasons that "an Arab-looking man heading toward a plane is statistically more likely to be a terrorist." Stuart Taylor, Jr., in the conservative *National Journal*, similarly invokes "statistics," arguing that "one hundred percent of the people who have hijacked airliners for the purpose of mass-murdering Americans have been Arab men." These arguments have no basis in the science of statistics. Statistical validity requires more than the likelihood that the suspect is of one race rather than another; it requires that the selected group contains a sufficient probability of return to justify the selection. As these pundits acknowledge, the statistical yield of terrorists from screening all young Arab men is likely to be "tiny" or "infinitesimal."

The very occurrence of September 11 demonstrated the profound incompetence of the FBI, the CIA, and the Immigration and Naturalization Service (INS). Yet America, in denial, seems incapable even now of facing the extent to which years of spectacular bungling by these agencies has left us dangerously exposed. The ethnicity, age, and sex were in fact *not* the "one identifiable fact" known about the nineteen September 11 terrorists. Some were already on watchlists but were missed anyway, while the conduct of others should have aroused suspicions. Even six months after the attacks, the INS unwittingly extended the visas of two of the dead September 11 terrorists. Congress has responded to the colossal failures of the FBI and the CIA by throwing more money into their already bloated budgets. The country thus reaches not for real security but for the habitual bromide of racial profiling, which diffuses and squanders investigative resources, undermining rather than enhancing public safety. Racial profiling is invoked, not for any proven effectiveness nor for lack of more sharply focused alternatives, but as a pacifier for a frightened public.

The notion that all members of the perpetrators' race or ethnic group are suspect, and therefore may be separated out for special treatment, has a familiar ring from an earlier era:

> [W]e cannot reject as unfounded the judgment . . . that there were disloyal members of that population whose number and strength could not be precisely and quickly ascertained. We cannot say that the . . . government did not have ground for believing that in a critical hour such persons could not readily be isolated and separately dealt with, and constituted a menace to the national defense and safety . . .

So did the Supreme Court, in *Korematsu vs. United States*, justify the World War II evacuation into concentration camps of 120,000 Japanese-Americans, an action for which the nation later confessed error and paid reparations. It is an all-too-common reaction to regard with fear and hostility all those of another racial or ethnic group. Reflexive actions, however, are not always beneficial. Civility and decency, not to say our genuine safety, frequently demand that we rise above our reactive fears and inclinations. That is in large part the function in a society of the rule of law.

THE RULE OF LAW

The Constitution was intended to limit the public's misguided passions against individuals and minorities by defining certain rights that are intrinsic. As Jefferson expressed it in the opening lines of the Declaration of Independence: "We hold these truths to be self-evident, that all men are created equal, that they are endowed by their Creator with certain unalienable rights, that among these are Life, Liberty and the pursuit of Happiness."

Civil liberties are the gift, the endowment, given us by "the Creator," not by the ACLU, not by the happenstance of "legal technicalities," not even by the Founding Fathers or John Locke's social compact. In short, and in less sectarian terms, certain fundamental rights come with the condition of being human—they come with the skin—and no one, no group, no sovereign, not even the people as sovereign, has the moral, the social, or the political right to deprive any one of us of those rights. Any effort to do so is illegitimate. It was the very purpose of our constitutional system and the Bill of Rights to establish a form of government in which the autonomy and integrity of the individual would predominate over the interests of the state, the collective society—the public. The philosophy is that the state exists for the preservation and advancement of the liberty of the individual, not the other way around.

The people retain ample means to protect themselves from dangerous individuals and groups. But the means must be within the confines of law—law which makes certain rights of the individual ironclad, no matter what the collective temptation to violate them. Moreover, the equality principle—won at the cost of a Civil War in which more American lives were lost than in all other wars combined—provides a baseline solution: If the threat is so great that the restrictions to be imposed on liberty are truly necessary and worth the hardships they entail, let them be borne by all, equally, regardless of race. If Arabs are to be questioned and frisked at airports, let us all be questioned and frisked in the same way. Equality has the built-in virtue that, if all are similarly burdened, the public will not tolerate unnecessary and excessive measures.

THE ANTI-DEMOCRATIC NATURE OF THE BILL OF RIGHTS

In late October 2001, six weeks after the terrorist attacks, I attended a presentation by Professor Arthur Miller at the forty-fifth reunion of my Harvard Law School class, in which a television journalist on a panel answered each issue on how to reconcile liberty with security by applying his "MOS" standard: What would the Man on the Street say? Unsurprisingly, on his scorecard, individual rights lost out to collective security every time. The man on the street will almost always say that he believes in civil liberties, *"but."* "I am all for civil liberties, *but,"* is the argument for racial profiling, the argument always made when rights are asserted in hard cases. People are in favor of the presumption of innocence, *but* against the pretrial release of suspects; in favor of freedom of speech and assembly, *but* against allowing Nazis to march in Skokie, Illinois; in favor of freedom of religion, *but* against permitting a Ku Klux Klan rally around a fiery cross.

The argument that civil liberties and racial equality are good, *but* not in times like these, reflects an ignorance or lack of faith in the very purpose of the Bill of Rights. The Bill of Rights is by design anti-democratic, intended to restrain reactions to the offensive, the unpopular, and the threatening; intended to stand as a bulwark against popular will when the public is most agitated; intended for stormy times, groups, and people, which is when the rights are most needed. Its purpose is to protect the individual and minorities from a tyrannical majority.

The question of whether the anti-democratic nature of the Bill of Rights is a sound and just concept is addressed in philosopher John Rawls's 1971 work, *A Theory of Justice*. Rawls asks what rights people would vote for if they had to work out such rights and laws under a "Veil of Ignorance." Under this veil of ignorance, Rawls theorizes, each person would have to decide, in a group vote, on the rights each of them would have, and what steps the collective group might take against each of them, without knowing in advance what his or her status and power would be in the society that would follow and function under these rules. Thus, each person would have to vote on the rules without knowing whether he or she would, for example, be in a racial, ethnic, or political minority, would be rich or poor, talented or untalented, highly intelligent or not, physically strong or weak, etc.

To protect self-interest one is thus forced to contemplate such potential vulnerabilities as being in an unpopular minority, or being erroneously accused of a crime, or otherwise being disliked or targeted by the group for punishment, restriction, or other action. Everyone is therefore impelled to gauge the best distribution of power and rights between the group and the individual, looking at it from both points of view. Rawls concludes that a rational person going through this process is most likely to end up where the Founders did, with a set of individual rights approximating those in the Bill of Rights.

THE SHOE ON THE OTHER FOOT: WHO WILL BE PROFILED NEXT?

Supporters of racial profiling need the Rawls "Veil of Ignorance" perspective. It is potentially dangerous to many of us to establish the precedent that members of a racial or ethnic minority may be treated differently. Being called out of line at the airport and sent to a separate area with all other members of one's ethnic group is of course not in the same league as being sent to a concentration camp. But surely it is more than the "pretty small imposition" and mere "inconvenience and embarrassment" with which Michael Kinsley dismisses it in his *Washington Post* article.

Consider the atmosphere generated around the lives of an ethnic group that is sorted out in public for special treatment. Dr. Martin Luther King, Jr., in *Letter*

From Birmingham City Jail, spoke of the black person's "being harried by day and haunted by night by the fact that you are a Negro, living constantly at tiptoe stance never quite knowing what to expect next, and plagued with inner fears and outer resentments." We are seeing and hearing the anguish of Arab- and Muslim-Americans, sudden pariahs in a hostile atmosphere currently driving some to change their family names. Consider, too, proposals for national identification cards as another security measure; surely, if Arabs are a special category, such cards would prominently identify the bearer's ethnicity. Given racial profiling and a terrorized public subjected to a few more bombings, how far would we be from requiring Arabs to wear yellow crescents, as Jews in Nazi Germany were once made to wear yellow stars?

This is a path we should not follow. It is appalling to contemplate that, after an act of Jewish terrorism in the United States, all young Jews would be specially screened at airports, or that, just because the suspect is white, all white people would be subjected to special screening in cities like Washington, D.C., where they are in the minority. Racial profiling is a dangerous standard, hazardous to us all.

THE NATIONAL SPIRIT: WHAT IS AMERICA?

Americans could benefit from looking at how another society responded when an ethnic group in its midst was targeted. Marcel Ophuls's 1970 documentary film, *The Sorrow and The Pity,* chronicles the shameful complicity of the French during the German occupation of the 1940s, including their cooperation in rounding up Jews for deportations to death camps. Another documentary film, *Weapons of the Spirit,* tells the story of Le Chambon-sur-Lignon, a small agricultural village in the mountains of Southern France, where five thousand Jews fleeing the Nazis were taken in and sheltered by five thousand Christians. This occurred organically, without a plan: Jewish families just started showing up, and the Huguenots of Le Chambon, with a history of persecution and concern for the scapegoat, took them in, one family at a time.

Forty years later, Pierre Sauvage, born in the town in 1944 to Jewish parents hiding there, returned to make the film. He asks villagers, now in their eighties, who had provided refuge, "What made you take in these people? Weren't you putting yourself in danger?" On camera we see an elderly lady shrug self-effacingly and answer, "We were used to it." A former school director explains, "It was the human thing to do." Eventually, the local Vichy prefect and the German army commander became aware of the presence of fugitive Jews, but for some unknown reason, both looked the other way. The Jews of Le Chambon escaped the Holocaust. Sauvage speculates that even the French prefect and the Nazi commander may have been caught up in the contagious goodness of Le Chambon. Bill Moyers, introducing the film, asks us to consider what each of us would have done if this had happened in America.

Of course, the anti-democratic and counterintuitive nature of civil liberties makes them unpopular. Opinion polls usually show that if the question is cast in a controversial context, about two-thirds of the public are opposed to any particular provision of the Bill of Rights. "Eternal vigilance is the price of liberty" is the adopted motto of the American Civil Liberties Union, and eternal vigilance—that is, an awareness by our political leaders, by our teachers, by our public commentators—has been lacking for a long time. The notion prevails that "civil libertarians" are a special interest group, and that civil liberties are an expendable luxury suitable only for calm times. Pierre Sauvage comments near the beginning of *Weapons of the Spirit* that when the crisis of the Nazi occupation came, Le Chambon found that it had the quality of leaders it needed and deserved. Our leaders, pundits, and other sculptors of the culture would do well to revisit the Jefferson Memorial and ponder the great man's warning, engraved on one of the walls: "Can the liberties of a nation be secure when the people have lost the conviction that those liberties are the gift of God?"

The system of civil liberties represents the highest qualities in law and government to which humans can aspire. As the philosopher Martin Buber maintains in his classic work, *I and Thou*, the challenge of being human is to rise above seeing people different from us as "the other," an object, a thing, an "it," and to see them instead as a part of an "I and Thou," a part of our very selves.

The Bill of Rights, civil liberties, and the primacy of the individual over the state are our most valuable heritage, our most unique and exalted national quality. They, more than mountains and free markets and consumerism, are what define our highest character as a people. We have shown in Afghanistan that we can defend our lives with weapons of war. Hopefully we can also preserve what we live *for* with weapons of the spirit.

Ralph Temple practiced law in Washington, D.C. for forty years, and was Legal Director of the D.C.-area ACLU from 1966–1980. He is now living and writing in Ashland, Oregon.

THE CHILLING OF DISSENT POST–9/11
by Chris Mooney

You don't have to be a head-in-the-sand, *Imagine*-singing, America-hating left-ist to be worried about the cracking down on political dissent—and even harm-less speech—that has occurred in this country since September 11. The California Democratic Congresswoman Barbara Lee, the lone representative to vote "nay" on a resolution authorizing the use of force, later received death threats. And now a slew of incidents further suggest a dark underside to our near-unanimous flag-waving and monolithic support for George W. Bush.

On September 23, 2001, the *Boston Globe* reported that Massachusetts Representative Marty Meehan was picketed by protesters for having criticized Bush's failure to return to Washington immediately during the crisis. According to the *Globe*, Meehan was widely quoted as saying, "I don't buy the notion Air Force One was a target. That's just PR. That's just spin." This apparently off-the-cuff remark sent right-wing radio talk-show hosts into a frenzy, leading to the recent mobilization against Meehan by the Massachusetts Republican Society, one of whose members explained, "This is a time to stand together." What's incredible about the whole affair is the utter innocuousness—nay, trivi-ality—of what Meehan said. Still, facing the forces of political homogenization, the congressman felt he had to apologize.

Meanwhile, conservative radio hordes—many of them whipped up by Rightwatch's good friend Rush Limbaugh—were doling out the same treatment to ABC newscaster Peter Jennings. Again, the issue was whether Bush should or shouldn't have returned to the White House immediately after the tragic attacks. Somehow it got out that Jennings, too, had criticized Bush. Ten thou-sand complaints later, the *Washington Post*'s Howard Kurtz reports, it turns out Jennings didn't even make the Bush-bashing remark attributed to him. That didn't stop Limbaugh from coming up with all sorts of clever attributions.

Limbaugh, relying on a friend's email message, denounced Jennings—"this fine son of Canada"—for "insulting comments toward President Bush." He said that "Little Peter couldn't understand why George Bush didn't address the nation sooner than he did, and even made snide comments like, 'Well, some presidents are just better at it than others,' and 'Maybe it's wise that certain presidents just not try to address the people of the country.'" If this is how Limbaugh sources his materials, then the notion that CNN might give him a show truly does have a unique place in the history of bad ideas.

One final example: The great Bill Maher of ABC's *Politically Incorrect* is also under fire for a . . . politically incorrect comment made post–September 11. This one is really disturbing because *Politically Incorrect* advertisers FedEx and Sears, Roebuck, and Co. pulled their ads from the show after viewers called to complain, thus threatening the continuation of Maher's program. [*Editor's note: Politically Incorrect was officially cancelled in May 2002.*] And what exactly did Maher say? He called U.S. military tactics cowardly. "We have been the cowards lobbing cruise missiles from two thousand miles away. That's cowardly. Staying in the airplane when it hits the building, say what you want about it, it's not cowardly." Only in a highly sensitive political environment could this comment provoke a scandal. But it was anathema to a Houston radio talk-show demagogue named Dan Patrick, who mobilized listeners to call in against Maher. As Patrick explained to the *Houston Chronicle:* "When you call our men in the [armed forces] cowards and our military policy cowardly, and when you call these hijackers 'warriors,' that should not be tolerated."

So, as of September 11, did criticizing George W. Bush, or simply speaking your mind in an unconventional way, become a lot more dangerous? Sure, this is a time when our nation has—perhaps rightfully—given up much of its characteristic partisan bickering. But it may also be a time when Congress, its civil libertarians cowed at last, finally manages to pass the idiotic but resilient flag-burning amendment. Are liberals really so off-base for fearing the way America tends to behave when it considers itself at war?

President Bush and many others have been chanting the mantra that we must not do just what the terrorists wanted, abandoning our democratic values and thereby letting them win. But as with repeated warnings about persecuting Arab- and Muslim-Americans, the current prevalence of this mot apparently says very little about how well it has registered.

Chris Mooney is a senior writer and online editor of The American Prospect. *This article originally appeared in* The American Prospect Online, *September 25, 2001. It may not be resold, reprinted, or redistributed for compensation of any kind without prior written permission from the author. Direct questions about permissions to permissions@prospect.org.*

SELF-EVIDENT
by Ani DiFranco

yes,
us people are just poems
we're ninety-percent metaphor
with a leanness of meaning
approaching hyper-distillation
and once upon a time
we were moonshine
rushing down the throat of a giraffe
yes, rushing down the long hallway
despite what the p.a. announcement says
yes, rushing down the long stairs
with the whiskey of eternity
fermented and distilled
to eighteen minutes
burning down our throats
down the hall
down the stairs
in a building so tall
that it will always be there
yes, it's part of a pair
there on the bow of noah's ark
the most prestigious couple
just kickin back parked
against a perfectly blue sky
on a morning beatific
in its indian summer breeze

on the day that america
fell to its knees
after strutting around for a century
without saying thank you
or please

and the shock was subsonic
and the smoke was deafening
between the setup and the punch line
cuz we were all on time for work that day
we all boarded that plane for to fly
and then while the fires were raging
we all climbed up on the windowsill
and then we all held hands
and jumped into the sky

and every borough looked up when it heard the first blast
and then every dumb action movie was summarily surpassed
and the exodus uptown by foot and motorcar
looked more like war than anything i've seen so far
so far
so far
so fierce and ingenious
a poetic specter so far gone
that every jackass newscaster was struck dumb and stumbling
over 'oh my god' and 'this is unbelievable' and on and on
and i'll tell you what, while we're at it
you can keep the pentagon
keep the propaganda
keep each and every tv
that's been trying to convince me
to participate
in some prep school punk's plan to perpetuate retribution
perpetuate retribution
even as the blue toxic smoke of our lesson in retribution
is still hanging in the air

and there's ash on our shoes
and there's ash in our hair
and there's a fine silt on every mantle
from hell's kitchen to brooklyn
and the streets are full of stories
sudden twists and near misses
and soon every open bar is crammed to the rafters
with tales of narrowly averted disasters
and the whiskey is flowin
like never before
as all over the country
folks just shake their heads
and pour

so here's a toast to all the folks who live in palestine
afghanistan
iraq
el salvador

here's a toast to the folks living on the pine ridge reservation
under the stone cold gaze of mt. rushmore

here's a toast to all those nurses and doctors
who daily provide women with a choice
who stand down a threat the size of oklahoma city
just to listen to a young woman's voice

here's a toast to all the folks on death row right now
awaiting the executioner's guillotine
who are shackled there with dread and can only escape into their heads
to find peace in the form of a dream

cuz take away our playstations
and we are a third world nation
under the thumb of some blue blood royal son
who stole the oval office and that phony election

i mean
it don't take a weatherman
to look around and see the weather
jeb said he'd deliver florida, folks
and boy did he ever

and we hold these truths to be self evident:
#1 george w. bush is not president
#2 america is not a true democracy
#3 the media is not fooling me
cuz i am a poem heeding hyper-distillation
i've got no room for a lie so verbose
i'm looking out over my whole human family
and i'm raising my glass in a toast

here's to our last drink of fossil fuels
let us vow to get off of this sauce
shoo away the swarms of commuter planes
and find that train ticket we lost
cuz once upon a time the line followed the river
and peeked into all the backyards
and the laundry was waving
the graffiti was teasing us
from brick walls and bridges
we were rolling over ridges
through valleys
under stars
i dream of touring like duke ellington
in my own railroad car
i dream of waiting on the tall blonde wooden benches
in a grand station aglow with grace
and then standing out on the platform
and feeling the air on my face

give back the night its distant whistle
give the darkness back its soul

give the big oil companies the finger finally
and relearn how to rock-n-roll
yes, the lessons are all around us and a change is waiting there
so it's time to pick through the rubble, clean the streets
and clear the air
get our government to pull its big dick out of the sand
of someone else's desert
put it back in its pants
and quit the hypocritical chants of
freedom forever

cuz when one lone phone rang
in two thousand and one
at ten after nine
on nine one one
which is the number we all called
when that lone phone rang right off the wall
right off our desk and down the long hall
down the long stairs
in a building so tall
that the whole world turned
just to watch it fall
and while we're at it
remember the first time around?
the bomb?
the ryder truck?
the parking garage?
the princess that didn't even feel the pea?
remember joking around in our apartment on avenue d?

can you imagine how many paper coffee cups would have to change their
design
following a fantastical reversal of the new york skyline?!

it was a joke, of course
it was a joke

at the time
and that was just a few years ago
so let the record show
that the FBI was all over that case
that the plot was obvious and in everybody's face
and scoping that scene
religiously
the CIA
or is it KGB?
committing countless crimes against humanity
with this kind of eventuality
as its excuse
for abuse after expensive abuse
and it didn't have a clue
look, another window to see through
way up here
on the 104th floor
look
another key
another door
ten-percent literal
ninety-percent metaphor
three thousand some poems disguised as people
on an almost too perfect day
should be more than pawns
in some asshole's passion play
so now it's your job
and it's my job
to make it that way
to make sure they didn't die in vain
sshhhhhh . . .
baby listen
hear the train?

Ani DiFranco, rather than signing a contract with a major record company, formed her own label, Righteous Babe Records. She has had great success due to her dedicated fan base and prolific touring.

PART 2

CONGRESSIONAL COMMENTARIES

SELECTIONS FROM HOUSE FLOOR STATEMENTS
by Congressman Jerrold Nadler (D-NY)

House of Representatives

October 12, 2001

Mr. Speaker, a month ago the United States was attacked, and in particular my district was attacked. I know or knew many people who were victims of that horrible attack, and I thirst to repay that attack and to make sure it will not happen again. But we can be attacked in many ways, and one of those attacks is to cause us to invade our own liberties as a reaction to the attack upon us, and that we must prevent.

Speaker after speaker on this floor today has described how this 187-page bill, seen by us only a few hours ago, with no opportunity to really look into it, to send out the text to law professors, to others, to really see the implications and to make intelligent judgments upon it, may very well be a danger to many of our liberties.

Well, we have to act in haste, we are told. Why? Because we must prevent acts of terrorism. Let us grant that assumption. Fine. But why should these provisions then extend to anything but terrorism? We can pass the bill today. I will not vote for it, but we can pass the bill today, give our government the powers it says it needs, that the president and the attorney general say they need to prevent terrorism and to defeat terrorists, but not grant that power with respect to everything else until we have had proper time to look into the question without the haste that this emergency imposes on us. And then we can say that these provisions should or should not, or some should and some should not, be extended to ordinary criminal investigations.

Let the terrorism bill proceed for terrorism now, albeit in haste, albeit hastily drafted, albeit not properly vetted. If that is the will of the body, let it be done for terrorism, but only for terrorism. And let us, for other things where the emergency is not immediate, take our time and do it properly.

So this motion to recommit simply says these extraordinary powers exist for terrorist threats, for investigations of terrorism, and not for others.

* * * *

Mr. Speaker, reclaiming my time, I agree with the other distinguished gentleman from New York. There are provisions that go too far in this bill, in my opinion; and there are things that are not in this bill that ought to be, again, after the wonderful work done by the distinguished gentleman from Wisconsin and the distinguished gentleman from Michigan and the committee as a whole, tossed out the window, a new bill, brand-new, emergency we are told.

Limit this to the terrorism and let us work regular order, the way this House ought to proceed, so we may examine whether these powers belong in the general criminal field. There is no emergency we are told about there. The emergency pertains to terrorism, so let us proceed on an emergency basis, which we are doing now, voting for this bill virtually sight unseen, proceed on that emergency only for the terrorism emergency. Limit the bill to the terrorism emergency and look at the rest in our own good time.

* * * *

Mr. Speaker, last year candidate George Bush pledged to seek repeal of the secret courts provision of the 1996 anti-terrorism bill because he claimed to understand that the law was passed hastily and that this provision at least endangered civil liberties without contributing to national security.

Now the president, the same George Bush, and the leadership of this House are insisting that we again enact hastily, and again in the name of national security and anti-terrorism, act so hastily as probably to endanger our civil liberties without necessarily helping our security.

The bill we passed in the Committee on the Judiciary was a balanced bill that would have enhanced our security without endangering our civil liberties. Now we have a 187-page bill with a lot of provisions in it.

What I am about to say I hope is accurate, but I cannot be sure, because we only had time to glance quickly through the bill. We have not had time to properly review it, to send it out to law schools, to send it out to civil libertarians to get comments back so we can make an intelligent judgment.

We cannot wait until Tuesday. We passed out the bill from committee last week. We wasted a whole week, but now we cannot wait three days. We must rush to judgment on this bill.

Let me give three provisions of this bill that look, to a hasty reading, dangerous.

Section 203 says that "secret grand jury information can be shared without a court order," upsetting all American legal tradition, "if notice is given to the court within a reasonable period after the sharing."

But, of course, the whole point of the current law is that a court, not some FBI agent, should decide if secret grand jury information is appropriate for sharing with other agencies. Now the FBI agent decides it on his own and tells the court later, and the court has nothing to do except to say thanks for the information.

Section 213 permits law enforcement to delay notification of search warrants in any criminal investigation. There may be justification for delaying notification of a search warrant sometimes, but in all criminal investigations? What does that have to do with terrorism?

Finally, there is a provision in the bill that essentially allows the attorney general—by stating that he has reasonable grounds to believe that there is someone here who is not a citizen and may be deportable—to start deportation proceedings within seven days, and once he does, that person can stay in jail forever. He can sue under habeas corpus, but if the court then says, "Okay, you can keep him in jail," it is not reviewable again ever.

So they can fling away the key and forget about him forever? Is that American justice, or is that the *Count of Monte Cristo?* We ought to review this bill carefully and not pass it today.

* * * *

November 16, 2001

We have learned through hundreds of experiences that it is only through the exercise of these liberties and these rights and affording people we think are guilty, people we think are terrible people, people we think deserve the most terrific punishment, nonetheless they get these rights, because every person deserves these rights, and only by giving every person these rights can we assure—with some assurance, we can't get it perfect—that innocent people will not be convicted and that the guilty and only the guilty will be punished.

The precedent for all this, the basis on which the administration says we can do this, we can trash our Constitution, is the case of the eight German saboteurs, where a Nazi U-boat landed eight German saboteurs in 1942 on Long Island. They weren't very good saboteurs. They were caught on the beach, walking down the beach, holding explosives, talking German. I didn't say they were competent. And they admitted—it was admitted that they were enemy agents; that they were soldiers in an enemy army, out of uniform behind the lines in the United States.

Under the law of war, you can prosecute such people in a military tribunal and the Supreme Court said so—upheld that. That's the standard law of war. To go from there to say that anybody in the United States other than a citizen, whom the president has reason to believe is a terrorist agent—based on that— can be tried in a military tribunal and not in a normal court, loses all rights of anybody. You know, the Constitution says "no person"—it does not say "no citizen"—shall be denied life, liberty, or property without due process of law. Every person is guaranteed a right of trial by jury for an infamous or otherwise capital crime. It doesn't say "citizen." To argue that the president on his own can determine if this person is an enemy agent and therefore could be tried under the law of war is to give the president unlimited power, which is nowhere granted by the Constitution or by statute or by the Congress.

And for the administration to try to do this without coming to Congress is a terrific arrogation of power. And it shows that this administration simply does not understand the American tradition of civil liberties and of due process of law. We must see that we are going to keep these conditions.

The administration protested. The United States government protested to the government of Peru, the Lori Berenson case in which the United States government said—we didn't say that she was innocent. We don't know that. We said she was tried by a secret military court and that's inherently an unfair procedure. Therefore, the United States protested to the government of Peru and said, "Give her a fair trial."

And now we are going to copy what we called the unfair procedures of the government of Peru.

These procedures belong in a Soviet state or a dictatorship, not in a free society. You can't have an unaccountable system. And I am joining, obviously, everyone else here in urging that hearings be held and that this system not be allowed to stand, because it is an insult, not only to the separation of powers in our government, but it is an insult to all our traditions of justice and due process. And we must not allow this war, this emergency, to eliminate everything we've gained in two hundred years of freedom.

Thank you.

* * * *

Let me add one more thing if I can—one thing of perspective I was just thinking of as I'm standing here. Historically and traditionally, political scientists wondered whether constitutional republics could stand times of stress and war and maintain their liberties and their constitutional systems.

Lincoln talked about that in the Gettysburg Address. The Civil War was a test of whether that nation can long endure, of a nation so conceived and so dedicated—conceived in liberty and dedicated to the proposition that all men are created equal—can long endure. We are now entering a test as to whether in this day and age the American constitutional system and our traditions of civil liberties can survive the combination of a war, because we were attacked, and some people in very high places who seem not to understand our traditions of constitutional liberty. And we will rise up and assert that we can fight a war and keep our civil liberties; fight a war, keep our constitutional traditions, and not junk them in the name of national security. We have to prove that because we are being challenged to that. We are being challenged to that not by Osama Bin Laden, but apparently by Mr. Ashcroft and his associates.

Jerrold Nadler (D) is serving his fifth term representing New York's eighth Congressional district, which includes "Ground Zero." He is a prominent member of the House Judiciary Committee and is the ranking member on the Subcommittee on the Constitution. He is also a member of the Commercial and Administrative Law Subcommittee.

FREEDOM VERSUS SECURITY ISSUES
by Congressman Bob Barr (R-GA)

September 24, 2001

A quote from Martin Luther King, Jr. hangs on my wall: "The ultimate measure of a man is not where he stands in moments of comfort and convenience, but where he stands at times of challenge and controversy"; so it is, too, with nations. The truest test of any system of government is not how it functions in times of peace and prosperity, but how it acts in times of national crisis. The terrorist assault on America last week will put this principle to the most difficult test it has ever faced.

America's mettle as a nation has been tested in past crises; in the vast majority we proved able to both respond to outside threats and preserve democratic principles. However, history shows our system is not always perfect, as we learned when thousands of loyal Americans were imprisoned during World War II, simply because they had Japanese parents.

Unlike every earlier test America has faced, no period of slow escalation and visibly rising international tensions preceded this crisis. This crisis came during a period of record calm and wealth, when threats against our lives seemed distant.

Our government must now make a series of extremely important decisions as quickly and effectively as possible. The most important will be deciding if—and if so, how much—our freedoms should be restricted, and our economy slowed, in order to protect our lives and property. This question will be directly presented to the American people as the Department of Justice seeks to expand its surveillance powers dramatically before the month ends.

Heading the wish list will be authority to conduct wiretaps that follow an individual across the country, accessing any phone he might use (including yours, should he or she happen to find themselves in your home or office and ask to borrow your phone), based on a single warrant. It may also expand the department's authority to conduct such surveillance without a warrant in situations it believes constitute an emergency.

Financial transactions are also certain to be a focus of the Justice Department proposal, since attacks such as these require substantial financial support in order to succeed. Based on past experience, these new powers will increase the amount of information financial institutions must report, and require them to profile their customers and report on any unusual deposits, transfers, or withdrawals. Additionally—and appropriately—the proposal will dramatically increase penalties for terrorism.

The process for obtaining search warrants may also be changed. For some time, federal law enforcement has desired the power to conduct secret searches of a suspect's business or home in order to obtain information without their knowledge: so-called "black bag" operations. The Internet will also be targeted for increased monitoring, through programs such as the FBI's Carnivore system.

As Congress considers these requests, I believe we must not stray from the fine balance between freedom and security created during centuries of court decisions and carefully crafted legislation.

However, there are some things we can, and should, consider. Clearly, our laws governing electronic surveillance, most of which were crafted prior to the 1990s, are severely out of date. This obsolescence hurts both freedom and security, by forcing law enforcement to guess its way through applying them to today's technology. We ought to review them.

The key to updating these laws effectively is modifying the technical language of statutes without changing the constitutional principles underpinning them. We should work to make the laws current without eliminating constitutional protections, such as judicial oversight and specific and limited search warrants.

We must also remember that electronic surveillance can actually make intelligence and law enforcement agencies less effective, by encouraging them to rely less on human intelligence and more on intercepted communications. Such an approach makes us highly vulnerable to attacks by economically destitute fanatics, who are less likely to communicate in ways accessible to surveillance. For this reason, I continue to urge aggressive recruitment of foreign agents and repeal of limitations on our ability to covertly eliminate international terrorists who threaten American lives.

Now, more than ever, we all want a country where we can live, work, and play in safety and freedom. We must remain mindful, however, that just as changes in our laws can make such a world more likely, they can also make it less likely.

The Communist dictatorship in Cuba, for example, faces virtually no threat from terrorism, but it also gives its citizens no freedom and has no significant economic output. As Congress debates the administration's proposed changes to criminal law, we must do everything possible to make America safer, without sacrificing the very freedoms we are fighting to protect.

Bob Barr (R), a former federal prosecutor, represents Georgia's seventh Congressional district. He serves on the House Financial Services, Judiciary, and Government Reform Committees.

COMMON SENSE, SECURITY, AND FREEDOM:
AN INTERVIEW WITH CONGRESSMAN BARNEY FRANK (D-MA)
conducted by David Silver

April 2002

DAVID SILVER: Congressman, what is wrong with the Patriot Act?

BARNEY FRANK: Well, there are a couple of things. I accept the need for more surveillance. We have this law enforcement problem. In a free society, particularly, the ideal method of law enforcement is deterrence; that is, you don't physically prevent people from doing things, you don't restrict people's movements in advance, because that gets the innocent as well as the guilty. You try to have a system in which there is a very high probability that if people do bad things they will be caught and punished.

The problem is, with suicide bombers, deterrence goes out the window. I mean, this is a difficult law enforcement problem. What do you do about people who are ready to kill themselves? You can't deter them.

That means you've got to put more emphasis on both—on prevention. Which means giving law enforcement more surveillance powers. It also means more restriction, to some extent, on our freedom; not absolute, but conditional, like more security checks at the airlines.

Now, so I was ready to support increased surveillance of cell phones, emails, etc. But we have this problem, which is that the FBI has been abusive in many ways in the past and we've recently seen that that's a continuing problem with Wen Ho-Lee, with some other issues.

So I thought the notion of a sunset clause was very important; I mean, you can put in other kinds of safeguards. And I did get an amendment in there that makes it easier for you to sue the government, win money if they release information about you that's personally damaging outside of a criminal context, like Hoover did to Martin Luther King. But still, the best way to regulate that is to give them a very powerful incentive not to abuse it, because unfortunately they have incentives to abuse it. And a short sunset was the best way to do that. When they went from two to four years—that was the major reason why I thought it was wrong.

Secondly, I worked very hard during the '80s—culminating in the act of 1990—to amend our immigration laws to remove restrictions on who could come here, because we didn't like what they thought, we didn't like the way they behaved personally. You couldn't come here if you were an anarchist, you couldn't come here if you believed in polygamy, you couldn't come here if you'd ever been mentally ill, if you were gay, or if you had various unpleasant political opinions. The exclusion section—I mean, we kept out Gabriel Garcìa Marquez, etc., etc., Graham Greene; it was an embarrassment. We cleaned that up.

Some elements of that bill could put that back in; that is, there are elements there that say that if you give to an organization that is subsequently declared to be a terrorist organization—without them proving in any way that you should have known that or could have known that—you could be excluded. So that one bothered me—that one bothered me as well.

DS: What about people who are in the country who have that problem?

BF: Well, it's similar, right. If you're an immigrant—it applies to immigrants. Whether as an exclusion or a deportation.

DS: What do you think is the necessary balance?

BF: We should legislate with safeguards—we did improve on the attorney general's bill. It's not what he wanted, which would have had some real problems. He wanted the power to hold people indefinitely, but there need to be safeguards.

I mean, if they follow the bill exactly as we intended, then I think it would be okay. That is, there is more surveillance. Part of the problem is that the FBI leaks about people and you want to try and deter that, but you can't be sure that they're going to follow it as it should be.

DS: Do you think part of it was just the visceral response—it was so close to the actual event. After all, politicians are human beings. A hasty bill was passed and later it couldn't it be ameliorated.

BF: Well, that's part of the sunset, right. That's part of the argument for the sunset, which is that it just expires at a certain date. And you have to start all over again. Now the relevance of that is that inertia is a very important part of the legislative process in America. It's hard, you know, you've got to get both houses and committees and things. So the sunset simply says, "The new powers that the FBI is given under this bill expire two years from today." And that's, as I said, the best incentive against abuse, because if they had a pattern of abuse, then people would be much less likely to renew.

DS: Do you think there's a particularly severe attack upon the very concept of habeas corpus in this bill? Or in other bills that have been passed in the last few years?

BF: Well, the attack on habeas corpus came earlier, in '96, with the crime bill. I mean, the Republicans did pass legislation seeking to restrict your access to federal court—habeas corpus, in that sense. The courts have not been fully responsive to it. In fact, the legislation that was passed in '96 after the Oklahoma City bombing was more restrictive and more abusive than what happened this time. Ironically, of course, a lot of that was aimed at immigrants when there were no immigrants involved in '96.

But I am not aware that there are any more significant restrictions on habeas corpus in the U.S. since this war. In general, things have been better than they have been in previous cases. I mean, there have been no Palmer Raids, no rounding up of Japanese-Americans, no McCarthyism. And, in fact, American citizens in particular have not suffered. I'm aware of only one case, for example, where there was government interference with people's freedom—this professor in Florida, who I think was a legal permanent resident who was fired for making anti-war remarks. But in general, there have been no cases that I'm aware of where the government has acted to kind of suppress speaking criticism.

There's no justification for any diminution in people's freedom of expression, their right to write or speak or organize politically. There has been some potential loss of privacy. And, on the other hand, it's a loss of privacy about which people are informed. You know, people should long since have recognized that emails are not exactly sacrosanct.

DS: Do you think the actual general public is more concerned about civil liberties at this point in time?

BF: Oh, it's much better, yes, I was very encouraged. I think we have been able to block some of what Ashcroft wanted to do with public support. When Ashcroft was pressing Congress to act quickly, I had as many people telling me, "Hey, don't rush into this," as saying, "Oh my God, protect me."

For instance, on the military tribunal, he hasn't abolished them obviously, but it has significantly changed from what he originally proposed. He went before the Senate and was mocking the notion that you would have trials. Well, he's now running two trials: John Walker Lynde and Zacarias Moussaoui. You know, he picked the district in which to have them, but they're still trials with all the rights and appellate procedures applying. So, yeah, I think the American public has shown a healthy unwillingness to be spooked. And it really is—it's better than it was in '96, interestingly. Fewer people were killed but we reacted worse to it. This time, the reaction was a little bit modulated.

DS: There's been some agreement between the ACLU and people like Bob Barr.

BF: He's a bit of faker. You know, he voted with them every time.

DS: He did vote for the Patriot Act.

BF: At every stage, absolutely.

DS: So what do you think that's about?

BF: Well, I think it's political—he's got a primary. I mean, he talked a better game than he fought. So he was being critical, but in the end we got very few Republican votes—well, in truth, it was really hard to get Democratic votes also. But we got very few Republican votes: Butch Otter and one or two others. They used tremendous Republican pressure to go along with the president at the time.

But while Barr did not follow through, the conservative distrust of government was hopeful.

DS: How do you feel about the question of racial profiling and the general public feeling about that? You know, people getting on a plane see Middle Eastern men and they get freaked . How do you educate people not to get paranoid?

BF: By talking. It's an old trick. You do it by talking. There's one way you do it, by the way, which is in a negative way, and it's to point out that if, in fact, we were to adopt a very strong profile and there were people determined to do us harm, what are they, morons? They'll find somebody who doesn't fit the profile. I mean, it's not like there are no blondes in the world ready to work with them. Or hair dye. Part of the problem with profiling is that people will come to rely on it excessively.

What we need to do is to check baggage and, I think, have an armed guard on the flight and secure the door and do a lot of other things. Profiling is a pretty weak reed to rely on.

I am not opposed to some degree of profiling with regard to airplanes and I think the answer with profiling is this: You've got to balance here. How much harm is being done to the individual versus how much damage could go with society? That's why pulling over black people driving cars is outrageous and unjustified. And pulling somebody over is scary and intrusive and has led to shooting—that's just outrageous.

On the other hand, being singled out for a kosher frisk getting on an airplane is—as the lawyers would say—de minimus. It's happened to me, because I often travel with a one-way ticket. I've had my shoes off three times in the last three days; it's happened to me flying back and forth. Frankly, that doesn't do any harm to you. It doesn't hold you up, because it holds up everybody equally. The plane doesn't take off until everybody's on it. But people say, "Well, it's insulting, because it means they suspect you."

I'll give you an analogy: As a gay man, I used to give blood and now I am not allowed to give blood by the Red Cross. I don't take that personally. There's a great harm of transmitting AIDS and not being able to give blood is not a serious intrusion. So I think the question of profiling is: What are you talking about by profiling? If you're talking about greater scrutiny of some people that does not disadvantage them, I don't have any problem with it. Once you get into disadvantaging people, then it's a mistake. And then there is the other point: That it's a very, very weak reed for law enforcement.

DS: So that's really a common-sense kind of attitude . . .

BF: Yeah, I think that's the best way to go.

DS: Do you think the public is more sensitive to civil liberties these days?

BF: I think the public, on the whole, is better informed, even with regard to the abusive treatment. After World War I and during World War I, Germans needed police protection. They were calling sauerkraut "liberty cabbage" and states made it illegal to teach German; that actually went to the Supreme Court. And, you know, you had the Japanese-Americans.

I think this time the public has behaved much better. There are always some abusive people. But look, you even had the local police departments siding with their local Arab and Muslim immigrants and saying, "I'm not going to round these people up." I thought that was an example of excessive profiling, not to mention a great waste of law enforcement time and money.

DS: Right. Do you think there's ever a time when preventive detention is appropriate?

BF: Preventive detention on a mass group basis? No, I think it's ineffective and outrageous. Now, if you were talking about preventive detention where you have a particular individual and you have very good reason to believe that he or she may have done something, in an extreme case that might be. But then, I don't know why you wouldn't charge 'em. I mean, "preventive detention," by the way, is another word for saying "denying bail." "We think you are the kind of person likely to do this, in the absence of any evidence that you've done anything." No, I think that's never justified.

DS: Why do you think the Senate was so overwhelmingly unified on the Patriot Act, except for Feingold?

BF: Well, I think Senator Leahy—who is a very good guy and we're very lucky he's there—made a strategic miscalculation, very well-intentioned. That is, his initial responses were all very good ones, which was to resist. And I think he may have miscalculated his political situation. That is, a couple of his Democratic colleagues were a lot more willing than he had anticipated to give in. And what happened was I think he got overextended politically, and thus was in a position where they were going to just disregard him, and that's where he lost his leverage.

DS: There are three issues here that we're talking about: civil liberties, privacy, and free speech. Could you delineate your opinions on all three?

BF: I think with free speech and freedom of expression, there is not the slightest justification for any impingement on them and I don't think there's been any. Unlike, again, the Palmer Raids and McCarthyism and even Vietnam. And I think we're doing all right—we can be very self-congratulatory about that.

Privacy, yes, we have authorized greater intrusions on privacy. And I am nervous about whether or not they will be abused. That's why I wanted a strong sunset. We had two in the House bill and then they went to none in the Senate bill and we only compromised on four.

DS: How easy will it be, on the exact day four years from now, for Congress to say, "Okay, let's do another four years"?

BF: Well, it's hard—and it depends. If we have had four years and there have been no abuses, they'll probably get it again. But that's the reason for having it. And then again, you would say, "Okay, let's do it for X years."

And then on the civil liberties—there's a bifurcation there.

American citizens have seen no abuse of their due process rights, legal permanent residents have seen some, and other people have seen significant ones. People who are here illegally by definition don't have legal rights under the Constitution, but they do have some rights as human beings not to be treated so badly. And I think that that's been where there's been the most abuse. People whom we have a right to kick out, we have treated more harshly than simply kicking them out.

DS: But, Guantanamo—that's a different story altogether.

BF: Totally different; I'm talking about people who are in the country.

DS: Yeah. Do you have problems with the way prisoners were treated there?

BF: On the whole, yeah. I think what bothers me is Rumsfeld saying that even if we can't show that they did anything wrong, we keep 'em forever. That's my biggest problem. The other thing you have with regard to Guantanamo—this is where some of the people lost the battle to say that they have no rights whatsoever. Americans get captured and the Pentagon weighed in there saying, "Wait a minute. We cannot set the precedent that will be used to allow mistreatment of Americans in uniform." That's a very powerful argument morally, politically, and intellectually.

Barney Frank (D) has represented Massachusetts' fourth Congressional district since 1981. In the 107th Congress, Frank serves on the Committee on Financial Services, where he is the senior Democrat on Housing Programs. He also serves on the House Judiciary Committee.

OUR LOSS OF CIVIL LIBERTIES IN A POST–SEPTEMBER 11 WORLD
by Congresswoman Maxine Waters (D-CA)

April 10, 2002

Since September 11, our country has been dealing with the catastrophic loss of life and the overwhelming loss of personal security that resulted from the terrorist attacks on the World Trade Center and the Pentagon. In the midst of these difficulties, we in Congress have sought to address the very real needs that have arisen. We have provided economic assistance to victims and to the airline industry. We have passed legislation that has as its goal the reduction of terrorism in our country.

But while we focused our attentions on these serious issues, the Department of Justice and the Bush administration made a series of rules and administrative orders that violate the Constitution, our beliefs, and our freedoms. They represent a huge step backwards for a nation that prides itself on having an open society with many freedoms. The administration did this in the name of fighting terrorism. It is high time that we look at these decisions and question whether they do more to hurt the foundation of this country than they do to fight terrorism.

First, the White House and the Department of Justice used strong-arm tactics to enact legislation that strips away traditional rights. The ironically named U.S.A.-Patriot Act was voted on in the House of Representatives a mere couple of hours after it was completed. The bill differed dramatically from the one which had been voted for unanimously out of the Judiciary Committee. That earlier bill, coming after long hours of work and compromise, represented a successful balance between law enforcement needs in dealing with terrorism and the individual's rights to civil liberties. It was that well-crafted bill that we thought we were going to be voting on in the House.

Instead, the Bush administration engaged in a variety of backdoor maneuvers to produce a bill dramatically different—and dramatically more draconian. We were left no time to evaluate and challenge the bill, despite its serious draw-backs. I did not vote for it, but some who were unhappy with it did, knowing that our country was desperate for some efforts at reducing terrorism.

The U.S.A.-Patriot Act fails the people of this country on numerous levels. It violates a number of constitutional protections, including due-process protec-tions, the right of freedom of association, and the right to be protected against unreasonable searches and seizures. Its detention provisions, of which there are several, violate due-process protections by virtue of the fact that they are not subjected to the sunset clause that applies to other sections of the bill. Thus, the detention provisions are less likely to be appropriately monitored and, if neces-sary, changed or eliminated.

This legislation limits the right of freedom of association. The U.S.A.-Patriot Act allows the secretary of state to designate either foreign or domestic groups as terrorist organizations if those groups have ever engaged in violent activity. That could include groups such as Operation Rescue, Greenpeace, and People for the Ethical Treatment of Animals. The penalty for assisting these groups would be deportation, regardless of whether the donor was aware that the group was des-ignated as a terrorist organization, and regardless of whether their assistance had anything to do with terrorist activities. Worse still is the fact that there is no notice requirement in the act. If the secretary of state changes a group's designa-tion, individuals who subsequently make donations, completely unaware of the group's change in status, may suddenly become deportable.

In addition, this anti-terrorism legislation erodes our Fourth Amendment protections against unreasonable search and seizure. Previously, law enforce-ment agencies were required to give notice before conducting a search. That notice was in the form of a search warrant, reviewed by a neutral and detached third party prior to issuance. The government did have the ability to delay notification in lim-ited situations. The act changed that to allow searches and, in some cases, seizure of evidence, without prior notice. This expands a previously limited authority so that it would be available for any kind of search and in any kind of criminal case.

The U.S.A.-Patriot Act also gives the Central Intelligence Agency an oppor-tunity to get back into the business of spying on Americans, an abuse by that agency that Congress has worked ardently to curtail. Specifically, it allows the CIA to gather or obtain a variety of information, including school records, financial transactions, Internet activity, telephone conversations, and material obtained from grand jury and criminal investigations. This information would be shared with the CIA even absent a court order.

Unfortunately, the hijacking of the U.S.A.-Patriot Act was not the only recent action by the Bush administration that violates our sense of justice and liberty. In November, we were informed that the Bush administration would begin using military tribunals to try persons suspected of terrorism offenses. Not only is this action grossly unconstitutional, but it also flies in the face of public stances this nation has taken against countries that use secret trials.

The constitutional issues raised by this action stem from the lack of authority to order military tribunals, to the astounding breadth of the order, to the use of military tribunals themselves. The administration has claimed that the president has the authority to order the use of military tribunals, yet the grounds it uses to support that assertion are shaky at best. Under the Constitution, Congress has the power "to define and punish . . . Offenses against the Law of Nations" (Article I, Section 8). The president does not have that power, nor does he have the power to declare war, which is also granted to the Congress.

During World War II, President Roosevelt used military trials in the case of eight accused saboteurs. There are two main differences between that situation and the current one. First, Roosevelt relied on the declaration of war Congress had given him. Second, Roosevelt also relied on specific statutory authority that permitted trials of enemy spies to be done by military commission—authority that was subsequently repealed.

Here, President Bush claimed that Congress' authorization of the use of military force gave him the authority to use military tribunals. However, that resolution does not include any language regarding military tribunals. Floor debate is similarly absent of any discussion about the use of military trials. President Bush also claimed that he had authority based on sections 821 and 836 of Title 10 of the United States Code. Unfortunately, he is misreading those sections. Section 821 merely says that if Congress authorizes the use of military tribunals, then they would not have to follow the same procedures used with courts-martial. Section 836 gives the president the power to establish the procedures that are to be used for military tribunals, but only after Congress has chosen to authorize them. In this case, Congress had not given that authorization.

In fact, the administration's action in declaring the use of military tribunals is a flagrant disregard of Congress' will. One of the few positive aspects to the highly flawed U.S.A.-Patriot Act is the fact that it does not permit indefinite detention of non-citizens. The administration's military tribunal order gives it that power which it had been denied in the earlier legislation. This directly contradicts the Supreme Court's ruling in *Ex Parte Milligan*, which held that the president cannot authorize detention without trial, absent preceding congressional action *(Ex Parte Milligan, 71 U.S. [4 Wall.] 2 [1866])*.

Putting aside the president's lack of authority to order military tribunals, we are faced with an order that is far broader than warranted. The order is retroactive, and has no end date. In essence, it would allow for the use of a military tribunal against any non-citizen located in the United States, or any individual anywhere else in the world, at any time. Not only is this overly inclusive, but it also contradicts the Supreme Court's recent ruling in *Zadvydas vs. Davis*, which held that the due process clause applies to all persons located in the United States, "whether their presence is lawful, unlawful, temporary, or permanent" *(Zadvydas vs. Davis, 121 S. Ct. 2491, 2500 [2001])*.

A further concern with the use of military tribunals is that they are only constitutionally permissible when applied to "unlawful enemy belligerents." That category, as defined by the Supreme Court, is much narrower than the entire group of people who could be accused of terrorism crimes. In general, military tribunals have been reserved for use against people captured in military operations zones. The president's order would not fit within those parameters.

We are told that these military tribunals are necessary to protect sensitive and classified information. Presumably that is supposed to assuage our concerns over the problems surrounding the president's order. Yet we have a system that has successfully tried and convicted terrorists in the past without destroying civil liberties. That same system has functioned well even when it was necessary to keep some information secret. If further safeguards are needed, the administration always has the option of requesting that Congress enact them.

In making the order, President Bush did not seem to consider international issues whatsoever. If he had, he would have encountered two significant realities. First, the state of international law is much improved over what existed in the World War II era. Numerous international laws and treaties now provide guarantees of fundamental due process to anyone imprisoned by the state. The United States is a party to several of these instruments. However, the military tribunal order fails to reach the standards set by the very agreements that the United States has ratified.

That problem notwithstanding, it appears that the Bush administration has forgotten the disapproval our State Department has had for other countries, such as Peru and Colombia, when they try civilians in military courts. With this order, the United

States has placed itself on par with those nations and with others, such as Nigeria and Egypt, that we have previously condemned for using special military courts.

The attack on civil liberties undertaken by this administration includes a host of other actions. On November 1, 2001, President Bush signed an executive order that would allow current or former presidents to veto the release of presidential papers. This was done, supposedly, in the interest of national security. Critics have said, though, that the Presidential Records Act of 1978, and other laws and regulations, already protect national security.

The attorney general has affirmatively stated that the Department of Justice will engage in racial profiling in determining who might be potential terrorism suspects. This same man had been speaking out against racial profiling in the months leading up to September 11. In fact, that racial profiling has occurred and continues to occur. Rounding up Arab-American men for questioning is counterintuitive. This is the very group of people who can potentially provide the most assistance to the government in its search for Bin Laden and al-Qaida leadership. Instead, these tactics ostracize and alienate.

In addition, the State Department agreed, at the insistence of the Bush administration, to impose more rigorous screening on visa applications from Arab and Muslim men from twenty-five countries. This screening will add an additional four weeks onto the time period that those applicants must wait to receive student, business, or tourist visas.

Attorney General John Ashcroft also gave the Bureau of Prisons the right "to monitor mail or communications with attorneys." Indirectly, this move takes away an individual's right to counsel, since clients will likely feel uncomfortable sharing the details of their case with their lawyers if they think those conversations are going to be monitored.

Perhaps the Bush administration thinks that the American people no longer believe in the freedoms on which this nation is based. Perhaps the Bush administration does not care about the liberties we all take for granted. It is that last possibility that should have the rest of us very concerned.

Maxine Waters (D) was elected in November 2000 to her sixth term representing California's thirty-fifth Congressional district. She is Chief Deputy Whip of the Democratic Party and serves on the Financial Services and Judiciary Committees. Waters is also the ranking member of the House Subcommittee on Financial Institutions and Consumer Credit.

A PRAYER FOR AMERICA
by Congressman Dennis J. Kucinich (D-OH)

Speech to the Southern California Americans for Democratic Action, delivered on February 17, 2002, in Los Angeles, California.

(To be sung as an overture for America)

My country 'tis of thee,
Sweet land of liberty,
Of thee I sing . . .
From every mountainside,
Let freedom ring . . .
Long may our land be bright,
With freedom's holy light . . .

Oh say does that star spangled banner yet wave
O'er the land of the free and the home of the brave?

America! America!
God shed grace on thee
And crown thy good with brotherhood
From sea to shining sea!

I offer these brief remarks today as a prayer for our country, with love of democracy, as a celebration of our country. With love for our country. With hope for our country. With a belief that the light of freedom cannot be extinguished as long as it is inside of us. With a belief that freedom rings resoundingly in a democracy each time we speak freely. With the understanding that freedom stirs the human heart and fear stills it. With the belief that a free people cannot walk in fear and faith at the same time.

With the understanding that there is a deeper truth expressed in the unity of the United States. That implicit in the union of our country is the union of all people. That all people are essentially one. That the world is interconnected not only on the material level of economics, trade, communication, and transportation, but innerconnected through human consciousness, through the human heart, through the heart of the world, through the simply expressed impulse and yearning to be and to breathe free.

I offer this prayer for America.

Let us pray that our nation will remember that the unfolding of the promise of democracy in our nation paralleled the striving for civil rights. That is why we must challenge the rationale of the Patriot Act. We must ask, why should America put aside guarantees of constitutional justice?

How can we justify in effect canceling the First Amendment and the right of free speech, the right to peaceably assemble?

How can we justify in effect canceling the Fourth Amendment, probable cause, the prohibitions against unreasonable search and seizure?

How can we justify in effect canceling the Fifth Amendment, nullifying due process, and allowing for indefinite incarceration without a trial?

How can we justify in effect canceling the Sixth Amendment, the right to prompt and public trial?

How can we justify in effect canceling the Eighth Amendment, which protects against cruel and unusual punishment?

We cannot justify widespread wiretaps and Internet surveillance without judicial supervision, let alone with it.

We cannot justify secret searches without a warrant.

We cannot justify giving the attorney general the ability to designate domestic terror groups.

We cannot justify giving the FBI total access to any type of data which may exist in any system anywhere such as medical records and financial records.

We cannot justify giving the CIA the ability to target people in this country for intelligence surveillance.

We cannot justify a government which takes from the people our right to privacy and then assumes for its own operations a right to total secrecy.

The attorney general recently covered up a statue of Lady Justice showing her bosom as if to underscore there is no danger of justice exposing herself at this time, before this administration.

Let us pray that our nation's leaders will not be overcome with fear. Because today there is great fear in our great Capitol. And this must be understood before we can ask about the shortcomings of Congress in the current environment. The great fear began when we had to evacuate the Capitol on September 11. It continued when we had to leave the Capitol again when a bomb scare occurred as members were pressing the CIA during a secret briefing. It continued when we abandoned Washington when anthrax, possibly from a government lab, arrived in the mail.

It continued when the attorney general declared a nationwide terror alert and then the administration brought the destructive Patriot Bill to the floor of the House.

It continued in the release of the Bin Laden tapes at the same time the president was announcing the withdrawal from the Anti-Ballistic Missile Treaty.

It remains present in the cordoning off of the Capitol. It is present in the camouflaged armed national guardsmen who greet members of Congress each day we enter the Capitol campus. It is present in the labyrinth of concrete barriers through which we must pass each time we go to vote.

The trappings of a state of siege trap us in a state of fear, ill-equipped to deal with the Patriot Games, the Mind Games, the War Games of an unelected president and his undetected vice president.

Let us pray that our country will stop this war. "To provide for the common defense" is one of the formational principles of America.

Our Congress gave the president the ability to respond to the tragedy of September 11. We licensed a response to those who helped bring the terror of September 11. But we the people and our elected representatives must reserve the right to measure the response, to proportion the response, to challenge the response, and to correct the response.

Because we did not authorize the invasion of Iraq.

We did not authorize the invasion of Iran.

We did not authorize the invasion of North Korea.

We did not authorize the bombing of civilians in Afghanistan.

We did not authorize permanent detainees in Guantanamo Bay.

We did not authorize the withdrawal from the Geneva Convention.

We did not authorize military tribunals suspending due process and habeas corpus.

We did not authorize assassination squads.

We did not authorize the resurrection of COINTELPRO.

We did not authorize the repeal of the Bill of Rights.

We did not authorize the revocation of the Constitution.

We did not authorize national identity cards.

We did not authorize the eye of Big Brother to peer from cameras throughout our cities.

We did not authorize an eye for an eye. Nor did we ask that the blood of innocent people, who perished on September 11, be avenged with the blood of innocent villagers in Afghanistan.

We did not authorize the administration to wage war anytime, anywhere, anyhow it pleases.

We did not authorize war without end.

We did not authorize a permanent war economy.

Yet we are upon the threshold of a permanent war economy. The president has requested a $45.6 billion increase in military spending. All defense-related programs will cost close to $400 billion.

Consider that the Department of Defense has never passed an independent audit. Consider that the inspector general has notified Congress that the Pentagon cannot properly account for $1.2 trillion in transactions. Consider that in recent years the Department of Defense could not match $22 billion worth of expenditures to the items it purchased; wrote off, as lost, billions of dollars worth of in-transit inventory; and stored nearly $30 billion worth of spare parts it did not need.

Yet the defense budget grows with more money for weapons systems to fight a Cold War which ended, weapons systems in search of new enemies to create new wars. This has nothing to do with fighting terror.

This has everything to do with fueling a military-industrial machine with the treasure of our nation, risking the future of our nation, risking democracy itself with the militarization of thought which follows the militarization of the budget.

Let us pray for our children.

Our children deserve a world without end. Not a war without end. Our children deserve a world free of the terror of hunger, free of the terror of poor health care, free of the terror of homelessness, free of the terror of ignorance, free of the terror of hopelessness, free of the terror of policies which are committed to a worldview which is not appropriate for the survival of a free people, not appropriate for the survival of democratic values, not appropriate for the survival of our nation, and not appropriate for the survival of the world.

Let us pray that we have the courage and the will as a people and as a nation to shore ourselves up, to reclaim from the ruins of September 11 our democratic traditions.

Let us declare our love for democracy. Let us declare our intent for peace.

Let us work to make nonviolence an organizing principle in our own society.

Let us recommit ourselves to the slow and painstaking work of statecraft, which sees peace, not war, as being inevitable.

Let us work for a world where someday war becomes archaic.

That is the vision which the proposal to create a Department of Peace envisions. Forty-three members of Congress are now co-sponsoring the legislation. Let us work for a world where nuclear disarmament is an imperative. That is why we must begin by insisting on the commitments of the ABM Treaty. That is why we must be steadfast for non-proliferation.

Let us work for a world where America can lead the way in banning weapons of mass destruction not only from our land and sea and sky but from outer space itself. That is the vision of HR 3616: a universe free of fear. Where we can look up at God's creation in the stars and imagine infinite wisdom, infinite peace, infinite possibilities, not infinite war, because we are taught that the kingdom will come on earth as it is in heaven.

Let us pray that we have the courage to replace the images of death which haunt us, the layers of images of September 11, faded into images of patriotism, spliced into images of military mobilization, jump-cut into images of our secular celebrations of the World Series, New Year's Eve, the Super Bowl, the Olympics, the strobic flashes which touch our deepest fears, let us replace those images with the work of human relations, reaching out to people, helping our own citizens here at home, lifting the plight of the poor everywhere.

That is the America which has the ability to rally the support of the world.

That is the America which stands not in pursuit of an axis of evil, but which is itself at the axis of hope and faith and peace and freedom. America, America. God shed grace on thee. Crown thy good, America.

Not with weapons of mass destruction. Not with invocations of an axis of evil. Not through breaking international treaties. Not through establishing

America as king of a unipolar world. Crown thy good, America. America, America. Let us pray for our country. Let us love our country. Let us defend our country not only from the threats without but from the threats within.

Crown thy good, America. Crown thy good with brotherhood, and sisterhood. And crown thy good with compassion and restraint and forbearance and a commitment to peace, to democracy, to economic justice here at home and throughout the world. Crown thy good, America. Crown thy good America. Crown thy good.

Thank you.

Dennis J. Kucinich (D) represents Ohio's tenth Congressional district and serves on the Education & Workforce and Government Reform Committees.

PART 3

ACLU VOICES

THE "SECRET" WAR AGAINST CIVIL LIBERTIES
by Anthony Romero

The war against terrorism in the United States is unlike any war we have previously fought: The enemy is diffuse, the targets are civilians, the threat is constant, and the war may never reach a decisive public end. There is also another difference: The impact on civil liberties is hard to ascertain or fully understand.

As we mark the first anniversary of the unprovoked, horrific terrorist attacks on our homeland, few Americans understand, or even want to hear about, the major changes that have taken place in our nation's laws, policies, and regulations. Many of our government's actions are veiled in a shroud of secrecy, and new rules and legislation confer additional surveillance and law enforcement powers that enable the government to shelter its actions from public scrutiny.

Many have compared the current environment to the Palmer Raids following WWI or the internment of Japanese-Americans during WWII, but unlike these crises, the current assault on civil liberties is largely hidden from the American public, historians, and even journalists.

PARALLELS TO OTHER NATIONAL CRISES

This is not the first time in American history that we have seen civil liberties sacrificed in the name of national security. Indeed, the ACLU was created in response to the gross violations of civil liberties that occurred during the Palmer Raids of 1918. The period following World War I was a time of great political and economic turmoil worldwide. The old world order was collapsing, and new social and revolutionary movements were underway. Millions of people were uprooted, disoriented, and frightened. In the U.S., cities were bursting with new immigrants who were poorly housed and working under terrible industrial conditions. A nascent union movement organized strikes that led to violent demonstrations and in some cases riots. Bombs exploded in eight cities, one killing its deliverer on the doorstep of Attorney General Palmer's house.

Law enforcement officials reacted immediately and drastically to the unrest. Over a period of two months they swooped down on suspected radicals in thirty-three cities, arresting six thousand people, most of them immigrants. The raids involved wholesale abuses of the law, including arrests without a warrant, unreasonable searches and seizures, wanton destruction of property, physical brutality, and prolonged detention.

While the public initially supported these actions in the name of law and order, popular opinion soon changed. Prominent lawyers like Felix Frankfurter charged that the abuses "struck at the foundation of American free institutions, and brought the name of our country into disrepute." It was precisely in this context that Roger Baldwin established the National Civil Liberties Bureau—which became the ACLU in 1920.

Baldwin and his fellow civil libertarians understood the critical role that the Constitution and the Bill of Rights fulfill in our society. "Those who have power," Baldwin observed, "call their wishes justice. Those who have not power call their wishes rights . . . You've got to have some law, or at least a living tradition to appeal to, or else you don't get anywhere." The Bill of Rights is that "living tradition."

The ACLU was thus forged in the crucible of the Palmer Raids, and then later tested by fire in 1942 when the nation once again surrendered itself to xenophobia. Claiming that the Japanese-American communities located on the West Coast were a national security risk, the federal government uprooted more than 120,000 people, many of them U.S. citizens, and held them in internment camps.

As public prejudice and hysteria mounted, the ACLU protested the internment to President Franklin Roosevelt. Arthur Garfield Hays, the ACLU's general counsel at the time, argued, "Our democratic structure is sufficiently elastic to reconcile the military necessity with the fundamental civil rights of the citizen." The ACLU lost that battle at the time, and it took the government more than forty-five years to acknowledge its wrongful actions and pay restitution to former internees.

A SECRET WAR ON CIVIL LIBERTIES

After September 11, the Bush administration refused to release crucial information about the fate of over 1200 immigrants it had arrested or detained. The

Justice Department responded to the ACLU's repeated requests for information by engaging in a game of hide-and-seek, withholding information that could prove that the vast majority of detainees had no connection at all to terrorism.

Lawsuits were filed in Michigan and New Jersey endeavoring to lift the veil of secrecy surrounding immigration hearings in those states. In an initial ruling, the federal district judge in the Michigan case insisted, "Openness is necessary for the public to maintain confidence in the value and soundness of the government's actions, as secrecy only breeds suspicion." In both pieces of litigation, the ACLU represented media outlets that were being denied access to the immigration hearings and were therefore precluded from providing information to the American public.

Two other lawsuits tried to compel the government to reveal the information on the detainees and end its secret war. One lawsuit was filed with sixteen other public interest groups and utilized the Freedom of Information Act, while a second suit utilized a New Jersey state open-records law to compel information on the detainees held in New Jersey facilities.

The lack of information on the detainees was also troubling since it would prove increasingly daunting over time to show that many of the detainees were denied their civil liberties and civil rights. Unlike the Palmer Raids or the internment of Japanese-Americans, which were fully documented by historians and civil libertarians, the September 11 sweeps were not. Moreover, unlike the Japanese internees who were free to go where they wished after their release at the end of the war, the September 11 detainees were largely deported or granted "voluntary departure" to their countries of origin.

Fearful that the historical record of civil liberties abuses would be lost with the deportation or departure of the detainees, the ACLU launched a campaign to chronicle and identify abuses of civil liberties. Consequently, we sent letters to the consulates of ten countries offering legal assistance to innocent people caught up in the government's crackdown on terrorism. Foreign officials were at first hesitant, not knowing who we were—and frankly surprised that an American organization was offering to challenge its own government.

The embassies and consulates did eventually provide the ACLU with names of detainees. In many instances, the ACLU even received the "a-file" number of the detainees—information that we suspect was provided to the embassies by the U.S. government itself. Ironically, this was the same information denied to the ACLU. We then hired a documentary filmmaker who used the information obtained from the consulates to contact family members or attorneys of many detainees. As a result of this outreach effort the filmmaker was able to interview dozens of detainees—some of them by using her ACLU credentials to gain entrance to two detention centers in New Jersey.

Among the stories she recorded was that of Mohammed Gondal, a forty-five-year-old Pakistani national who had spent 125 days in jail, had not been charged with any crime connected to terrorism, but who had suffered a heart attack during his confinement:

> I am not a terrorist. I have no idea why they won't release me . . . They tell me they will release very soon. They sending me back. Waiting for Washington, clearance letter . . . My health is very bad . . . Got heart attack . . . I was very healthy . . . now I can think anytime get heart attack and die . . . They can investigate me. I'm not afraid from investigate. I'm worried about my health . . . Before, very nice country, very peaceful. I like it. Now, I think I not come ever back.

She was also able to speak to Mohammed Zaman, who had lived in the United States for several years and worked as a limousine driver until he "lost everything" while being detained:

> I work in this country seven years, I don't have any criminal record. Why they treat me like this? . . . I just like to live in this country because I like this country. I love this country . . . This country give me more than other country . . . We are human. Where is human right? Just only on paper . . . Some police people very nice. Some police officer call us terrorist. Why? . . . We are hard worker . . . we work seven days a week. How can I go terrorist?

And then there was Iqbal Tihar, another Pakistani national who has been struggling since 1992 to get legal permission to stay in the United States:

> I'm two months, sixteen days in jail . . . I don't want to go back to Pakistan, I like America. Good people, good life, good everything. My daughter is U.S. citizen, I want to stay here, is good life. You can eat good, you can make good money. Three months I bought a car. In my country, I work whole life, cannot buy a car. I work whole life, cannot buy a house. Here I can do everything.

Some commentators argue that violation of immigrants' rights is an acceptable imposition to insure the national security. Others agree that since immigrants are not citizens they cannot expect to be afforded full civil rights and civil liberties. Still others argue that immigrants do present an increased danger to the nation and its values.

Yet these arguments fail to take into account that our freedom has been the main draw for immigrants since the formation of our country. Many immigrants, including the September 11 detainees, have worked, lived, and paid taxes in the United States. While it is true that non-citizens are denied certain civic rights, such as the right to vote, the fact is that many of the constitutionally guaranteed rights apply to citizens and non-citizens alike. For example, the Fifth Amendment guarantee of due process makes no distinction between individuals, and instead is very clear that "No *person* shall . . . be deprived of life, liberty, or property, without due process of the law." Therefore, any denial of due process has to be of concern to every American, for when the rights of any are sacrificed the rights of none are safe.

America affirmed the international scope of its ideals in 1948 when it became party to the United Nations Declaration of Human Rights, which claimed in part, "No one shall be subjected to arbitrary arrest, detention, or exile," and, "Everyone is entitled in full equality to a fair and public hearing." Yet recent actions by the U.S. government have failed to live up to the ideals it championed in the U.N. declaration. Arbitrary arrests and detentions without fair and public hearings were the primary concern of civil libertarians after September 11.

As we take steps to prevent terrorism we must reinforce the premise that a government "of" the people and "by" the people must be visible *to* the people. Government has an obligation to protect the safety and security of its citizens, but it has an equally important responsibility to safeguard the freedoms and liberties that are the cornerstones of American democracy.

Too High A Price?

Admittedly, the terrorists who attacked the United States on September 11, 2001, took insidious advantage of American liberties and tolerance. They lived in our communities and enjoyed our freedoms. That does not mean, however, that those freedoms are at fault.

President Bush understood this point at the start. In his first address to the nation following 9/11, Mr. Bush said that America was targeted for attack because we are the brightest beacon for freedom and opportunity in the world. And no one, he emphasized, "will keep that light from shining."

Unfortunately, within days of the president's affirming the need to keep freedom strong, his administration, with the support of Congress, sought and eventually gained an expansive array of new powers that threaten to undermine the system of checks and balances so essential for the protection of civil liberties.

As a result, laws and regulations enacted in the aftermath of September 11 now permit the government to:

> 1) Detain non-citizens facing deportation based merely on the attorney general's certification that he has "reasonable grounds to believe" the non-citizen endangers national security. In other words, the legislation confers new and unprecedented detention authority on the attorney general based on vague and unspecified threats to national security.

Although the law requires that immigration or criminal charges must be filed within seven days, these charges need not have anything to do with terrorism, but can be minor visa violations of the kind that normally would not result in detention at all. Furthermore, the government has bypassed the seven-day limit in several instances by holding individuals as "material witnesses." This loophole allows individuals to be detained for months without any criminal charges being brought against them and also places a gag order on their attorneys to prevent them from discussing the case. In a ruling against using the material witness statute for grand jury investigation, New York Judge Shira A. Scheindlin stated that interpreting the law in such a broad manner "poses the threat of making detention the norm and liberty the exception." In addition, this rule allows the government to detain citizens as well as immigrants.

> 2) Search our homes, rifle through our effects, all without providing us the opportunity to scrutinize the search warrant until several days after the search. The new law refers to this infringement on due process as "delayed notice" searches. The ACLU has dubbed them "sneak and peek" searches.

The ACLU is often asked what is so objectionable about such searches, especially since law enforcement agents are still required to obtain a search warrant. Our answer is that the secretive nature of such searches makes them ripe for abuse. In fact, agents frequently get it wrong. They may have the wrong name on the warrant, the wrong address, or the wrong judge may have signed the warrant. Without a way of catching these mistakes until after the search has been completed, it is often too late to assert your constitutional right to be left alone.

> 3) Minimize judicial supervision of law enforcement wiretap authority by permitting law enforcement to obtain the equivalent of blank search warrants, and by authorizing intelligence wiretaps that need not specify the phone to be tapped nor be limited to the suspect's conversations. In addition, the new law extends lower surveillance standards to the Internet.

Authorities can require a telephone company to reveal numbers dialed to and from a particular phone simply by certifying that this information is "relevant to an ongoing criminal investigation." This is far less than the probable cause standard that governs most searches and seizures. The new law extends this low level of proof to Internet communications, which, unlike a telephone number, can reveal personal and private information, such as which Internet sites an individual has visited. Once that lower standard is applied to the Internet, law enforcement officers would have unprecedented power to monitor what citizens do online, thereby opening a "back door" on the content of personal communications.

> 4) Monitor confidential attorney-client conversations in any case in which the attorney general finds that there is "reasonable suspicion" to believe that a particular federal prisoner "may" use communications with attorneys or their agents "to further or facilitate acts of terrorism." In short, the Justice Department, unilaterally, without judicial oversight, and with no meaningful standards, is to decide when to monitor the confidential attorney-client conversations of a person whom the Justice Department itself may be seeking to prosecute.

What makes this regulation even more disturbing is that it is completely unnecessary. The Department of Justice already had legal authority to record attorney-client conversations by going before a judge and obtaining a warrant based on probable cause that the attorney is facilitating a crime. With the new regulation, the power to record attorney-client conversations has been relocated from the independent judiciary into the hands of the attorney general.

5) Enhance the power of the FBI to spy on Americans for "intelligence" as opposed to criminal purposes, and to share highly personal information with the CIA and Department of Defense—all without meaningful restrictions on how the information is used or redistributed.

These new allowances are a step back to the '60s and '70s when the FBI and CIA used intelligence gathering and smear campaigns to dishonor Dr. Martin Luther King, Jr. and anti-war demonstrators. In the words of the Church Committee which later investigated the FBI's practices, the intelligence agencies had "adopt[ed] tactics unworthy of a democracy, and occasionally reminiscent of the tactics of totalitarian regimes."

CONCLUSION

Some have commented on the transformative nature of 9/11. It is hard to disagree that our country has changed in some significant way now that it is no longer immune to the furies of foreign events. But we must also be reminded of the transformative nature of 1776, 1787, and 1791—the Declaration of Independence, the signing of the Constitution, and the ratification of the Bill of Rights. For Americans, these must remain the key transformative events, shaping how we see the world and what we understand our role in it to be.

Our democracy is built squarely on principles of transparency, free speech, and due process of law. These great principles encourage each and every one of us to speak up in the firm conviction that by so doing, we strengthen our nation. Therefore, when Americans question whether the new anti-terrorism laws are upsetting the system of checks and balances that is fundamental to our democracy, they are fulfilling a civic responsibility. And when others decry the detention of hundreds of immigrants for reasons that have nothing to do with the September 11 terrorist attacks, they are performing a necessary task. Democracy has many great attributes, but it is not a secret or quiet business.

Anthony D. Romero is the sixth executive director of the ACLU. Previously, he was a Ford Foundation executive and public-interest attorney.

AMERICA: "LAND OF THE FREE"?

by Norman Siegel

I was born in 1943. I became politically aware in the '60s and I still am proud to be referred to as "a child of the '60s." I remember my New York City teachers at John J. Pershing Junior High School, New Utrecht High School, Brooklyn College, and NYU School of Law teaching about the principles and values embedded in our constitutional system. They spoke about freedom of expression, freedom to be judged by your acts and not on the color of your skin, your religious beliefs, or your financial status. They spoke of the right to be free from unreasonable stops and searches by law enforcement officials. The concepts were exciting to me then, and they are the values that I have identified as American values for over a half-century.

As a civil rights law student, I traveled south in the summers of 1966 and 1967. I later worked as an ACLU lawyer. During that time, many Southern African-Americans and some Southern whites worked together for equality and freedom. I recall the chant "Freedom Now!" and a glorious era of many dreams being dreamed, and some dreams being fulfilled.

From the '60s Southern civil rights movement sprung three decades of progressive movements for women, gays and lesbians, mentally ill people, the physically impaired, and senior citizens. America was marching to the call of freedom.

Unfortunately, in these early days of the twenty-first century, after the September 11, 2001 attacks on the World Trade Center in New York City and the Pentagon in our nation's capitol, I can't help but be concerned about the diminishing value being placed on the principles of freedom that I—we—cherish.

The 9/11 attacks put our national security and safety into question. It forced us to evaluate the issues of freedom and security, liberty and order. We are committed to investigating, identifying, prosecuting, and convicting—with due process, of course—all who are responsible for the 9/11 attacks. The difficulty we face is determining the means to achieve that goal. And as we proceed toward the objective of preserving our society, we ponder whether we can reach the desired result without losing our most cherished freedoms.

In the aftermath of 9/11, our government—in our name—has initiated a series of policies to counter terrorism. Some of those policies threaten the bedrock principles of freedom upon which our country is founded. Some policies may upset the carefully crafted balance of power between the executive, legislative, and judicial branches of government that were established by our Constitution; they demonstrate a troubling trend toward increased government secrecy, and they put into question due process and privacy rights that are so much a part of our identity. Many of these policies were instituted without prior notice and with little or no consultation, even with Congress.

These actions, taken together, should have alerted Americans to the possible erosion of fundamental freedoms. The lack of public discussion, both before and after these policies were announced, is most troubling, especially in an open, democratic society. I would have hoped that the America that marched for freedom in the '60s would have asked more questions and would have engaged in more vigorous debate about whether or not these policies are the best response to concerns raised in the aftermath of the attack.

Perhaps most troubling is the fact that many of these policies were implemented without advance notice or discussion, even with Congress. In addition, the policies themselves often provided for increased government secrecy. Open government is essential to let us know what our government is doing in our name, and consequently to enable us to hold government accountable. When the government operates secretly, we lose the ability to ensure that it is, in fact, acting properly. Similarly, even if the government is acting properly, secrecy can only breed distrust.

The secrecy also can directly affect the ability of individuals to assert their rights. For example, the government has refused to release the names of most of the post–9/11 detainees who are currently held in the U.S., and has vigorously opposed Freedom of Information Act requests and litigation seeking that information. It is essential to learn the names and locations of persons who are being held, because without the information we cannot ensure that their rights are being respected and that they have meaningful access to a lawyer. If their names were available, family members, lawyers, and civil rights organizations could contact detainees to offer counsel. Instead, we hear reports of obstacles that prevent detainees from hiring and consulting with lawyers. For example: Some detainees have been permitted one call per week to try to retain an attorney; a detainee who requested an attorney was provided with a list of sixteen organizations, only two of which offer legal counseling to detainees; and attorneys trying to reach clients have not been able to obtain information concerning where their clients are being detained.

The America that I—we—learned about as students is not a place in which people are confined, held in secrecy without the ability to seek counsel for advice concerning their rights.

This information is also needed to ensure that the actions of the government are justified. The detentions are being defended on the grounds that they are necessary to prevent further terrorist attacks, when, in fact, it appears that most detainees are being held for violations of immigration regulations that had no connection to the events of 9/11. A large number of the detainees were eventually released and have presumably been cleared of presenting a terrorist threat. Don't we have a right to know whether the government has been engaged in a narrowly targeted investigation with appropriate respect for the rights of suspects, or a broad dragnet of Middle Eastern immigrants that has scooped up innocent people? If we do not know who was detained, or why, how can we properly make that assessment? How can we determine if the government's actions are both appropriate and effective?

Another example in which the rules specify a right integral to our system of justice and freedom, but then limit that right, is the prohibition against double-jeopardy. The rules provide that the defendant cannot be tried a second time on a charge once the commission's finding becomes final through approval by the president. While in a civilian trial a "not guilty" verdict ends the process, the rules here appear to allow a "not guilty" finding to be sent back for further proceedings by the presiding authority, the review panel, the secretary of defense, and by the president, before it becomes "final." Consequently, the sort of double-jeopardy protection provided by the military tribunal rules is not the protection envisioned by our system of justice and freedom.

Whether the military tribunals are operated openly or in secret, they may lack many of the safeguards provided in our civilian courts to avoid unjust convictions. But for those tribunals that are operated in secret, the public will have no means to evaluate whether or not the proceedings are fair and meet our

American standards of justice. Should we as a society accept a system that operates in the darkness when a person's freedom is at stake?

Detentions and military tribunals are examples of policies already in place. But the changes our society may face are much more broad and sweeping. We cannot anticipate all that may be proposed, but the post–9/11 climate already seems to be inviting expanded surveillance powers to the government. Video surveillance in public places, facial-recognition software, expanded government power to monitor our phones and emails, and national ID cards are some of the proposals that could dramatically limit our privacy and anonymity. Some of these ideas have been proposed and rejected in the past, but are now resurfacing. Taken together, these and other proposals could move us further in the direction of the society imagined by George Orwell in 1984 than any of us would have contemplated.

In the spring of 2002, the National Parks Department in Washington, D.C. announced that it would install video surveillance cameras at places such as the Lincoln Memorial and the Washington Monument. Local government officials stated that they were planning to install hundreds of video surveillance cameras throughout the District of Columbia. The surveillance cameras appear to be a permanent fixture in the Capitol. They seriously undermine our long-honored tradition of free movement and may jeopardize the right of anonymity in our daily lives.

After the September 11 hijacking of the two jumbo jets that crashed into the World Trade Towers, authorities at Logan Airport in Boston decided to install the facial-recognition software video surveillance cameras. Though inviting in theory, the technology, at least at this time, does not seem to work. Studies report high instances of both "false negatives" and "false positives," meaning that the technology could, according to an ACLU statement, "miss a high proportion of suspects included in the photo database, and flag huge numbers of innocent people—thereby lessening vigilance, wasting precious manpower resources, and creating a false sense of security."

We need, at a minimum, to have public discussions and hearings on the use of video surveillance cameras in public places, facial-recognition technology, and other invasive measures intended to increase our safety. If we conclude that such measures will be effective in increasing our security and permit them to be employed, we need to develop guidelines to minimize their intrusion on our free association, anonymity, and other essential freedoms.

Equally troubling is the real possibility of the introduction of national identification cards, an idea we have previously rejected. However, post–9/11 the atmosphere is ripe for the advocacy of these cards. National ID cards are not likely to increase our safety and may, in fact, create a false sense of security. America has never been a place in which the government is permitted to stop people and demand that they show "papers." We should all be concerned about a system that would effectively create a government database on everyone, with identifying information and, inevitably, details about our activities and movement.

The erosions of our rights and freedom, and the speed and secrecy with which they are being carried out, are troubling and raise concern that the nation could face additional violations of our basic freedoms in the future.

Reaction to the erosion of freedom post–9/11 has been surprisingly quiet and cautious. Many members of Congress have been reluctant to speak or act in opposition to an administration in a time of crisis. A fearful public has not yet rallied to resist, seeming to accept the notion that we must sacrifice freedom to achieve safety.

Consequently, the question becomes: What can we do?

First and foremost, we need not choose between safety and freedom. The Declaration of Independence describes both "life" and "liberty" as inalienable rights. The Preamble to the Constitution states that it was established both to "provide for the common defense" and to "secure the Blessings of Liberty to ourselves and our Posterity."

These times require that we be ever vigilant and ever strong in protecting freedom. Be outspoken—no matter how unpopular or controversial the issues are. It's part of the tradition that makes America *sui generis*. Please remember, we don't lose our precious freedom with a big bang over night. We lose our freedoms incrementally, often quietly, one day at a time.

The horrific attacks on September 11 and the deaths of over three thousand innocent people have created a changing world. Yet we should remember our history to guide us through these difficult times. In the Southern civil rights movement when we fought for freedom and equality, the third branch of government—the judiciary—intervened in various matters to remind the executive and legislative branches of government of their constitutional limitations. The important role of the federal courts in the civil rights movement was essential to our success in protecting and enhancing the principles of freedom and equality.

The federal courts once again will most likely be asked to intervene on some of the Bush administration's policies that raise serious and substantial issues relating to our fundamental freedoms. Indeed, these requests have already begun and probably will continue in the future. Americans should welcome this needed check and not be critical or threatened by possible judicial involvement.

September 11 has forced me to reflect on American history and freedom.

I never knew how we as a nation could intern 120,000 Japanese-Americans— without visible and vocal opposition.

I never knew how we as a nation could go through the McCarthy period in the early '50s—without visible and vocal opposition.

I now know.

It's when people of goodwill become silent and even quiet. It's when people of goodwill look the other way, rationalize and minimize what their government is doing in their name.

History will judge the government by how it responded to the 9/11 attack, and history will judge *us* by our willingness to question, to challenge, and to speak up when necessary to defend freedom.

Years from now, historians and our children will ask us if we were aware of the secret detentions, military tribunals, eavesdropping of attorney-client conversations, and other encroachments on our freedoms. Eventually, we will also be asked what we did in the face of these violations of freedom. Hopefully, all of us will be able to answer the questions satisfactorily. Hopefully, we will be able to say we spoke up in opposition to encroachments on our freedoms and helped keep America the "land of the free."

Norman Siegel is a civil rights–civil liberties lawyer and the Executive Director of the Freedom Legal Defense and Education Project. From 1985–2001, he was the Executive Director of the New York Civil Liberties Union. Mr. Siegel wishes to express his appreciation to Marina Sheriff for her assistance in the preparation of this article.

CASUALTIES OF WAR: ANTI-TERROR HYSTERIA
by Ramona Ripston

Reason is the first casualty of war. When we are attacked, reason is replaced by fear. Reason is a higher function of dispassionate reflection and cost-benefit analysis, the interplay of memory and probability. Fear is a biological instinct. Left unchecked, fear dissolves those bonds of trust, compassion, and mutuality which are essential for a civil society to survive.

When the hijacked planes of September 11 flew into the centers of American power and security, terrorists plunged fear into our hearts. This, of course, was their intention. The terrorists wove instability and doubt throughout our country. The most taken-for-granted actions—stepping on a plane, opening the mail, standing in a crowd—became a test of nerves. Most of us had never faced a crisis quite like that. When faced with a crisis we need all the powers of wisdom and good judgment we can muster. Yet that is precisely when these attributes fail us. Or we fail them.

We cannot delude ourselves that our only threats come from abroad. We must acknowledge that the democratic values that make us proud to be Americans are under attack from the very people who are supposed to protect those values. Justice Louis Brandeis once warned us that "the greatest dangers to liberty lurk in insidious encroachment by men of zeal, well-meaning but without understanding." Time and time again, Justice Brandeis has been proven right. The sad truth is that in times of war, while others have threatened America's interests, it was our own government that betrayed our values. We pride ourselves on our ability to come together in times of crisis, but all too often we turn against each other. We have let fear turn our neighbors—of whatever race, religion, age, or class—into phantom enemies.

History has shown us exactly what not to do. In the days after September 11 we needed the sensible and sober leadership of our elected officials. What we got instead was the U.S.A.-Patriot Act, which made us a country of secret searches, secret surveillance, secret evidence, secret trials, and limited due process, where the very act of going to pray can bring you under government scrutiny. Representative Barney Frank lamented that "this was the least democratic process for debating questions fundamental to democracy I have ever seen. A bill drafted by a handful of people in secret, subject to no committee process, comes before us immune from amendment."

The destruction of so many lives on September 11 highlighted the vulnerability of our aviation system and the weaknesses of our security, and Congress—rightly, if belatedly—acted to address some of the problems by passing the Aviation and Transportation Security Act (ATSA). The law includes numerous provisions rationally intended to increase aviation security, such as deploying air marshals on flights, expanding screening of passengers and baggage, enhancing the training of flight and cabin crew, and providing for federal control of the screening function. However, Section 111 of ATSA adds a new and unwarranted precondition for employment as an airport screener: United States citizenship.

As a direct consequence of this provision, thousands of lawful permanent residents of all nationalities who are currently employed as airport screeners—many of whom in the process of becoming naturalized citizens, and many of whom with perfect personnel records and routine commendations for their good work—will be summarily fired from their jobs without any process whatsoever to determine whether their continued employment would genuinely pose a security risk. These women and men are prohibited by ATSA from eligibility to reapply as federal screeners, notwithstanding that some have worked for more than ten years at their present employment. Those screeners who are citizens, on the other hand, are eligible to become federal screeners.

The vulnerability of our aviation security system was well known long before the tragic events of September 11. Private security corporations have amassed huge profits while ignoring safety. In particular, concerns have long existed about the ability of screeners to detect weapons and other dangerous objects. An FAA study from as far back as 1979 attributed poor screener performance to three factors: high employee turnover, low pay, and inadequate training, all of which combine to leave few skilled and experienced screeners on the job at any given time. Numerous subsequent reports by the United States General Accounting Office (GAO) and by presidential commissions have identified precisely the same factors as being principally responsible for screeners' performance problems. For example, the GAO recently reported that during the twelve months between May 1998 and April 1999, turnover averaged 126 percent among screeners at nineteen large airports, and one airport reported turnover as high as 416 percent. None of these studies have cited citizenship as relevant to security personnel performance. The citizenship of a screener does not control how well they are paid, how adequate the training, or how well their supervisors manage airport security. And yet, in a thoughtless reflex, non-citizens, the very people with the least influence over the system, many of whom have worked hard with little resources, are being singled out.

This is a moment when reason has been trumped by fear. This is a moment when rational policy-making has been replaced by reckless posturing. This is a moment, when, again, we are turning against each other. Non-citizens are being made scapegoats, they are being asked to pay for the sins of those who should have known better. This is wrong. The first step in scapegoating someone, the first step in fighting an enemy—external or internal, real or imagined—is to dehumanize them. I want to rehumanize three of the people who have been unjustly treated like enemies. I want to give you profiles of some of the Americans we are now turning into scapegoats. I want to introduce you to three of your neighbors.

Let's start with Alba Reyes. Like most Americans, Alba's roots lie in a foreign country. Alba was born in El Salvador. Life was probably fairly normal until her seventh birthday. Most of us have warm memories of our birthdays, especially when we were young, surrounded by presents and bows, family and friends. Over the years those memories may fade. Alba will never forget her seventh birthday. That is the day her father, the town mayor, was killed by the El Salvadoran army. Alba's mother, who was in the U.S. at that time, wanted her children to escape the civil war that had just claimed their father's life. She wanted the children safe here in the U.S., but she wanted them here legally. So the girls stayed with their grandparents in El Salvador until their papers were approved. It took four years.

Finally, when Alba was eleven, she moved to the United States with her mother and older sister. She has lived here ever since. Born in El Salvador, the U.S. is where she went to high school and college. Born in El Salvador, the U.S. is where she grew from a child into a woman. Born in El Salvador, the U.S. is her home. Two years ago, this young woman, who dreams of one day becoming a nurse or elementary school teacher, applied for a job as an airport screener.

Sixteen hours of classroom lectures and videotape viewing, forty hours of certification training, and passing grades on two written tests later, Alba joined the screener force at Los Angeles International Airport, working the graveyard shift from 10 p.m. to 6 a.m. for $8.97 per hour. (For those who might wonder how a single woman can survive in one the most expensive cities in the U.S. on only $8.97 per hour, don't be alarmed—she later got a raise to $9.24 per hour.)

That hefty wage turned out to be insufficient, so Alba took a second job. Finishing her screener work at 6 a.m., Alba would drive home and have about an hour to shower, change, and eat before reporting to work at 9 a.m. as a cashier at a Sears department store. On some days, Alba changed and slept in her car between jobs. As you can imagine, the work schedule took a toll. As Alba recalls, the sleep depravation meant that she "could not think as fast and your brain is slow." This was even harder at Sears, where she was dealing with money.

While at the store Alba focused on money, at the airport she focused on safety. Alba rotated between a variety of vital security tasks: looking for weapons, monitoring baggage X-ray machines, watching over secure areas, staffing metal detectors, and searching people with "the wand." All of these duties are expected. What Alba did not expect, what shocked her then and what angers her to this day—what should anger all of us—is the security company's utter disregard for security.

What Alba witnessed was faulty equipment left unrepaired for days at a time, vulnerable security personnel left with no radios to use in case of emergency, lack of follow-up on problems, and a total absence of the federal government. "I never saw the FAA until after September 11," she says. Alba also recalls the lax efforts to test the screener staff. "Once you were certified you got an occasional test. But it was always the same test," she remembers. The screeners would look for grenades or guns which were "just put in the bags by themselves, not hidden. The tests were a joke." Alba never discussed her citizenship status or that of her co-workers, it was irrelevant to how well the screeners did the job or how poorly the security company was run.

Alba could never understand the casual attitude of her employer. "I tried to do the job best [I could] because people can die. I knew it was serious. My supervisor didn't take it seriously," Alba says, still incredulous. "My family travels a lot and I worry about their safety."

While million-dollar companies cut corners and the federal government ducked responsibility for keeping us safe, this low-paid, overworked immigrant worried about our security. Now, she and thousands like her are scapegoats for our collective failure and fear. Alba welcomes the federalization of screeners as necessary for "taking into account the importance of security and paying attention to flaws," but is angry at the hypocrisy of those who would blame others for their own negligence. "They are trying to find someone to blame to cover themselves. The workers struggled for a living wage, struggled to get respect."

Through all of that, however, Alba seems more mystified than outraged. And she is still loyal to her adopted home. She has reapplied for citizenship (an application form in 1999 was lost due to a bureaucratic mishandling) and stresses, "I feel like my whole life is here."

Nevertheless, some are saying that because she is not a citizen she is not really one of us, she is "other," she is an "outsider." But Alba looks around and all her friends are citizens. Her boyfriend is a citizen. She feels like one of "us." Perhaps she should feel that not being a citizen makes her less of an American. Perhaps she should care less about the U.S. than the citizen congressmen and citizen CEOs who failed this country. Or, perhaps she knows better than that.

Let's now travel up the coast about four hundred miles to Daly City and across two generations to meet Vicente Crisologo. A sixty-eight-year-old native of the Philippines whose brother died fighting alongside U.S. troops at Battan in World War II, Vicente arrived in the United States three years ago at the invitation of his son, who is a U.S. citizen. "My wife also wanted to move to the U.S. because she suffers from asthma and she believed that her health would be better here," he recalls. "After a year on a tourist visa, I decided that I wanted to become an American citizen, and I filed for permanent immigration status and obtained my green card. I intend to file for citizenship as soon as I am qualified to be a real member of the U.S. citizenry, so I can vote and participate in American society without limitations."

In addition to his son and daughter-in-law, Vicente also has two children who live in the U.S. In the short time he has been here Vicente has immersed himself in the civic life of his community. He serves as a member of the board of trustees of the Daly City United Methodist Church and is a former member of the Senior Citizens of Daly City. He is also the interim president of the ITS-SFO unit of Local 790 of the Service Employees International Union.

A man of varied background, Vicente worked for twenty-five years for the United Pharmaceutical Company, ran his own printing business, and studied law in the Philippines. He is a trained and licensed security guard and now works as a screener at the San Francisco International Airport (SFO). At SFO, screeners are assigned three different areas of responsibility: screener, special service, and customer service. "As screeners, we inspect passengers and carry-on luggage at the screening checkpoint," Vicente explains. "When we do special service, we are assigned as guards to secure the airplane when it is parked and to make sure that no one passes through without proper identification. Sometimes, we do random luggage checks at the gate too. Customer service usually means helping passengers who need wheelchairs or other special assistance.

"The screener job is not easy," he says. "In fact, it is not really one job, but many. Screeners rotate through six different stations: reading the X-ray monitor; guarding the metal detector; hand-wanding passengers; checking for passports and boarding passes; operating the itemizer, which is an explosives-trace detector; and loading bags onto the conveyor belt. We usually have about three seconds to view the items as they pass through, and the system would be much better if all the pressure wasn't on a single person. No screener is supposed to work close to the X-ray machine for more than thirty minutes at a time, because of radiation, but sometimes the rotations are not made on schedule. Although the job can be very stressful, I find it to be quite rewarding, and I have enjoyed meeting people from around the world." Indeed, Vicente estimates that eighty percent of the screeners at SFO are not citizens.

Like Alba, Vicente is concerned that security policy is neither well-crafted nor closely monitored. He notes that "it seems that FAA policies change almost every day, and it is not easy to keep up with the changes. For example, after September 11, we were told that FAA policy did not allow passengers to carry lighters onto the plane. Then we were told that lighters *were* allowed on planes, but no more than two. Next we were told that passengers could only bring *one* lighter onto the plane. I don't understand why *any* lighters should be on an airplane, but we have to follow the guidelines."

Also like Alba, Vicente is convinced that eliminating non-citizen screeners will in fact make the U.S. less safe. He is emphatic that "if all non-citizens are fired from their screener jobs at SFO, safety will be worse. This job cannot be learned in the wink of an eye. It takes at least six months to learn to do the job well, and there must be experienced screeners around to train and supervise. Just because the new screeners will be citizens does not mean they will know better how to do the job."

Like many clear-headed people, Vicente sees the absurdity of the belief that eliminating those with security experience will improve security. He is also justifiably outraged at the hypocrisy of the policy. "Have the people who wrote this law forgotten that their ancestors came to this country as immigrants too? Screeners are as loyal to this country as anyone because we are trying so hard to become citizens, and we know we can be deported if we make any mistakes."

I want to return to Los Angeles, where Jeimy Gebin has lived since she was six years old. But first, let's go back even further and return to El Salvador, where Jeimy was born and where the army threatened to kill Jeimy's father if he refused conscription.

Jeimy's father was luckier than Alba's. He came to the U.S. and eventually got his children here as well. The adjustment to life here took time. When she started school in Los Angeles, "the kids teased me because I didn't speak English. But I learned. When you're young it comes easy." After high school Jeimy decided she wanted to "give something back" to her new country and enlisted in the U.S. Army. "I joined the army because I wanted to make something of myself and because I love this country. You can't go fight for this country if you don't love it." Love for the U.S. notwithstanding, Jeimy's mother, probably like most mothers, was nervous about her young daughter joining the military.

Jeimy was not nervous, however, showing a typically American "can-do" attitude: "When I set my mind to something I just want to accomplish what I have to. You just have to prepare yourself mentally." Stationed in South Carolina, Virginia, and Georgia, her army service was "a good experience. I made a lot of friends. We never discussed our backgrounds or if we were citizens. We just accepted each other." In the army she met her husband, also a soldier. Her husband, an American citizen born in Hawaii, joined the army at the behest of his grandfather, a World War II POW and recipient of the Purple Heart. "I had wanted to go to college," he recalls, but one of his grandfather's dying wishes "was for me to join the army. When he passed, I thought it was my obligation." Jeimy's husband watched for enemy fire in the Kuwaiti desert, rose to the rank of sergeant, returned to the U.S., and met Jeimy.

When their tour of duty was finished, the couple and their baby moved to Los Angeles to be with the rest of her family. While Jeimy moved to L.A. to be with her family, she yearned for the homey atmosphere and slow pace of small-town America. "I'm not comfortable here anymore," she says of the town where she grew up. She would like to go back to the south. "I loved it down south. It's cleaner there, the people are nicer. It's a nicer place to raise kids. The schools are nice, they are not overcrowded. There are more school activities for the kids." She dreams of getting an affordable house with a front yard and a garage. Friendly neighbors, good schools, and a nice house with a yard: Jeimy may have emigrated here, but her American dream sure sounds like that of any other American.

And like a typical American, she was stunned by the events of September 2000. On September 11 Jeimy's brother woke her up and told her to turn on the news. She watched the destruction in New York "frightened" and "baffled." Soon after, she applied to be a security screener. Her application was subjected to a background check—work experience, references, fingerprints—the things you might expect would be relevant to genuine security concerns. Her citizenship was not one of them. Jeimy went through the same type of training as Alba, training she deemed "too easy" based on her military background. Eventually, the honorably discharged veteran was offered the job for $9 per hour. She knew that the job, not unlike the army, might be risky, might put her in harm's way. But, as she says, "you just hope that nothing happens to you."

Her shift started about the time that Alba's would end. Her work day, on the high-volume day shift, was quite different from Alba's. "Busy, busy, busy," is how she describes the average day in which she might screen one thousand pieces of luggage. When Jeimy started, the heightened alert made the job "very stressful. Everyone was very edgy. Security was tight. You had to check practically everyone who came in." Not everyone appreciated that. She endured yelling and insults from people not used to being scrutinized. Jeimy had a hard time comprehending the lack of gratitude from so many people. "You would think that people would understand that I am trying to keep [them] secure." Such was not always the case. "Do I look like a terrorist?" passengers would shout. To which Jeimy would respond, "Do you think I'm a psychic? To me, everyone is a suspect until you are cleared. I don't know what terrorists look like." Exactly.

Like Alba, Jeimy rotated every thirty minutes between X-ray machines, metal detectors, and bag checking. She was surprised to see that tight security was not the norm for the job, but she kept at it. "I make sure I do my best because at night I want to sleep. I want to know that I didn't let anything bad happen." Her work quickly earned her a promotion to supervisor, "because they know I do a good job and care about doing it right. I make sure that things get done." That kind of commitment and leadership skills would be lost to us if Jeimy and others like her unfairly lose their jobs.

Jeimy heard about the challenged citizenship requirement on the news. She never expected citizenship would be an issue, especially because of her time in the armed services. "There are a lot of military personnel who are just residents. If there's a safety issue, why isn't [citizenship] a requirement" for the military? she sensibly asks. "It's really insane." Jeimy thinks federalizing the screener force was a good idea, but like her co-workers she is both shocked by the foolishness of the citizenship requirement and infuriated by its unfairness. "I was very angry when I heard that non-citizens would be fired from the job. I can't believe they let me serve my country in the military, but they don't think I can be an airport screener. I want to fight this law. It's personal." Although she feels personally targeted, she has not let that sway her commitment. There have been scares at LAX airport leading to evacuations, but Jeimy and her co-workers have had to stay in the terminal. "We're sitting ducks." That's the job.

One of the more outrageous elements of this current scapegoating scheme is the people it overlooks. Airline pilots, airplane mechanics, food service workers, and cargo and baggage loaders all pose a potential security risk, yet the ATSA does not require citizenship to serve in this capacity. And as Jeimy points out, "the craziest part is that if I get fired, I can go enroll in the National Guard and be back in the airport, with a gun, two weeks later, standing behind the screeners and doing nothing. It's just awful to think about what they're doing." In fact, Jeimy is planning to serve her country again by joining the Air National Guard.

Having worked for the legal acceptance so many of us take as a birthright, Jeimy, whose citizenship request is being processed, has a keen appreciation of the irony of her situation: "I think a lot of U.S. citizens take things for granted. They take their jobs for granted, their country for granted, even their freedom. The screeners who aren't citizens don't take any of that for granted. We know how important it is to have a good job with good pay and to be thankful. It's not right the way we're being treated. This law won't make anyone safer, but it will hurt a lot of good, hard-working people."

Jeimy's husband is equally passionate, especially when he compares what is happening now to his time in the military, which, he argues, "takes whomever because they are putting their life on the line. Everybody works, everybody's the same. We're all part of the same team." He adds that if the armed services applied the same citizenship requirements, people would be shocked to see "how many people they'd lose." He sees the moral contradiction quite clearly, adding that the aviation law "pisses me off. If you dig hard enough you'll find a lot of non-citizens dying for their country in wartime. The government doesn't question them then, it shouldn't turn on them now."

That is the point, after all: Turning on each other will not make us safer, only smaller. Closing ourselves off from others does not make us stronger, it makes us weaker. We face tremendous challenges ahead. Let's learn from our history, and proceed with wisdom gleaned from our experience. Let us not do anything today for which we will have to apologize to our children tomorrow. Let us remember the values that brought people like Jeimy, Alba, and Vicente here. Let them remind us of the meaning of *e pluribus unim*—out of many, one. For Jeimy, as for Alba and Vicente, the bottom line is, "I am an American and no one can tell me anything different."

Ramona Ripston is the Executive Director of the ACLU of Southern California.

THE DANGER OF REMAINING SILENT
by Donna Lieberman, with Wickham Boyle

In the aftermath of the attack on America which occurred in New York City—our backyard, the bastion of diversity—many of us felt compelled to revert to our most basic instincts: escape, self-protection, fantasies of vindication, even vengeance. There was a rush to clutch symbols to assuage our terror: We flew flags, lit candles, sang hymns, anthems, and even old protest songs.

On September 11, 2001, there was unimaginable, earthshaking terror in downtown Manhattan where the New York Civil Liberties Union has its offices. The building vibrated and staff ran, limped, and cried their way uptown to homes and safety. Our offices were closed for nearly a week—off-limits. The security in the reopened building at 125 Broad Street was intense. And in the days and weeks afterwards we startled at loud noises or paper floating down. Our lives had been altered.

From those who would lead came ominous declarations that a new era was upon us; this new era would require militant watchfulness. The message was quite explicit: Public safety could be secured only by surrendering certain liberties and freedoms. And should we fail to heed this new reality, we would do so at our peril.

The NYCLU staff barely had time to hug friends and colleagues on our first day back at work before we received word that the governor had summoned the New York state legislature into an emergency session to enact the "toughest anti-terrorism legislation in the country," and would vote before the end of the day. Gathered around our large conference table, poised to analyze whatever was on the legislative agenda, determined to provide a thoughtful, reasoned response, we were stymied. The legislature was meeting in closed session, advocates could not get in, legislators could not get out. And neither the NYCLU nor anyone else could find out exactly what our representatives were discussing.

That was when we realized that whatever we said about the legislation, we had another message to get out: process counts. The legislature must follow its own rules and legislate in the open, out of reason and sound policy—not fear.

Nonetheless, on September 17, following a closed-door session, New York enacted the Anti-Terrorism Law, creating several new crimes, including the dangerously vague "soliciting support for terrorism," using a definition of terrorism that encompasses "intimidation or coercion of civilians or units of government," and expanding the list of state death-penalty offenses. It was acknowledged on both sides of the aisle as "better-safe-than-sorry legislation." As our Senate leader Joseph Bruno said, we would rather "overreact in terms of protecting potential victims and not worry . . . about coddling potential criminals," than be unsafe.

Only one senator in the entire state objected: Tom Duane, whose district, ironically, includes "Ground Zero," and who had been denied the opportunity to speak during the session!

It was not only politicians, however, who warned us that the rights and liberties we had so recently considered fundamental to American democracy had become, somehow, dangerous. Supreme Court Justice Sandra Day O' Connor, speaking to students at NYU, warned that "we're likely to experience more restrictions on our personal freedom than has ever been the case in our country."

BACK TO THE FUTURE

It seems we have once again been seized by fear of the subversive, the invader, the "un-American." But we hear little about the colossal failures of the national security apparatus in the months and years prior to September 11, 2001. Instead, with a minimum of public debate, we enact extraordinary expansion of state police powers. We see misguided efforts to round up suspects who by virtue of race, color, religion, or national origin are tainted with a presumption of guilt. A poll conducted by the *National Law Journal* finds that two-thirds of Americans approve of the police engaging in "racial profiling"—what we called, in the old days, guilt by association.

MY FREEDOM YES, YOUR FREEDOM NO

Our Constitution was amended to include a bill of rights precisely so that legal protections were afforded those who found themselves among the unpopular or despised. These protections were deemed essential in the face of what is often a tendency to tyranny on the part of the majority.

As one scholar has observed, we have always had a curiously ambivalent attitude toward the Constitution and the Bill of Rights. It has often been a self-centered approach: my freedom, yes; your freedom, no. In every era there are those—members of the privileged majority or the well-insulated minority—who would suspend the rights of due process and equal protection when invoked by the unpopular, the despised—the other guy.

South Asians, Middle Easterners, and Muslims have found out just how easy it is to become the other guy after September 11.

In November, a Pakistani-American who is a longtime community leader and has a friendly, first-name relationship with his local police precinct and elected officials, was so terrified of the sudden hostility that he feared even coming into lower Manhattan for a meeting. He made the trip—his first in two months—accompanied by his Imam. He was not alone—Sikh cabbies were afraid to go to work; children in chadors feared going to school; ordinary people stayed home for days.

Here in New York, scores of South Asian and Middle Eastern immigrants are being detained at the Metropolitan Detention Center—sometimes on the most minor of visa violations. For weeks, many were denied access to lawyers, telephones, family. Not until the NYCLU, the Legal Aid Society, and others intervened in November did the Bureau of Prisons provide them accurate information about legal resources and assure regular phone privileges and family visits. By that time, too many families had stories far too reminiscent of "the disappeared." And the conditions of detention are sometimes draconian. Some detainees are held in the Segregated Housing Unit—locked up twenty-three hours a day. Meanwhile, the presumption of innocence is turned on its head: none, even those who ask to be deported, are released without clearance from the FBI.

Even among citizens the basic rules of law enforcement appear to be suspended after 9/11, when it comes to the other guy. An American citizen from Pakistan returned to New York after a visit to his native country only to be visited by an FBI agent, who asked to "borrow" his passport. There were no allegations of wrongdoing and no basis to take the passport. Only when the NYCLU intervened did the agent return the document.

Tough times create difficult choices. It is a lot easier to adhere to lofty principles in times of relative peace, but it is far more difficult when fundamental beliefs are in conflict. And more difficult still when we feel that our personal safety is at risk. These times put us to the test. Too often, we seem incapable of fully recognizing how vital are the constitutional protections of fundamental rights and liberties—until it is *our* rights that have been suspended.

How quick we are to condone these suspensions of individual liberties. A Lebanese-American woman published an op-ed piece in the *New York Times*— one of the most influential editorial pages in American journalism—arguing for racial profiling: "I understand why people want to profile Middle Easterners. If they do even I will feel safer. It will be unpleasant, yes, but we have to do it to be safe." Of course, the writer is an affluent academic, traveling with what she described as her "fair-haired, blue-eyed" husband. The next day an article in the *Times* wondered, might she have been so willing to be stopped and questioned had she not been an upscale professional, so fluent in English, so comfortable dealing with imperious authority figures, or traveling with a fair-haired, blue-eyed husband?

Three weeks after the attacks, there was a bizarre incident just blocks from the site charged with grief and loss. William Harvey chose to pass out leaflets singing the praises of the person most people believed to be responsible for the horrific attacks. There is no one more hated than he in this country. But our Constitution says that expression deserves the most fundamental protection. You can say his name, sing his praises. Nonetheless, Harvey was arrested and, months later, when cooler heads should have prevailed, a judged refused to throw out the case. The judge rationalized that a man could be arrested for that most basic of First Amendment exercises—leafletting—because the near-violent reaction of the crowd that gathered was entirely predictable! And so we have, in the post–9/11 world, the unprecedented judicial sanction for criminal enforcement of vetoing a heckler's rights for "bad speech."

The perversion of the First Amendment was repeated—and again ratified by a court—with regard to a Times Square incident around the same time. Members of the Black Israelites, a sect that has been preaching in Times Square for years, were arrested for inciting to riot because they praised the terrorist attacks and shouted at the gathering crowd, "We've got something for your asses." Here too a judge improperly removed classic expressive activity from the protections of the First Amendment. He refused to dismiss the charges because "praising the tragic deaths of thousands of innocents at the hands of terrorists and wishing for more carnage while the threat of attacks loomed over the city cannot be considered 'an expression of a political nature.'"'

Indeed, for a while after 9/11 there were some who thought it legitimate to ban all protest activity. Organizers of a peace demonstration scheduled for October 8, 2001, were told by police that there was a ban on demonstrations. But in fact New Yorkers were demonstrating all over the place. There were prayer vigils, makeshift shrines where mourners gathered, and every fire station in Manhattan had a crowd gathered in silent demonstration. When the NYCLU stepped in, the police department quickly reversed the ban and issued the permit. One can only wonder whether it had anything to do with the fact that a permit had already been granted for the Columbus Day parade the following day!

America has responded to the attacks with a surge of patriotism and patriotic displays. But one person's patriotism can quickly become another's act of oppression. On October 17, 2001, the New York City Board of Education decreed that the Pledge of Allegiance must be recited "at the beginning of every school day and at all school-wide assemblies and school events." The NYCLU quickly pointed out that every student and teacher has a constitutional right not to say the Pledge, a right that endures even—or especially—in these intense moments of fear for our national safety. Even a ten-year-old has the right not to speak. The law requires that the Pledge be voluntary, and the schools' chancellor issued guidelines to that effect. But protecting the minority amidst the swell of patriotism is easier said than done. Young teachers, for example, particularly those who don't have tenure, feel like they cannot say no. If they are intimidated, imagine how the children feel. But what choice do they have? To say no, they must publicize their personal beliefs to teachers and peers, and risk the taunts, ostracism, or even discipline for being "the other guy." Some schools have resisted or created opt-ins that do not marginalize the children who choose not to participate, but other schools that once thrived on the ethnic, racial, and religious diversity of their student body are being torn apart by the issue.

True patriotism is not about requiring—directly or by peer pressure—that we all intone the words of the Pledge. The words mean precious little if in the name of patriotism we wrap ourselves in the flag and destroy "the principles for which it stands." We all have to become activists and champions of the underdogs. It starts with thinking, and then questions and moves forward. Ronald Dworkin in a February 28, 2002, article in the *New York Review* sums up our responsibilities: "Of course we are frightened of the power of suicidal terrorists to kill again, perhaps on an even more massive scale. But what our enemies mainly hope to achieve through their terror is the destruction of the values they hate and we cherish. We must protect those values as well as we can, even as we fight the terrorists. That is difficult: it requires discrimination, imagination, and candor. But it is what patriotism now demands."

Donna Lieberman is the Executive Director of the New York Civil Liberties Union.

Matt Groening created the gigantically successful animated TV series, "The Simpsons."

PART 4

THE INVESTIGATORS

THE MISUSE OF "INTELLIGENCE" IN THE NAME OF SECURITY
by Michael Isikoff

Presidential counselor Karen Hughes had every reason to believe she was going to make big news when she entered the White House pressroom on the morning of January 29, 2002. Briefing the media on President George W. Bush's upcoming State of the Union address, Hughes had come armed with a new intelligence report about the purported size of Osama Bin Laden's terrorist network. "We have learned that up to 100,000 people have been trained as killers in the camps of Afghanistan and are now spread throughout the world," Hughes said. Those comments were startling by any measure. Never before had any administration official provided such a frightening estimate for the size of the hidden al-Qaida enemy in the war on terrorism. Hughes's numbers were taken straight from a critical passage in the final draft of Bush's speech, which warned about a vast army of "dangerous killers" who, in the wake of the military campaign in Afghanistan, had now dispersed throughout the world "like ticking time bombs." The reporters dutifully took down Hughes's comments—and ran with them. "Bush says up to 100,000 terrorists threaten America," ran the headline on one wire service report that moved that day.

There was one small problem with Hughes's comments that morning: They were wrong—by a country mile. Indeed, that afternoon, as government officials first started reviewing an advance text of the president's speech, there was considerable consternation within the office of Central Intelligence Agency director George Tenet. "We saw that 100,000 figure and it kind of leapt out," recalled one CIA official. Soon enough, the CIA's press office began getting phone calls. Where had this figure come from? Was there some new discovery suggesting that al-Qaida forces were far bigger than anybody had previously imagined? The awkward truth was the agency had nothing to back up the president's claims. The CIA's own best estimate was that the number of al-Qaida fighters who had been through Bin Laden's training camps in Afghanistan was between 10,000 and 15,000—less than one-sixth the number in Bush's speech. CIA officials delicately informed senior White House staff of the problem. Although it went barely detected at the time, in the hours before Bush's speech, White House speechwriters hastily revised Bush's address to refer instead to "tens of thousands of trained terrorists" who are "still at large."

Trying to make sense of what the U.S. government says about the war on terrorism is hard enough given the extraordinary levels of secrecy the Bush administration has imposed an every aspect of the conflict. But as an example of the misinformation that abounds in this most unusual of wars, Hughes's comments are especially revealing. One senior White House official later insisted, on background, that Hughes's figure was technically "accurate" because 100,000 was indeed the intelligence community's estimate for the total number of fighters who had been training in Afghanistan since 1979. Bush himself had apparently heard that figure in an intelligence briefing in December and was taken by it. Vacationing at Camp David in the weeks before the speech, the president had begun to throw the 100,000 figure out to top aides as evidence of just how big a challenge the country still faced. But, as some administration officials later acknowledged, using figures dating back to 1979 made no sense, at least in the current context. It covered a substantial chunk of time when the CIA was itself arming and training the mujahideen guerrillas trying to free the country from Soviet occupation.

As it turns out, there was reason to question even the CIA's figures on these matters. A few days after Bush's speech, for example, I met in New York with Prince Turki Bin Faisal, the former chief of Saudi intelligence. A cool and urbane Georgetown graduate, Turki knew the Bin Laden network as well as anybody. For years his agents had tracked the number of Islamic militants crossing the Pakistani border to enlist in Bin Laden's training camps. Turki was baffled as to where any of the U.S. government's figures were coming from—including the CIA's. The Saudi's own estimates on the number of hard-core al-Qaida fighters, he told me, were no more than 2,000 to 3,000—and the figure was probably lower than that in the aftermath of the U.S. military operation in Afghanistan. As Turki saw it, Bush officials were seriously overstating the magnitude of the terrorist group. "I think President Bush has to justify his request for homeland security," he said.

* * * *

The confusion and misreporting about the dimensions of the Bin Laden network don't stand in isolation. Since the September 11 attacks on the World Trade Center and the Pentagon, a number of Bush administration claims about the war on terrorism have turned out to be wildly inflated, if not flat out wrong. Were there really subterranean networks of al-Qaida cells still operating on U.S. soil in the days after the September 11 attacks? Had Bin Laden's operatives actually acquired sophisticated biological and chemical weapons that they were about to unleash on American cities? And what about the putative role of foreign governments in the September 11 attacks? Did Mohammed Atta, the ringleader of the hijackers, really meet with an agent of Saddam Hussein's intelligence service in the months before the attacks? At one point or another all these claims have been confidently asserted by senior U.S. government officials and prominently reported on cable TV news networks and in the country's biggest newspapers. And all of them, under closer scrutiny, have proven to be at a minimum, highly suspect.

None of this is meant to suggest that the threat of terrorism isn't deadly serious, or in any way to minimize the horrific human toll of the events of September 11. Nor is it necessarily evidence of government deception—at least at first. Certainly in the days after the attacks there was considerable, and entirely justifiable, alarm over the prospect of more terrorist assaults. But over time the Bush administration's penchant for secrecy, along with its clear political self-interest in keeping the terrorist threat fresh in the public's mind, has tended to cloud many of the most important issues surrounding the conflict. The questionable and sometimes overly alarmist claims by top administration officials illustrate more than just the shaky nature of U.S. "intelligence" about our terrorist enemies. They also show how easily that intelligence can be manipulated for political purposes, especially when so much of the "war" is being waged outside the public orbit, under the all-smothering cloak of "national security."

At least part of the initial impulse toward secrecy, it should be noted, stemmed in no small degree from embarrassment. When the first two hijacked airplanes slammed into the World Trade Center towers, the U.S. intelligence community was caught flat-footed. Electronic intercepts from al-Qaida operatives suggesting an upcoming "big attack" had been misread. (NSA analysts assumed the cryptic conversations referred to an assault overseas, most likely in the Pacific Rim.) In late July, the CIA alerted the FBI that two known al-Qaida operatives (who later turned out to be among the hijackers) had slipped into the country. The bureau launched a probe—and couldn't find them. In mid-August, FBI agents in Minneapolis arrested a French Morrocan named Zacarias Moussaoui on immigration charges when a local flight school reported he showed a suspicious interest in learning how to steer large airliners. After learning, from French intelligence about his radical Islamic ties, the agents became convinced he was plotting a terrorist attack with a jumbo jet. One even jotted down in his notes his fears that Moussaoui was planning to crash an airplane into the World Trade Center. The agents requested a national security warrant to crack into Moussaoui's computer and search his personal belongings. They got turned down by FBI lawyers in Washington.

* * * *

In the days after September 11 the Bush administration took an unprecedented series of measures to respond to the threat—most of the details of which have been almost entirely shielded from public view.[1] Within hours of the attacks, the Justice Department, under the direction of Attorney General John Ashcroft, initiated the most sweeping law enforcement dragnet since the Palmer Raids in the days after World War I. Federal agents fanned across the country and began locking up hundreds of foreign nationals on only the vaguest suspicion of "links" to terrorism. Senior FBI officials talked about upwards of one thousand suspected terrorists still residing in the country. The *Washington Post,* in a front-page September 23 story, reported that government officials had identified "four to five al-Qaida" cells that officials believed were still operating inside the country and might well be planning further attacks.

The arrests of a handful of these suspects seemed to lend credence to such fears. On September 12, for example, FBI agents in Forth Worth, Texas boarded an Amtrak train and arrested two Indian nationals, Mohammed Jaweed Azmath and Ayub Ali Khan. Federal officials said they believed the two men might have been part of the September 11 plot. The evidence: They were carrying hair dye, a wad of cash, and box-cutters purportedly similar to those used by the hijackers. "The FBI Holds Men Travelling with Knives," read the headline in the *New York Times.* Other arrests—of Middle Easterners in Chicago, Detroit, and even Iowa City—produced similar coverage, all of it suggesting that the subjects might in some way be connected to the September 11 attack or to Bin Laden's al-Qaida underground.

But tracking what became of these and hundreds of others arrested in the Justice Department dragnet soon became next to impossible. In conducting its roundup the Justice Department relied to a degree never before seen on a little noticed provision in federal law authorizing prosecutors to arrest and hold suspects indefinitely as "material witnesses"—without ever charging them with a crime or holding any public hearings on the evidence that purportedly justified their incarceration. Most others were arrested on minor immigration charges and herded into county jails and detention centers—again, with no public explanation of their "link," if any, to terrorism.

An emblematic example is Mohammed Irshaid. A Jordanian-born civil engineer who worked on construction projects in the New York area, Irshaid had lived in the United States for twenty-two years. He was the father of three young children—all of them American citizens. In the aftermath of September 11, some business competitors—irate that Irshaid's company had won a lucrative bridge overhaul contract—called up the FBI and raised suggestions that Irshaid might have terrorist ties. Within days, a team of FBI agents showed up at his office and led him away in handcuffs. "It was absolutely the most humiliating thing to happen to me in my life," Irshaid later recalled. Irshaid, who only a few weeks earlier thought he was close to getting his long-cherished green card, soon found himself locked up in a holding pen in the Passaic, N.J. county jail with three dozen other Muslim men. When the men asked to hold on to their food trays so they could observe the Ramadan fast and eat after sundown, the jail guards contemptuously denied their requests. "I don't care about fucking Ramadan," one guard shouted, according to Irshaid's account. Irshaid remained in the holding pen for nearly a month—with no charges ever filed against him. "With all due respect to Mr. Ashcroft," Irshaid said, after he was finally released, "if somebody wants to accuse you of something, they should tell you what it is."

In fact, the Justice Department went to unprecedented lengths to insure there could never be any public accounting of such cases. On September 21, in a move ordered by Ashcroft, the nation's chief immigration judge, Michael Creppy, emailed a directive imposing "special procedures" on the cases of any individuals detained as a result of the September 11 roundup. Their dockets were to be isolated and specially coded—with access barred to members of the public. (INS computers were to be programmed to read, "WARNING

WARNING WARNING," if anybody tried to check on the status of any of these cases.) Hearings were to be conducted behind closed doors. "No visitors, no family, and no press," the Creppy memo instructed. The Justice Department—again under orders from Ashcroft—refused even to release the names of those being held.

By late November more than eleven hundred had been detained. When pressed for an explanation for his refusal to release the names of those being held, Ashcroft left the clear impression that many of them were Bin Laden operatives, and that public disclosure of their identities would jeopardize the "war" effort. "I do not think it is responsible for us, in a time of war, when our objective is to save American lives, to advertise to the opposing side that we have al-Qaida membership in custody," Ashcroft said on November 27, 2001. "We might as well mail this list to the Osama Bin Laden al-Qaida network as to release it."

But how many "al-Qaida members" did the Justice Department really have in custody? As the political heat began to build and reports of mistreatment of the prisoners began to escalate, the department started releasing hundreds of the detainees, implicitly acknowledging it had been unable to find any evidence that tied them to terrorists. In the meantime, new information began to emerge that cast doubt on the reputed guilt of some of the more widely publicized suspects. A roommate of Azmath and Khan, the two Indian nationals arrested aboard the Amtrak train, stepped forward to point out that the men had worked in a newsstand and the box-cutters found in their possession were standard tools of the trade. In December, federal prosecutors charged the men with credit card fraud—wholly unrelated to al-Qaida or Bin Laden. Another highly publicized case involved Abdallah Higazy, a man who was secretly jailed as a material witness after an aircraft radio was allegedly found in a hotel room he occupied near the World Trade Center on September 11. Higazy spent four weeks in jail. Then he was released, after another hotel guest came forward to say the radio was his.

So it went out in case after case. Many of the "detainees," like Mohammed Irshaid, the civil engineer, were entirely innocent—victims of mistaken identity or ethnic prejudice. A grab bag of charges was filed against some of the suspects—for lying to federal investigators, for forging driver's licenses, for visa violations, and for other petty frauds. A few of them had, apparently unwittingly, aided the September 11 plot by providing the hijackers with false IDs or driver's licenses in exchange for cash. And yet by mid-May, more than eight months after the attacks (and shortly after a federal judge in Detroit found the Creppy memo unconstitutional), the most striking statistic was wholly unnoticed by the media: Not a single suspect arrested in the Ashcroft-ordered mass roundups had been charged with a terrorism-related crime.[2] If the Justice Department's actions had led to the arrest of any al-Qaida terrorists inside the United States, it had yet to produce the evidence.

* * * *

Ashcroft's questionable assertions were replicated in the furor over the threat of biological and chemical weapons. The idea that Bin Laden was plotting a biological or chemical weapons attack had been a staple of reporting since the early days after the attacks. The *New York Times* reported on October 10 that Bin Laden operatives in one of the al-Qaida training camps in Afghanistan had "experimented on dogs, rabbits and other animals with nerve gases" and that "aerial surveillance photographs" showed chemicals and poisons had been tested on "animals tethered to outdoor posts." The intelligence reports seemed, at first, to confirm the accounts of at least one FBI cooperating witness—Ahmed Ressam, an al-Qaida operative arrested trying to cross the border from Canada in 1999—that he had personally participated in the poisoning of dogs at one Afghanistan training camp. But Bush himself ratcheted up the ante considerably with a genuinely frightening passage in his State of the Union speech. Reciting a chilling litany of discoveries by U.S. military personnel in the caves of Afghanistan—including "diagrams of American nuclear power plants and public water facilities" and "surveillance maps of American cities"—the president mentioned that our troops had also found "detailed instructions for making chemical weapons."

This was all scary stuff, to be sure. But once again, there turned out to be somewhat less than first met the eye. Most of the new material Bush was referring to, U.S. officials later acknowledged, had been downloaded off the Internet and could not be connected to any identifiable terrorist plots. (That doesn't mean there weren't any. It just means the authorities simply didn't know.) More importantly, as the *New York Times* first reported in a March 19, 2002, story, U.S. officials searching through captured al-Qaida sanctuaries in Afghanistan were unable to find any evidence that the terrorist group had ever actually acquired chemical or biological weapons.

While it was clear that some Bin Laden operatives had researched the subject, sophisticated testing of soil samples and other material found at al-Qaida training camps showed no traces of anthrax or any other biological or chemical agents. "They were reading college textbook level stuff," a senior CIA official told me months after Bush's nationally televised address. "But there have been no smoking guns in terms of live viruses or samples of chemical weapons." What about the previous and widely publicized reports of aerial surveillance photos showing dead animals—the purported victims of biological warfare experiments? "I've been looking for those photographs for a year and, as far as I can tell, nobody here has ever seen them," the official said. The best explanation for the earlier reports, the official explained, was that there were a few U.S. surveillance photographs showing what appeared to be "stakes" outside the training camps and "some people speculated they might have once had animals on them."

The murky nature of "intelligence" in the terrorism war—and its potential for misuse—was even more graphically illustrated by the widely publicized reports that Mohammed Atta, the leader of the September 11 hijackers, had flown to Prague in April 2001 for a clandestine meeting with an Iraqi intelligence agent. This story got its greatest bounce in October when the Czech Interior Minister was reported to have "confirmed" that such a meeting took place. "Today's confirmation raises fresh questions about whether Iraq's foreign intelligence arm in recent years established secret ties with al-Qaida," the *New York Times* stated in a front page October 26, 2001, story, which also quoted "federal law enforcement officials" as pinpointing Atta's trip to Prague has having taken place between April 4 and April 11, 2001. *Times* columnist William Safire went even further, proclaiming the Atta meeting in Prague an "undisputed fact connecting" Saddam to September 11. These reports were no small matter. They provided powerful ammunition to those inside the administration (led by Deputy Defense Secretary Paul Wolfowitz) pushing for a preemptive military strike to topple Iraqi dictator Saddam Hussein. Months later, when Vice President Dick Cheney flew to the Middle East on a futile mission to enlist Arab government backing for an attack against Iraq, a "senior U.S. official" on the trip referred to "meetings that have been made public" between Atta and Iraqi intelligence.

There may well be plenty of reasons to worry about Saddam Hussein. But there were also plenty of reasons to be skeptical about the accounts that Atta had met with one of Saddam's agents. From the outset, the reports of the encounter were unusually sketchy and devoid of detail. The Czech intelligence officials who appear to have given birth to the story claimed to have learned of the meeting because they had the Iraqi intelligence agent in question, a mid-level "diplomat" named Ahmed Khalil Ibrahim Samir al-Ani, under surveillance. But it soon became clear the Czechs also had no photographs of al-Ani in the presence of Atta. Their "source" turned out to be an informant in Prague's Middle East community who saw Atta's picture in the paper after September 11 and "remembered" seeing such an individual meeting with al-Ani five months earlier. (This after-the-fact "ID" was all the more problematic given that, at the time of the meeting, Atta was a wholly unknown figure to any Western intelligence or law enforcement agency, much less to the general public.) Then there was the question of timing. Airline records showed that Atta did indeed first enter the United States on a flight from the Czech capital to Newark, New Jersey in June 2000. But the Czechs placed the meeting between al-Ani and Atta nearly ten months later, in April 2001. When the Immigration and Naturalization Service searched their records for Atta's entries and exits from the United States, they could find nothing at all for the period he supposedly flew to Prague.[3] Nor were there airline tickets or any other records showing Atta in the Czech Republic at the time. There was, on the other hand, plenty of evidence—including car rental and hotel records—showing Atta was in Virginia Beach and Florida during that period. Indeed, after reviewing the available data, both the FBI and CIA concluded that the event simply never happened. "We looked at this real hard because, obviously, if it were true, it would be huge," one senior U.S. law enforcement official told me. "But nothing has matched up." Another U.S. official who works closely with the Czechs was even more blunt: "The whole story is bullshit." But given the administration's interest in keeping up the heat on Saddam, these and other U.S. officials saw little advantage in publicly stepping forward and setting the record straight.

Indeed, in Washington there has been little reason to set the record straight on much of anything related to September 11. The war has been a personal and political triumph for President Bush. In his initial speeches to the country, the president articulated the public's justifiable sense of anger and outrage over the attacks. The routing of the Taliban regime from Afghanistan seemed to vindicate Bush's strategy. When the president's poll rating soared, the White House's political self-interest in maintaining public attention on the conflict became painfully apparent. Bush's top political advisor, Karl Rove, gave the game away last January when he outlined the White House's political strategy for the 2002 elections. "We can go to the country on this issue," Rove said, because the public "trust(s) the Republican Party to do a better job of protecting and strengthening America's military might and thereby protecting America." At the time, Democrats cried foul, insisting—in the words of House Democratic Whip Nancy Pelosi—that "We stand side by side with President Bush on the war on terrorism." But the real lesson to be learned from Rove's remarks may be slightly different. It was a lesson that was learned time and again throughout the darkest days of the Cold War: When national security and politics become intertwined, truth and public accountability are among the biggest victims of all.

Michael Isikoff joined Newsweek *as an investigative correspondent in June 1994. His exclusive reporting on the Monica Lewinsky scandal gained him national attention in 1998. His 2002* Newsweek *piece on pre–9/11 knowledge of terrorist aims was seminal in the inquiries into what the government did and did not know prior to the 9/11 attacks.*

ENDNOTES:

1. To date, the public has only learned a small fraction of the far-reaching steps that were undertaken by administration officials during this period. Consider, to pick only one heretofore unpublicized example, the legal steps that the Bush administration took to place the country on a war footing. Within a few days after the attacks, lawyers inside the Justice Department began drafting a series of secret legal opinions that concluded the country was in a "state of armed conflict." The opinions authorized the president to invoke his powers as Commander in Chief—not just to deploy military troops abroad but to create secret military tribunals and take whatever other measures he sought fit to defend the country without any consultation with Congress. These opinions by the department's Office of Legal Counsel were likened by one administration official to a formal "declaration of war." But they were stamped classified, and were never shared with congressional leaders. As of this writing, the OLC opinions—the legal underpinnings for the entire war on terrorism—have never been made public.

2. The Justice Department, it should be noted, did have two genuinely accused al-Qaida operatives in domestic custody, but the apprehension of neither can be attributed to actions the Justice Department took after the September 11 attacks. One was Robert Reid, the British Islamic militant who was apprehended by airline personnel over the Christmas holidays when he tried to light explosives attached to his shoe. The other was Moussaoui, the reputed twentieth hijacker, who, as previously noted, had actually been apprehended before

the attacks even took place. Yet a third suspect, Enaam M. Arnaout, the head of a Chicago-area Islamic charity, was arrested in late April and charged with perjury when he denied in a lawsuit that he had any connections with al-Qaida.

3. Atta flew to Madrid on January 4, 2001, and returned to Miami six days later. He flew to Spain again on July 8, 2001, and returned to Atlanta on July 19. There were no recorded trips in April.

"PATRIOCHIALISM": SEPTEMBER 11 AND THE DEATH OF DEBATE
by Michael Tomasky

Here, off the top of my head and in no particular order, are a few things I've thought since September 11 but have not said publicly:

> —While I supported the strike against Afghanistan and al-Qaida and am certainly not a doctoral candidate in the Noam Chomsky School of International Affairs, the fact is that the United States has repeatedly pursued policies in the region that have contributed to the rise in anti-American fundamentalism;

> —Until our governmental leaders can undertake a public and at least reasonably frank debate about those policies, hatred of the United States in the region will not diminish;

> —Generally speaking, I'd wager that most New Yorkers—this excludes, obviously, those who were directly affected by the attacks—actually "got over" the event some time ago, long before the media began to acknowledge that doing so could be possible, and appropriately moved through the next stages of mourning and on to other matters, as the press of life insists we must;

> —While the courage of the firefighters that morning was staggering, and properly made people stop and think about the nature of a job with demands that include running headlong into burning rooms and stairwells with the knowledge that you might not come out, I couldn't help but think of another, altogether less noble legacy of the FDNY as I perused the pictures of the deceased, who included a grand total of twelve African-Americans or Latinos out of 343 lost;

> —The concert organized last fall at Madison Square Garden by Paul McCartney carried powerful and repulsive vapors of something that I will be polite and call jingoism;

—The "Tribute of Light," the light shafts beamed toward the heavens from the erstwhile footprints of the two World Trade Center towers as a temporary memorial, was mediocre and seemed to preoccupy the heart or mind of no one in my personal experience—I did not have a single friend or acquaintance who ever said something like, "By the way, have you seen that beautiful Tribute of Light?"—despite its being unanimously hailed in the press, even though the best Herbert Muschamp could do in the *New York Times* by way of citing historical precedent for the display was to name a corporate logo (Twentieth Century Fox), a piece of utility-company propaganda (the "Tower of Light" at the 1964 World's Fair), and, I kid you not, a design by Albert Speer used at the 1934 Nuremberg Rally (hey, he said it, not me).

These six assertions cover some disparate territory, but what they have in common is this: While matters of constitutionally protected opinion, and therefore not subject to "censorship" in any legal sense (at least, so far), they are nevertheless expressions of views that would have been or still would be considered rude, uncharitable, outrageous, or even unAmerican by lots of people, and certainly by the major media, at some point since the attacks. They express points of view or concerns that haven't had much of a hearing in the mainstream media since September 11. I suspect many people agree with at least one of the above assertions; I have heard people privately chortle about the way the newspapers feel obliged to insist that New York is "still reeling" from the attacks, which is perhaps true fiscally but no longer emotionally, and, as I said, I know that the "Tribute of Light" underwhelmed people. But to broach such sentiments in public has been at best difficult and at worst impossible. One hears only—and hears, and hears, and hears—the agreed-upon storylines. And so, an extra-legal censorship; a media-inspired censorship; a censorship not enforced actively by proscription, but agreed to passively, through laziness, reflexive stupidity, lack of imagination, and fear that any assertion that deviates from the accepted narrative will be taken as evidence of lack of patriotism, support for terrorism, or both.

Exaggeration? Admittedly, my first two assertions, critiquing American foreign policy, have found voice. But lamentably, these views have been expressed only in left-wing publications. This only proves my point. To contend, for example, that U.S. support of the Shah and his SAVAK helped give rise to Khomeini—already the fundamentalists' leader in 1964, when he was banished from Iran by the Shah, an act undertaken with U.S. support that only increased his popularity—represents a point of view that is hardly radical. It is a view that finds its distant echoes in the Truman men, devout Cold Warriors all, who were trying to stabilize Muhammad Mossadegh's reformist regime, efforts that ended in 1953 when Dwight Eisenhower took office and decided to topple it and move our dice to the Pahlevi side of the board. It is a view, then, that should not be consigned to journals on the fringes of accepted opinion, where everyone reading already agrees and where no one else is persuaded. In a better world, the American media would have seen to it that the average, semi-informed American should have learned some of this history since September 11.

Oh well. At least *someone* is making the first two assertions—I happen to disagree with much of what they have to say, and in fact find some of it quite loony, but on balance I suppose I'm glad they're saying it. But with regard to the last four assertions, and dozens like them that might be put forth about the way we are all being coached to think and talk about September 11, almost no one is making them. True, saying some of these things might have been inappropriate in the attack's immediate aftermath. Last November would not, for example, have been the best time for a New York City newspaper to run an expose on the historical, institutional racism within the fire department (it fought integration in a sometimes grotesquely ugly way in the late 1970s and early 1980s; still just 2.7 percent black, a number that by all accounts is dropping, it lags far behind the New York Police Department in minority recruitment). *Newsday* columnist Les Payne is one of the few who dared do so, in one column that ran in late January, fully four-and-a-half months after the attack. He found himself on the business end of vituperative—and, it should be said, defensive—mail for days.

But fine—even leave the FDNY out of it, if you like. As to the rest, why has it not been possible to say that that concert was awash in an appallingly mean-spirited xenophobia that was completely antithetical to the better traditions of rock 'n' roll music? Why can't we—politely, but firmly—say that most of us citizens have been ready for some time now to debate the aims of this war, the wisdom of moving against Iraq, and what the hell the Bush administration proposes to do about the Israelis and Palestinians? Why can someone like the *Washington Post's* Ceci Connolly—not a commentator, mind you, but an "objective" reporter—go on television after Al Gore's April speech to Democrats in Florida, in which he asserted the Democrats' right to criticize the White House, and say that Gore's making this obvious and very American point "just doesn't seem appropriate right now," as heads all around her nod? Why does any person or thing remotely tied to September 11 enjoy the broadest immunity from not only criticism, but from virtually any commentary that diverges even gently from the accepted storyline?

We are living out the Information Age Paradox, which, bluntly put, is this: More voices actually equals *less* diversity. We were told, with the dawn of all-news cable stations and the World Wide Web, that the cacophony of voices and viewpoints would result in a great, hectic symphony of debate, in which every conceivable point of view would become known to the layperson. Well, we got the symphony, but it's something short of hectic; in fact, with few exceptions, every instrument is playing the same note. The *New York Times* writes essentially what the *Washington Post* writes, and most other papers follow suit; CNN, trying to keep pace with Fox, apes it; all those television screaming matches sound the same. The result is that, instead of ten people saying the same thing, as was the case in the media stone age when *Agronsky & Co.* had the chat field to itself, now we have one hundred people saying the same thing. And one hundred people are, well, much louder than ten people, and they make it that much harder for the one who's trying to say something different to break through the wall of noise.

A contemporary definition of media diversity: If you get tired of the dark-haired Irish guy praising George W. Bush on one channel, no problem; turn to the other channel and watch the blond-haired Irish guy do it.

* * * *

Since September 11, the Paradox has manifested itself as something I call "patriochialism." It fuses, as the portmanteau suggests, the power of American patriotism with the never-to-be-underestimated potency of New Yorkers' parochialism. It is the chief view of the world we get now in the American media, and in large part it is the only view we get.

Patriotism is, of course, a good thing. I am a patriot. But nothing is good when it feels coercive and enforced. And in the current case, patriotism has been transmuted into a diktat holding that supporting your country means supporting the current administration. Consider this fact, revealed in mid-April by Tom Daschle and Dick Gephardt: Of the total number of live political events the cable channels covered in a three-month period studied by the Democratic National Committee, ninety-four percent of such events featured Republicans.

That is a very big deal indeed—Filipino TV during the Marcos years could scarcely have been more efficient—and it is being done, whatever the networks say, under cover of patriotism: The president is speaking, we are at war, and so on. The events covered include speeches on domestic policies that have nothing to do with war, and even fund-raising events, the broadcast of which shows Bush under the friendliest circumstances possible. This disparity in coverage is astounding, and it amounts to telling viewers, "The president is your leader; these other guys, who really shouldn't be opening their mouths with the nation still reeling and all, aren't worth your time."

But wasn't it always this way in wartime, and probably even worse? Well, in 1800, when John Adams passed the Alien and Sedition Acts, yes, worse; during the Civil War, yes. But in our century, not so. During World War I, it is true that the Wilson administration revoked the second-class mailing privileges of pacifist and radical publications. But with regard to political debate among elected officials—it was fierce. A bill Wilson sent to Congress just before America's war declaration seeking the authority to place mounted guns on American trading ships (this was a response to a recent German ratcheting up of aggression on the high seas) was killed by filibuster. When Wilson did get his war declaration a few weeks later, six senators and fifty members of the House opposed it. Those are not huge numbers. But imagine that Bush had sought a formal declaration of war in the last seven months, and imagine that six senators and fifty House members had opposed him. You can also imagine what objects of calumny those fifty-six would be. (Congresswoman Barbara Lee of California, the lone House member to vote against an open-ended war authorization for Bush, was repeatedly denounced as unpatriotic in the press, and has received death threats.)

In World War II, Franklin Roosevelt got his war declaration (almost) unanimously, but he was hardly immune from partisan attack. After Pearl Harbor, Robert Taft, one of the GOP's leading senators, delivered a speech in Chicago that was a spirited defense of dissent as patriotism and a fairly scathing attack on New Deal Keynesianism—not in April or June of 1942, after the initial shock of the attack had faded, but on December 19, 1941! "Too many people," Taft said, "desire to suppress criticism simply because they think that it will give some comfort to the enemy to know that there is such criticism. If that comfort makes the enemy feel better for a few moments, they are welcome to it as far as I am concerned, because the maintenance of the right of criticism in the long run will do the country maintaining it a great deal more good than it will do the enemy . . ."

And here's the thing: Taft's speech was hardly covered in the press. It was not news, then, that a leading senator should possess the right to disagree with the president, twelve days after the most deadly attack ever on American soil or not.

Again, imagine with me the media reaction if Tom Daschle had given such a speech last September 23. We have gone *backwards*, folks. We get there faster, in ever more technologically dazzling ways; but backwards is the direction.

As for the parochialism part of my equation, we confront the New York view, sustained chiefly by the tabloids, that geography is destiny, and that anything that happens in New York, from a nightmarish terrorist attack to a supermodel scraping her knee outside a club, is rendered vastly more important and layered with extra meaning simply because it happened here. Now obviously, the Trade Center attack was a monstrously important event. It dominated the papers for weeks, and of course it deserved to. During those weeks, I read some fine reporting, and genuinely moving stories, like Jim Dwyer's gem in the *Times* about a window cleaner, trapped on a high floor with several other people, who used his squeegee to break through a wall so that everyone could survive. But the geo-snobbery of New York was also on constant display in those weeks. It was not enough to pay homage to police officers' and firefighters' many acts of courage; rhetoric had to emphasize that they were the world's best, clearly the intrinsic moral superiors of police officers and firefighters anywhere else. New Yorkers were better and more generous than people anywhere else. Our mayor was the maximum leader, and it would verge on blasphemy for anyone to suggest that any other mayor in America could have done what Rudy Giuliani did.

Ah, the mayor. Undeniably, his comportment in the crucial days right after the attack was brilliant. But I have heard a lot of people—by no means just left-wingers or Rudy-haters, some relatives of mine, for example—say things like, "Most big-city mayors probably would have been about as good." They do not say it with animus or resentment. It's just an observation, which any number of regular citizens can make, but which, in the media, cannot be considered. We have no way of knowing whether this sentiment is true. My own suspicion is that most municipal administrations would have been more or less the Giuliani administration's equal in terms of setting up emergency services and so on, but that Giuliani's manner (he does thrive on crisis) provided a certain level of succor that could well have proved beyond the talents of most mayors. But the point would have been made in a month, or even two. Seven, eight months later, we're still hearing it. Are we two-year-old children who need to be told something 862 times for it to register?

Just as the national media tailored patriotism to become the equivalent of support for the Bush administration and the brooking of no dissent, so did the media in New York convert the city's tragedy into a narrative of infantilization, by which we became completely subservient to our leaders, Giuliani especially, and were assumed to be unable to move through the grieving process in a mature way. These are New Yorkers we're talking about?!

Thus, patriochialism: the belief, fueled and reinforced by the major media, that September 11 means that we should just obey our leaders and banish from our minds any but the simplest and most plangently homiletic thoughts. If anything has emerged in the national character since the attacks that is fundamentally unAmerican, it is this—the idea that we should all think the same way. But the funny, or frightening, thing is how many people, intelligent people, have decided to agree. Why? One supposes there is a need for heroes. There is also a need, or at least a perceived one, to vanquish once and for all the ghosts of Vietnam—I can't be the only person who sees in the media boosterism of Bush's policies a yearning on the part of Boomer-generation editors and reporters to do penance for their opposition to the Vietnamese war by being gung-ho for this one. And, finally, most people cannot be persuaded to believe they live in a country where propaganda can work. When people think propaganda, they think Josef Goebbels; it doesn't occur to most people that there exists a wide range of subtler shades, and that some of those gradations can indeed take hold in a country where the major media are owned by the likes of General Electric and the Disney corporation.

So there is censorship, and then there is censorship. For the generally understood, statutory variety, there is at least potential remedy in the courts. For the kind I'm writing about, there is only time—an eventual reexamination of presumptions that will once again recognize the value of dissent, criticism, robust debate, critical thought, constant questioning of our leaders (that is, our servants), an insistence that pious blandishments do not, in a democratic society, suffice as answers. I have to say I'm not holding my breath.

Michael Tomasky has been the "City Politic" columnist at New York *magazine since 1995. His work has appeared in the* New York Times Book Review, *the* Washington Post, Harper's, The Nation, *and many other publications.*

HOW THE MEDIA THREATENS CIVIL LIBERTIES
by Danny Schechter

Civil liberties are really about exercising the liberty to be civil, that is, to participate in the discourse in civil society. The First Amendment that prohibited Congress from making laws against freedom of speech also implies support for the right to speak, perhaps even the democratic duty to do so.

Most debates about civil liberties focus on governmental abuses and Big Brother laws that intrude on our privacy and censor what we can read, see, or hear. But what happens to these issues as power shifts from public to private, and in an era of globalization from national governments to less accountable international bodies and multinational corporations who operate beyond the reach of U.S. law and tradition?

In today's environment, commercial imperatives and democratic cultural requirements are clashing. In an advertising-dominated media, the real message is, as media historian Bob McChesney points out, "Shut up and shop." Increasingly, for structural reasons as well as elitist corporate agendas, participation from the public is not welcome. No wonder election-day turnout is going down as citizens realize that they are valued more as consumers than as voters.

Just as these forces and new global realities have reframed many political debates and options, they are restructuring the civil liberties challenge even though many of its advocates continue to act as if nothing has changed in the way we have to think about the threats to free expression.

A recent Nation Institute forum on the subject illustrated the problem. Prominent journalists, advocates, and even the president of the American Civil Liberties Union spoke articulately about the new threats to civil liberties in the post–September 11 environment. Critiques were offered of the draconian terms of the U.S.A.-Patriot act, and the growing suspension of legal protections of immigrants, especially of Arab descent, in the name of fighting terrorism. These details are no doubt frightening in their implications.

But:

Most Americans don't fully appreciate these dangers in large part because they are not being told about them. The serious and well-documented concerns about illegal detentions, ID card abuses, harassments of dissenters, and profiling may have been mentioned, but are rarely followed up on, rarely treated with the depth and seriousness they deserve. And Americans are not being told about them by the one power center in American life that, in my view, currently poses the greatest threat to the exercise of our civil liberties.

Our media.

On its face, this may sound preposterous in a country that boasts of the freest media in the world. How can it be that freedom of speech is being menaced by freedom of the press?

Has the traditional conflict between the First Amendment and government abuses given way to a deeper but often invisible intra-First Amendment conflict between the right, needs, and interests of the public to have its say, and the power and priorities of our communications system to muzzle and/or restrain its voice?

Oddly enough, I had to raise the question of the media role from the floor after the civil liberties panel had concluded (which, ironically, was moderated by the media maven Phil Donahue). The audience applauded, and at least two people took up my line of questioning. Yet the civil liberties traditionalists didn't even have this aspect of the issue on the agenda. Once it was raised, they all jumped in with personal testimonies to its importance.

In the aftermath of the attacks of September 11, it was common to hear journalists and pundits alike say we were at a turning point, as in "the world will never be the same." But, since then, not only has our commercial-dominated media system remained largely the same, but it has steadily narrowed and limited a national conversation about the parameters, logic, and effect of the U.S.-sponsored global "war on terrorism" that followed.

WAR IN THE MEDIA

After the attacks on the World Trade Center and the Pentagon, millions of people worldwide gravitated toward—even glued themselves to—their TV sets and every means of available communication to keep informed and stay in touch. The media mediated an alarming and often alarmist global conversation in the aftermath of the shockwaves and trauma, as we all discussed what we heard and the latest rumors.

The networks went wall to wall, 24/7, with an unprecedented news-a-thon without commercial interruptions or any break in the news flow. Throughout much of the news media there was a note of self-congratulation about all the comprehensive stop-the-presses coverage. "For all that we lost on September 11 as Americans and human beings," enthused Tad Bartimus in the *American Editor*, the publication of America's newspaper editors, "we journalists regained our relevance and credibility. All media outlets became information clearinghouses; every journalist became a storyteller. Collectively we rededicated ourselves to informing, reassuring, and comforting a transfixed nation holding vigil in a communal living room."

True enough, that is how many journalists felt, and with some justified sense of pride and exhaustion. But also true was that the acres of print and hours of TV time also showcased institutional flaws and shortcomings that turned journalism into a limited and not totally trustworthy guide to understanding the meaning of rapidly unfolding events.

Americans who worried about the impacts on our civil liberties, or who protested hate crimes and roundups of suspects on ethnic grounds, found themselves largely shut out of the discourse, marginalized and unable to have much of an impact on public opinion.

Institutional trends within the media to downgrade serious news and global coverage, and to promote, in its place, a fusion of news-biz and showbiz known as "infotainment," had been underway for years with the consequence of depoliticizing politics itself.

Soon after the initial attacks, TV reverted to form with a type of terror-tainment. Out came the graphics and stirring music as coverage became packaged with titles like "America Under Attack," "America Rising," and "America Fights Back." On the networks and in the written press an ideological mobilization took form as the attack provoked an ongoing global war against terrorism. The effects were soon noticeable as patriotism-influenced punditry and jingoism-informed journalism.

PATRIOTIC CORRECTNESS IN EFFECT

As a period of "patriotic correctness" began, self-censorship and corporate censorship snapped into place. There was a flurry of incidents—editorial writers fired for raising the wrong questions, editorial cartoonists dropped, and advertisers pulling out of a comedy show whose host made a remark that offended a conservative talk-show big mouth who mounted a campaign to drive the program off the air.

The signals had been sent. The media began marching in lock step with the government, with dissenters hard to find. A hypercompetitive and fast-consolidating media system has time and again its bottom-line free market concerns ahead of its responsibility to protect and vitalize the marketplace of ideas.

It was in the immediate aftermath of the events that I began somewhat obsessively tracking the news coverage from many sources, and its consequences in all of its variations and conformity, on a daily basis. As the editor of the world's largest online media issues network with 960 affiliates and 90 advisors led by Walter Cronkite, Mediachannel.org (http://www.mediachannel.org), I was able to read/watch/monitor coverage across borders and mediums, online and off. I began writing about the media differences and similarities, omissions and errors, attitudes and outlooks, in a daily column posted in my own writer-edited weblog. I am known in the biz as the "News Dissector," and am one organizer of the Globalvision News Network which now aggregates news content and context from hundreds of news providers on seven continents, with the goal of offering more diverse reporting.

We found that despite the media mantra that "the world has changed forever," and while some institutions and security practices changed a lot, media approaches changed the least. There was more news, of course, but much of it stuck, like a needle on a record, in the "As" (Airplane attacks, Anthrax, and Afghanistan), never reaching the rest of the alphabet, except for a few Os (Osama, Omar). At year's end, the *New York Times* devoted a major story to "Headlines From the Cutting Room Floor," referring to "key stories that were overlooked, or that might have played out differently had the world's gaze not been fixed on terrorism." (The *Times*, of course, helps fix the gaze.)

The news not in the news included the Florida presidential election, a watershed moment in American democracy. That story disappeared as "the debate shifted from 'Who won' to 'Who cares,'" acknowledged the "newspaper of record," institutionally a member of the consortium of news organizations behind a mysteriously delayed media review.

Imagine: The most disputed election in U.S. history became a footnote, rating just a few headlines, as a larger question about the content of our democracy was swept under the rug. There were many more underreported stories that weren't pursued at all in the nonstop news stream that I reported on in my column. The problem was not just the government's largely successful attempts to limit information, but the media's unwillingness to challenge or flout them.

ONE NATION UNDER TELEVISION

Why is this important? Because we live in "one nation under television," where the media is the nation's town hall and political nerve center, where the news anchors are national symbols, and the TV news screen functions like the church in which we all worship. Terrorists know that the media has more power than most politicians, especially the power to reinforce a national mood. That's why Osama Bin Laden spent so much time (and money) making videos. And that's also why politicians want the media to play the role of megaphone and rally the people to support their leaders in this hour of need.

The late media writer Ed Diamond wrote about a colleague of the political columnist Walter Lippmann (1889–1974), who he accused of "always dredging up basic principles." Noted Diamond in his book, *The Tin Gazoo:*

> "That won't do in daily journalism," the colleague explained, and offered this metaphor: A piano has eight octaves, a violin three, and a bugle only four notes. "Now if what you've got to play is a bugle," the friend concluded, "there isn't any sense in camping down in front of piano music." "You may be right," Lippmann replied. "But I am not going to spend my life writing bugle calls."

Sadly, few voices in the media understand that they have a duty to play more than bugle calls, too—especially in wartime when bugle calls rouse warriors and silence critics. One of the problems, given the lack of international coverage over the years, is that you can't blame most people for not being critical or aware. As longtime propaganda analysts Ed Herman and David Peterson write: "Thanks to the effectiveness of the U.S. propaganda system, U.S. citizens by and large are caught within the epistemic bind of not knowing that they do not know."

We live down in a mediaocracy, where the media is no longer a separate "fourth estate" functioning as an independent watchdog, but, rather, is an active participant in the policy and electoral debate. Government and media tend to synergize and interact with shared assumptions and common messages, especially on national security steps. Our mediachannel reported on three ways that this silent merger operated in tandem. There were three planks in Washington's media strategy:

First, keep critics off the air. (And not just videos of Bin Laden or al-Jazeera, which "coincidentally" had its Kabul office bombed). It soon became clear that the media were allocating little space for domestic critics, much less harder-line opponents of the policy. While administration officials condemned the ideological fundamentalism of the Taliban, a certain ideological intolerance began to be practiced in our own heavily male-dominated homeland media. Fairness and Accuracy in Reporting (FAIR) noted on November 2 that forty-four columns in the *Washington Post* and the *New York Times* stressed a military response, with only two suggesting diplomatic and international law approaches.

Second, bring the press on board. Despite a tightening of information policies and the total exclusion of reporters from most battlefields, there has been nary a critical word heard from many of those who have been loudest in defense of freedom of the press. Even a champion of freedom of the press like Walter Cronkite said he was willing to countenance a censorship board of some kind, if camera crews were allowed in to cover the war in Afghanistan. (They weren't for months and his proposal went nowhere.)

Will government media managers soon boast about what a great job they did, as they did ten years ago in the aftermath of Desert Storm? Then, Michael Deaver, President Reagan's PR honcho, was ecstatic, contending, "If you were to hire a public relations firm to do the media relations for an international event, it couldn't be done any better than this is being done." Hodding Carter, President Jimmy Carter's former chief flack, seconded the emotion: "If I were the government, I'd be paying the press for the coverage it's getting."

Yet the press—and this was a television story above all else—did not have to be paid. Pete Williams, the man who "handled" media for the Pentagon during the Gulf War and was rewarded with a job on NBC News, put his finger on it: "The reporting," he boasted to his superiors, "has been largely a recitation of what administration people have said, or an extension of it." Is this true today? Not totally. Happily, there are still some exceptions, like Seymour Hersh, who catch the Pentagon in blatant lies, as happened recently in conflicting stories about casualties U.S. troops suffered on the ground.

Third, get the West Coast studios to jump in. On the day this column was written, media moguls and movie-studio heads strategized with White House aide

Karl Rove on how they can do even more than they already have to boost the war effort. Tom Cruise is just one star who has met with the CIA; according to MSNBC.com, "He was emphatic about presenting the CIA in as positive a light as possible."

The military is quietly infiltrating Hollywood as· well. The little-known Institute for Creative Studies at the University of Southern California brings top Hollywood talent into secret contact with top military officials. The think tank received funding of $45 million from the U.S. Army in 1999. According to the *Sunday Herald*, "One of the few members named publicly, by the Hollywood newspaper *Daily Variety*, is Steven de Souza, co-writer of the hit 1988 action movie *Die Hard*." Michael Macedonia—of the Army's Simulation, Training, and Instrumentation Command—said: "You're talking about screenwriters and producers. These are very brilliant, creative people. They can come up with fascinating insights very quickly."

While movieland is key because of its global reach, the cooperation of the TV networks is vital for the engineering of consent on the domestic front. The networks have their own reasons to cooperate. Remember that while war unleashes devastation and death on people, it delivers ratings and brings life to television. War is often the big story (when sex isn't) and a defining moment for many journalists. It's the story that permits news departments to mobilize their "troops"— that's what ABC called employees when I worked there—and show off their high-tech deployments. Many reporters who make it to the top do so because of war reporting. Ask Peter Arnett, Cristianne Amanpour, or even Peter Jennings—no disrespect intended—if being under fire helped or hurt their careers. The answer is obvious. Less obvious is the relationship between our bloated defense budget and war coverage.

The Pentagon uses and manipulates TV's military boosterism to hype adventures, secure appropriations, and sell weaponry.

WORLD VIEWS

The problem in an age of globalization is that harnessing domestic media is no longer enough. The fact is that coverage outside the United States seeps back in, and despite the government's media strategists, is growing more critical and less cheerleading by the day. Growing skepticism in influential media outlets overseas is worrying to policy-makers here. On November 11, the front page of the

New York Times carried a long piece by Elizabeth Becker called "In the War on Terrorism, A Battle to Shape Opinion," reporting on the Bush administration's new strategies. The article acknowledges that the administration has enforced "policies ensuring that journalists have little or no access to independent information about military strategies, successes, and failures." But it also notes that public opinion worldwide, led in part by the press, increasingly opposes U.S. policies.

The Arab press is hostile. The Asian media, unconvinced. Over sixty percent of the people in Tony Blair's Britain, the only real partner the U.S. has in its leaky coalition, say they want a bombing pause. Half of Italy agrees. The German press is critical. Reports the *Times*, with understated candor way at the bottom of a story that consumed an acre of print, "European journalists have also become suspicious that the American news media have been co-opted by the government or at least swept up by patriotism." One German writer calls this a "Post-Vietnam Patriotic Syndrome." To massage this problem, the Bush administration has hired PR firms and created a task force for coordinating U.S. and U.K. communications directors with daily conference calls between the White House, London, and Islamabad.

As these strategies are put in effect, and as they quietly manage media practices, the space for the exercise of free speech narrows.

Hence: Crude censorship is not the main problem today. The media is.

My question is: What will it take for the civil liberties movement to recognize that it has a common interest with the growing media-reform movement? When will it begin educating its members and constituencies that freedom of the press must not be interpreted as freedom only for the press-lords and their monopolistic über-merged companies?

Criticizing media practices is not censorship. It is the work of saving democracy.

Danny Schechter, two-time Emmy Award winner, is the Executive Editor of Globalvision's Mediachannel.org and the author of The More You Watch The Less You Know *(Seven Stories Press, 1997) and* News Dissector: Passions, Pieces, and Polemics, 1960–2000 *(Akashic Books, 2001).*

THE KNOCK AT THE DOOR
by Eve Pell

> *"I think this conflict is going to require a suspension of freedom and rights unlike anything we have seen, at least since World War II."*
>
> —Marlin Fitzwater, press secretary to former President George H. W. Bush

A month after the attacks of September 11, while working out at his San Francisco gym, sixty-year-old retiree Barry Reingold mouthed off about the Bush family's links to the oil industry. Someone overhead his comments and called the FBI. Shortly afterward, two agents showed up at Reingold's condo to question him about possible links with terrorists. He declined to be interviewed. "But we have to file a report," the agent complained.

Kate Rafael, a member of an international peace group, spoke at an anti-war vigil in San Francisco on September 24. Soon after, an FBI agent left a message on her answering machine. After Rafael contacted an attorney, she says, the FBI agent then threatened to label Rafael a "non-cooperating witness" and issue her a subpoena. "I'm a Jewish lesbian," she told me. "About as unlikely an al-Qaida terrorist as you'd find."

A.J. Brown, a student in North Carolina, found agents at her door eager to inspect the "unAmerican activity" they had been told was taking place in her apartment. She did have a poster on her wall featuring George Bush and a hangman's noose, and that was what concerned them. But the poster was a protest against the large number of executions Bush had authorized as governor of Texas, and in no way a threat to the president. Nevertheless, the two agents, one from the Secret Service and one from the FBI, questioned her for forty minutes.

After September 11, President Bush shifted FBI priorities away from the investigation of crime to emphasize the prevention of terror. But, in the pursuit of this necessary goal, civil libertarians believe that agents sometimes go wide of the mark, inflicting collateral damage on Americans' constitutional rights to free speech.

Both the president and the attorney general have issued statements that appear to equate dissent with disloyalty. "Americans . . . need to watch what they say, watch what they do," said presidential press secretary Ari Fleischer, in remarks criticizing *Politically Incorrect* host Bill Maher. The president, speaking in Portland, Oregon, echoed that mind-set when he said, "Anyone who espouses a philosophy that's terrorist . . . I assure you, we will bring that person to justice." Such statements trouble Chip Berlet, senior analyst at Political Research Associates in Boston: "This administration's definition of terrorism does not differentiate between a pacifist nun and a terrorist bomber," he says.

So perhaps it is not surprising that since September 11, agents are knocking on the doors of some citizens—with no apparent connection to terror or the Middle East—who criticize the Bush administration or the war.

While the need to prevent terror is obvious, there is concern—even among conservatives—that the biggest investigation in FBI history may have the unintended effect of chilling criticism of White House policies.

In past times of crisis, our leaders often encroached on civil liberties in the name of patriotism. Just twenty years after the American Revolution, a Vermont congressman was tried for sedition after he lambasted President John Adams's "grasp for power" and "thirst for ridiculous pomp." In the Civil War, in a situation cited by President Bush to legitimize his own use of extraordinary powers, President Lincoln suspended the right of habeas corpus. During World War I, administration critics, most notably Eugene Debs, were jailed for criticizing government policy. After the Second World War, the Smith Act, targeted at Communists, was used to prosecute dissenters. More recently, during the Cold War, FBI and CIA agents spied on, infiltrated, and disrupted political protest groups.

Back in the Reagan administration, then–FBI Director William Webster had a discussion with Congressman John Conyers about dissenters who criticized U.S. policy in Central America and were contacted by the bureau. Webster said he couldn't image why anyone would object to such a visit. Conyers answered something like this: "I don't know what neighborhood you come from, sir, but in my neighborhood a visit from the FBI can result in the loss of a job or something else you don't want to happen."

Between September 11 and April 1, the Center for Investigative Reporting, using information from lawyers, civil liberties groups, and the Internet, found more than a dozen individuals across the nation—all citizens who are neither of Middle Eastern origin nor linked to violence—who had been contacted by law enforcement agents after expressing a dissenting view. (Most of those contacted by the agents had criticized U.S. policies from an anti-war, anti-corporate, pro-environment perspective. Interestingly enough, the right-wing groups whom the Center called reported no such contacts.)

But there is no way of knowing the full extent of this phenomenon, partly because some who were contacted remain silent for fear of adverse consequences. This fear worried some people we found, including a woman who opposes the administration's Cuba policy, and a lesbian pacifist. They refused to discuss the incidents at all, even when guaranteed that their identities would be protected.

Their fears are not completely unfounded. Last November, Green Party member Nancy Oden, who criticized the war in Afghanistan, arrived at the airport in Bangor, Maine, headed for a conference in Chicago. In an interview, she described being singled out for special search, then stopped by an armed soldier in the airport and forbidden to fly because her name showed up "on a list" on the airport computer. Grabbing her arm, the soldier proceeded to harangue her about politics and the war. "The war on terror is spilling over into a war on dissent," she said.

The real question at the heart of this issue is this: At what point does the intrusiveness—and perhaps carelessness and overzealousness—of the FBI investigation begin to have corrosive effects on Americans' freedom to criticize the government without fear of the knock on the door, the visit at work, the name on a list. To one person, such consequences may seem minor—to another, hugely frightening.

Political Research Associates analyst Chip Berlet warns that the freedom to speak out is no small thing: "This administration's reaction to dissent is what the Founders tried to protect us against with the Constitution and the Bill of Rights." As the Supreme Court has written, this freedom is "the matrix, the indispensable condition of nearly every other form of freedom."

Eve Pell works at the Center for Investigative Reporting in San Francisco, California. For further information about the Center for Investigative Reporting, visit their website at www.muckraker.org. Pell is also the author of a book on free speech and censorship, The Big Chill *(Beacon Press, 1984)—alas, not nearly so successful as the movie of that name—and has written about civil liberties issues for many years. She is a nationally ranked senior runner.*

AGAINST A TWENTY-FIRST-CENTURY STAR CHAMBER
by Jeremy Voas

No journalist ever covets the prospect of making news. We'd rather observe and chronicle the newsmakers, and rightly so.

Yet in the wake of the terror attacks of September 11, 2001, the government began arresting aliens and barring public access to the process of their adjudication. It became clear that something had to be done to pry open the lid that had been capriciously clamped on.

That's why I lent the name of the publication I edit, the alternative newsweekly *Metro Times of Detroit*, to a lawsuit that challenged the constitutionality of the government's star chamber proceedings.

My publication joined U.S. Representative John Conyers (D-Detroit) and the *Detroit News* to force the light of public scrutiny onto the shadowy actions of our government. The American Civil Liberties Union filed the case on our behalf. Other newspapers filed similar complaints. The detention and attempted deportation of a Michigan resident provided the avenue for the challenge.

Rabih Haddad, forty-one, a citizen of Lebanon, was arrested December 14 in front of his wife and four children at their apartment in Ann Arbor. The U.S. Immigration and Naturalization Service accused Haddad of overstaying his tourist visa. Haddad, who holds an advanced engineering degree from the University of Nebraska, has lived and worked in the U.S. off and on for twenty years.

The fact that he had dutifully applied to remain in the United States under an amnesty program did not stop the INS from throwing him into solitary confinement and barring his family, the public, and the press from his "removal" hearings. The government even forbade Haddad from attending the hearings—he watched and listened via closed-circuit TV from his cell.

The immigration judge presiding over his case denied bail to Haddad. Haddad's attorney says the judge cited Haddad's ownership of a firearm, and we must take his word for it. The judge has not publicly justified her decision and the hearing at which bail was denied was conducted in secret. That's because the INS, acting on orders from U.S. Attorney General John Ashcroft, has arbitrarily (and unconstitutionally, in my view) decreed that such proceedings must be closed in the name of national security. To allow the public and the press access would compromise the investigation into the terror attacks.

Which is, of course, rubbish.

Ashcroft's edict to close all immigration hearings involving virtually anyone of Middle Eastern descent inspired a September 21 memo by Chief Immigration Judge David Creppy that states, in part:

> The attorney general has implemented additional security procedures for certain cases in the Immigration Court. Those procedures require us to hold the hearings individually, to close the hearings to the public, and to avoid discussing the case or otherwise disclosing any information about the case to anyone outside the Immigration Court . . .
>
> Each of these cases is to be heard separately from all other cases. The courtroom must be closed for these cases—no visitors, no family, and no press.

No way.

Sweeping actions like Ashcroft's are, in a word, unAmerican. They undermine public confidence in government and further reduce the United States to the plane of the radical and allegedly barbaric regimes we seem intent on bombing and/or reforming and/or exploiting.

The attorney general's overzealous acts have even rankled his own subordinates within the INS. The nation's 221 immigration judges have asked Congress to free them from Ashcroft's yoke. They desire an independent immigration court under a separate executive branch agency, instead of the Justice Department. Such reform would clip Ashcroft's wings, removing him from the position of being both chief prosecutor and chief judge.

The government insists that Haddad's case is purely an immigration matter.

Which is, of course, more rubbish.

Haddad, you see, helped found a nonprofit organization called Global Relief Foundation (GRF) in Chicago a decade ago. Since then, the GRF claims to have raised more than $20 million for emergency relief, education, and aid to people in twenty-two countries, including Chechnya, Albania, Jordan, Iraq,

China, Ethiopia, and the Palestinian-occupied territories.

Haddad's friends say he had forsaken his engineering aspirations to devote his life to Islam. In addition to his work for GRF, he served as a leader of a mosque in Ann Arbor, a position from which he publicly decried the carnage wrought on September 11. He made numerous appearances before civic groups in the months following the terror attacks to explain the tenets of his faith to many uninformed Americans.

The government says it suspects that GRF has funneled money to terrorist organizations. Yet it does not have enough evidence to add the group to a list of 168 organizations suspected to be directly linked to funding terrorism. It insists that Haddad's detention in solitary confinement is not related to the investigation of GRF, which, not coincidentally, had its Chicago-area offices raided and its assets frozen on the day of Haddad's arrest.

Our participation in the lawsuit against Ashcroft, et al. should not be viewed as an endorsement of Haddad, his immigration status, or the GRF.

The truth is, we simply don't know.

But we—and you—have a right to find out. Hence, the lawsuit.

It's a travesty—a stain on the flag—that it's taking litigation to learn what our government is doing in the people's name. Fortunately, we have found one sympathetic ear. On April 3 in Detroit, U.S. District Court Judge Nancy Edmunds ruled in our favor, declaring the INS closed-hearing policy unconstitutional and ordering the INS to open future hearings in Haddad's case. Edmunds also said the government must turn over evidence introduced and transcripts of his prior hearings.

The government refused to do so and is appealing Edmunds's ruling, which states in part, "It is important for the public, particularly individuals who feel that they are being targeted by the government as a result of the terrorist attacks of September 11, to know that even during these sensitive times the government is adhering to immigration procedures and respecting individuals' rights. Openness is necessary for the public to maintain confidence in the value and soundness of the government's actions, as secrecy only breeds suspicion as to why the government is proceeding against Haddad and aliens like him."

It's poetic justice that Edmunds was appointed to the federal bench by the first President Bush.

Jeremy Voas is an editor at the Detroit Metro Times.

EXCERPT FROM "GET YOUR WAR ON" BY DAVID REES

David Rees is the creator of "My New Fighting Technique is Unstoppable" and "My New Filing Technique is Unstoppable." He lives in New York City with his wife.

PART 5

LOOK AT IT THIS WAY . . .

WHAT THE HELL DO I KNOW, ANYWAY?
by Robert Greenwald

As a director and producer of theatrical and television films, I am of course accustomed to criticism, insults, and attacks. I was nonetheless taken aback at the venom of the response when people learned that I was editing this book.

Who was I to question our government's actions in the wake of September 11?

"The times are too dangerous." "We need only one voice." "We need only military or government experts." "You are helping the terrorists." "Yes, we need civil liberties, but not at the risk of our lives." Etc., etc., etc.

In my world of film and television, I saw a ferocious kind of self-censorship quickly setting in. Suddenly everyone was an expert on what the "public" wanted or didn't want. And the immediate consensus was clearly that nothing critical of the United States should or would pass muster. Anything deemed "unpatriotic" that was "in the can" was delayed or shelved. New ideas and projects in the works were examined under a microscope—with a lens of fear and concern and second-guessing.

The decision-makers with the power to dictate what audiences watch determined that the people—a generic, unified, patriotic "PUBLIC"—did not want to see anything challenging the actions of our government. And so we had Danny Glover getting attacked, Bill Maher castigated, and a disc jockey fired—all in the name of "giving the people what they want."

The idea of a book on civil liberties began to have a very real and specific connection to my life, and the lives of my children. And as time has progressed, we have seen that, indeed, mistakes are being made. Surprise—government officials, FBI leaders, and CIA workers have all made mis-steps and miscalculations. So the need for the non-experts to question, probe, and poke, with humor, music, and poetry—to hoist the flag of democracy—has become essential. (See, for example, the contributions in this volume from Steve Earle, Ani DiFranco, and Matt Groening.)

It is true: I don't know what the hell I'm talking about. But that doesn't mean that we don't need as many people as possible, in as many ways as possible, asking questions about things *they* too don't understand. It would be a tragedy if all the poets, artists, cartoonists, composers, and authors were silenced.

What the hell do I know? I know that now is not the time to shut up.

Robert Greenwald has produced and/or directed more than forty-five television, cable, and theatrical films, including the award-winning NBC-TV movie The Burning Bed, *and the recent theatrical film,* Steal This Movie, *about Abbie Hoffman. Through his newly formed "Public Interest Productions," Greenwald is executive producing* Unprecedented—*a documentary about the 2000 election. Greenwald is on the Board of Directors of "A Place Called Home," a gang-prevention program in South Central Los Angeles, and of the Venice Community Housing Corporation, which provides low-income housing in Los Angeles. He also works with "Homies Unidos," a gang-violence prevention and intervention program with projects in El Salvador and Los Angeles.*

ALL I AM SAYING IS GIVE WAR A CHANCE:
THE PRIVATE CORRESPONDENCE BETWEEN MICHAEL MOORE AND GEORGE W. BUSH
by Michael Moore

After the attack and mass murder of September 11, 2001, I spent a lot of time in front of my television set waiting for our revenge—massive, all-out, relentlessly bloody revenge. But nothing was happening. Was W a bigger wimp than his father? What kind of message were we sending to the rest of the world by not immediately going somewhere and bombing somebody, anybody, to smithereens?

Fortunately, by the first week in October, the rockets were red-glare and true Americans all across the fruited plain were cheering The Leader on—including me . . .

October 5, 2001

Dear George W,

It's about time! I was beginning to worry that you didn't have it in you, that you might take off on Air Force One again and spend the day hiding in Omaha. But finally, at last, the bombs are raining down on Afghanistan and, as Martha Stewart would say, that's a damn good thing.

Oh, don't get me wrong—I deplore war and killing and violence. But, hey, I'm a pragmatist, I know where I live. This is America and dammit, somebody's ass had to get kicked!

You, our Leader, are a former part-owner of a baseball club, and you could have easily waited one more day until the baseball season was over. But no! You have your priorities straight! Poor Barry Bonds—will anyone even remember what he did a month from now? (At least Fox had the good grace to get the football game back on the tube within an hour of the war's start! They KNEW none of us could stomach looking at Stepford Drones from Fox News for the rest of the day.)

I have tried to tell all my fellow liberals, lefties, Greens, and working stiffs, plus those lovable Gore voters and all the other recovering Democrats, why I think this war on Afghanistan is good for us. Feel free to use ANY of these reasons in convincing the American people why you are doing an honorable thing . . .

1. We Now Have Network Unanimity in Coming Up With a Name for This War. It has been so confusing the past four weeks, what with all the networks calling the battle we are in by so many names: "America's New War," "America Under Attack," "America Fights Back," and "America . . . Why You Hate Us So?" Finally, the media has settled on just the right moniker: "America, Pissed and Proud."

I like this because it shows our complex makeup. It says, essentially, that we are "pissed"—but then, it also says we are "proud." We are not a one-dimensional people. "America Strikes Back" sounded too much like "The Empire Strikes Back." "Empire" is a scary word, and there's no use reminding the rest of the world that we call all the shots.

2. We Can Now Go Back to What We Were Doing. I don't know about you, but nearly four weeks of anxious and tense anticipation of what would happen next was starting to wear me down. I thought nothing could top spending the entire summer agonizing over who the father of the baby was on *Friends*.

The last four weeks were worse than a bad classic-rock drum solo. NOW we have resolution. NOW we know the ending—the bombing to bits of a country so advanced it has, to date, laid a total of eighteen miles of railroad tracks throughout the entire country! How very nineteenth-century of them! I hope our missiles were able to take them out. I don't want this thing going on forever. Best that we obliterate them before they come up with some smart idea like the telegraph.

3. Dick Cheney Has Been Moved Into Hiding Again. That can only help. The further this mastermind can be kept from you, George, the better. He's like that creepy friend of your dad's who has taken a bit too much of a shine to you. Wait—he *is* that creepy friend of your dad's! Anytime I hear they have transported Cheney out of town and into a bunker in the woods, I feel safe.

4. Rush Limbaugh, Bill O'Reilly, and Orrin Hatch Will All Be Fighting This War for Us! These are all honorable men, men of their word, men who would not expect someone else to fight their

battles for them. They have all called for war, revenge, blood—and, by God, it is blood I want them to have! Now that we are at war, let us insist that those who have cried the loudest for the killing be the first to go and do just that!

I would like to see Rush, Bill, Orrin, and the rest of their colleagues head down to the recruiting station and join the U.S. Army. Sure, I know they are no longer young, but there are many jobs they will be able to do once they get through the Khyber Pass. Surely these men would not expect our sons and daughters to die for something that they themselves would not be willing to die for? To make it easy, guys, you can just go to the army's website right now! (http://www.goarmy.com/index02.htm) Get your butts over there to Afghanistan and *defend a way of life that allows companies like Boeing to get rid of 30,000 people* while using the tragedy in New York as their *shameful* excuse for their actions.

5. Really Cool War Footage. It's been way too long since we've been able to watch those cruise missiles and smart bombs with their little cameras on them sail in and blow the crap out of a bunch of human beings. This time, let's hope the video is in color and that it's attached with a miniature set of Dolby microphones so we can hear the screams and wails of those Afghans as our shrapnel guts them into strips of bacon. Oh, and let's pray the video can be loaded into my Sony Playstation!!

6. Better a Permanent War Than a Quickie One. Orwell taught us about this. The Leader, in order to control the population, knew that it was necessary for the people to always believe they were in a state of siege, that the enemy was getting closer and closer, and that the war would take a very long time.

That is EXACTLY what you need to tell the people, George. You need to continually whip us into such a state of fear and panic that we will gladly give up the cherished freedoms that our fathers and those before them fought and died for. Who wouldn't submit to searches, restrictions of movement, and the rounding up of anyone who looks suspicious if it would prevent another September 11?

In order to get these laws passed that will *strip us of our rights*, you must constantly remind us that we are in a LONG and PROTRACTED war that has no end in sight.

As I'm sure you must agree, there are many upsides to this war. Sure, the Emmys got canceled again, and, as a nominee this year, I already found out that I wasn't getting one of those little gold people so who cares if I can't walk down the red carpet in my Bob Mackie gown? I don't even wear a gown—I wear pants, ill-fitting pants at that! Yesiree, I say, BOMBS AWAY! Bombs bursting in air! We are all WHITE WITH FOAM!

And please, dear George, do not get distracted by the fact that the last time a Bush took us to war and got a ninety-percent approval rating, he was toast and a ghost the following year. You can surely do better than that!

Yours,
Michael Moore
#1 Fan of the Texas Air National Guard

* * * *

In less than two months, the Taliban were defeated. OK, maybe they just shaved off their beards and said they weren't Taliban anymore. I dunno. Nonetheless, I felt compelled to send another letter to the White House and congratulate W for his heroic efforts on behalf of freedom-loving people everywhere north of Tallahassee . . .

December 18, 2001

Dear George, Conqueror of Evildoers,

Hats off to you, sir, for a job well done! The Soviets tried for ten years to do what it took you only two months to accomplish in Afghanistan. How did you do that? It's funny how a couple months ago there were all these Taliban, and now—there aren't any! You must be some kind of super magician—almost as good at disappearing acts as ol' Osama (or, as they say on the Fox Nuisance Channel, "Usama"—I like their spelling better, "We put the 'U.S.A' in U.S.Ama!"). He did exist, didn't he? I would hate to have gotten myself all worked up over the wrong evildoer! I loved that last tape of his, the home video of his sleepover with that sheik. What a party animal, that guy!

And how 'bout that Northern Alliance! Thanks to them, my weekly supply of heroin will finally be reinstated. Whoo-hoo—and just in time for New Year's Rockin' Eve! Those Taliban simply did NOT have the best delivery system for the stuff, kinda like why you never see Beman's gum anymore—poor distribution and shelf placement. According to the *New York Times*, the Northern Alliance has put all the poppy farmers back to work, and they are promising a "bumper crop" by spring.

But Mr. Bush, I am most impressed with how you have used those who died on September 11 to justify your lining the pockets of your rich friends and campaign contributors. Your "Economic Stimulus Bill"—pure genius! You actually got the House of Representatives to pass a bill eliminating the law that said corporations have to pay at least a token minimum tax every year.

See, most people forget that back in your daddy's day (when he was VP), thousands of companies were able to lawyer their way out of paying any taxes at all! Then a law was passed to stop that. Now you got the House to agree to give all these corporations back ALL the minimum taxes they have paid since 1986!! That's $140 billion of givebacks ($1.4 billion to IBM, a billion to Ford, $800 million to GM, etc.). And you got this passed, all under the guise of "September 11"! How do you get away with this without the American public whoopin' your behind? Man, you are THE MAN!

Oh, and tell your top sheriff, Big John Ashcroft, that his refusal to let the FBI look at the files of the gun background checks that the Justice Department keeps—to see if any of the terrorists or suspected terrorists purchased weapons in the past two years—boy, that took some balls! Even though checking those files might turn up information that could protect us in possible future attacks, Ashcroft was more concerned with not upsetting the NRA than in helping his own FBI catch the bad guys. Now that's what I call getting your priorities straight. Big John may have lost his Senate seat last year to a dead guy, but he sure as heck ain't gonna lose me as a huge admirer!

Well, I better go before someone from the Office of Homeland Security mistakes me for someone who needs to be "interviewed"! Rest assured, I'm doing my part for the country by shopping my sorry ass off in this week before Christmas. Buy! Buy! Buy! Tora! Tora! Tora! Whoo-hoo, Prince O' Peace!! Fight Team Fight! Go get 'em, George, Jr.—we're counting on you to kill all evildoers!

Yours,
Michael Moore
Thirteenth in Line to the King of Afghanistan

p.s. By the way, sir—you'll beat that Enron rap, just like you beat all your other raps! Chin up! Who needs "energy traders," anyway? I never saw that job on the list from my high school counselor!!

Michael Moore's recent book, Stupid White Men . . . and Other Sorry Excuses for the State of the Nation *(Regan Books, 2002), reached the top of the* New York Times Book Review *chart. His 1989 documentary about General Motors,* Roger and Me, *was a huge success. He was formerly Executive Editor of* Mother Jones *and is a frequent guest on many network and cable talk shows.*

CIVIL LIBERTIES AND BARE BREASTS: ME AND MY JOHN POST–SEPTEMBER 11
by Janna Malamud Smith

My fantasy life has taken a bizarre turn post–September 11. I've started dreaming about a protest march. I call it the Million Babe Bare-Breasted March on the Justice Department. I've now talked it up enough that at least one male in my household is calling it the Million Boob March. This pithy handle in turn caused a friend to observe the good news: If the name holds, we'll need only 500,000 women to travel to Washington (give or take our mastectomied legions) and parade up Pennsylvania Avenue, blouses, bras, and, very possibly, vanity flung to the wind. In case you wondered, our mission is to rip the curtains from the two female statues of justice in the Great Hall of the United States Justice Department that Attorney General Ashcroft or one of his minions ordered covered. We are going to liberate them, allow them to show tit; to flash again: fried eggs on glass.

I take their confinement very personally. I resent it just the way I resent the Taliban forcing Afghani women to wear burqas. Indeed, I admit there were days this past winter when I felt a little confused about where, sexually and puritanically speaking, the Taliban ended and Attorney General Ashcroft began. Their opposite worldviews seem to have uncanny unconscious common ground. Not long after the Taliban idiotically (and tragically) exploded the ancient Buddhas from the rock face in Bamiyan, John Ashcroft's department spent $8,650 (merely idiotically; first time tragedy, second time farce) buying curtains to cover over the two statues, "Spirit of Justice" and "Majesty of Justice," that since the 1930s have welcomed visitors into the U.S. Justice Building.

The bit of bare breast one statue sported apparently made the attorney general uncomfortable. John, big guy, I hate to be the one to drop this idea on you, but democracy *is* uncomfortable. Power can be opposed. Read accounts of early American presidents—George Washington, John Adams—and they have moments of gnashing their teeth, cursing that no one treats them like kings. Rightly so. Democratic is not just the NRA and Enron-graft buying you office, democratic is messy: it's dis and backtalk. The bare-breasted, ogled g-string girl can walk out of the strip joint into the great public hall, jump onto a platform, and have her say. She can run for office. She can sell her john-list to the *Enquirer*. Girls have rights. Enemies of all stripes have rights. It's a brave new world, John. And its delicate, hard-won liberties are precious.

Oh, I know that curtains aren't dynamite. And it may well be that such fine points are the mundane but exact definition of what distinguishes a democratic country from a totalitarian one. I can appreciate that. What's more, I understand perfectly that if I had attempted to publish this piece in Afghanistan under the Taliban, I'd have been killed. Or, at best, had fingers chopped off—like women caught using nail polish. I comprehend the chasm between liberty and unliberty, especially as a woman. *Vive la différence,* I say. Indeed, I feel grateful to my fore-bears who had the courage and desperation to pack their bags and jump onto boats so that I could be born here. I recite with pride the opening of the Declaration of Independence; and I believe that the Bill of Rights is our glory. I say these things not out of braggadocio, but sincerely, even urgently; I am trying to stake out a patriotism based in neither jingoism nor blind obedience.

More to the point, will the best, most inspiring aspects of our country survive the current fight against terrorism? Civil liberties tend to get constricted during times of war, but how much today is really justified by, or efficacious against, external danger? Right now, the chemotherapy that the administration is aiming at the terrorist cancer seems too poisonous for the job: new limits on attorney-client privilege, new prisoner-of-war rules at Guantanamo, new self-proclaimed mandates to sweep up and question anyone whose skin has melanin, new military tribunals, new warnings about what constitutes disloyalty. But more than any single act there's an appalling "we're good/they're bad" entitlement. Whatever invaders this chemo kills, the drug is inadequately selective, the collateral damage ugly, leading me some days to ponder the quality of life post-cure.

Reading David McCullough's biography of John Adams, I started to wonder if American democracy, however flawed and compromised it's always been, will someday be recalled as a brief moment between tyrannies. What if, when the Bostonians tossed the taxed tea into the harbor, the British had had modern surveillance techniques and DNA testing? I've read enough colonial history to appreciate that the guys flinging Red Rose resembled George Bush as much as

Abbie Hoffman. Yet, what if Ashcroft had been the Crown's attorney general in Massachusetts in 1770 and had possessed all the privacy-invading wiretaps and other high-tech spy resources he now has? Sam Adams would have been hanged as a traitor, and god knows what eventually would have become of John A., or George, or Thomas J.

Privacy is necessary for democracy; secrecy harms it. Writing a book about privacy several years ago, I learned indelibly, as Alan Westin observes in his classic treatise *Privacy and Freedom,* that the essential method of totalitarianism is to keep its own actions secret while putting everyone else under surveillance. Ashcroft is a curtainer. He wants to hide things that should be visible, and at the same time spy on others. He's a peephole man. He's an elder peering into Susannah's bath. What a tragedy it would be if our post–September 11 fear made us into unwitting totalitarians as we sought to protect the American way. What if we killed the girl-liberty we loved by jealous rants, stalking, and paranoia that, Othello-like, finally placed her in a deadly, suffocating stranglehold? As long as you're dating me, baby, you're not going out in public like that. Cover your breast! And speak only when I tell you to!

What will become of the extraordinary First Amendment if we stop using it? If, fearful, we censor ourselves into passive silence and complicity? If we fail to appreciate how much the price of liberty is, indeed, eternal vigilance? If we stop trying, however imperfectly, to speak truth to power? In perhaps the most staggering moment of his tenure to date, on December 6, 2001, the attorney general righteously pummeled the feeble Senate panel that had called him to testify; he had the audacity to declare that questioning leaders' judgments during a time of war was a tactic that could "only aid terrorists." His interlocutors immediately went belly up, and in their supine state could manage only loud sucking noises for the rest of the encounter. My dear senators, you have failed me miserably. Whatever happened to the loyal opposition? Power avoids corruption only through dialectic and resistance. Impudence is safety. Irreverence is respect.

Even before September 11, in January 2001 when George W. Bush was inaugurated and my husband and I went to Washington with friends to protest the instatement of a president who had not won an election, you had to wonder about liberty. We were permitted to march along a carefully designated route. But military helicopters swooped in low over our heads to intimidate; heavily armed soldiers blocked our way if we sought to approach the day's events;

snipers stood above us on rooftops. My husband teaches high school. I'm a psychotherapist and social worker. We're middle-aged and a little creaky. What is so frightening about us or our compatriots that we required armed guards and corrals? For all the John Wayne posturing of the guys in power, stronger leaders would have known to welcome us, would have blessed our presence: two, four, six, eight, it's democracy we celebrate. Underneath the simian grunts and hunk chest-pounding, one fears one is observing frightened men.

There is something almost gorgeously primitive about hanging a curtain over a breast. It's not unlike sticking pins in a voodoo doll, or eating a piece (let's not say which) of your enemy to consume and assume his power. And primitive is the name of the current game. Black and white. Good and evil. Them and us. Yes, there is evil. Yes, it must be opposed everywhere. But isn't it really one of life's great mysteries? How does it take root in a person or nation? What let the world remain indifferent as Belgian overlords slaughtered millions of helpless, enslaved Congolese? Why did no one care when the Turks killed a million and a half innocent Armenians? And on and on. What sets a genocide in motion? What makes a terrorist pick up a box-cutter? How can we stop these terrible human behaviors? Have we no tools but guns, bombs, prisons, and censorship? "When all you have is a hammer," someone said, "everything begins to look like nails." Or, as Pogo so rightly observed, "I have seen the enemy, and them is us." Yes, some safety resides in military strength. But it is one strand of a complex braid which includes social justice, empathy for the other's perspective, a large appreciation of shades of gray and subtleties, protection of civil rights, and an ability to appreciate one's own contribution to creating a situation. What's more, safety comes from encouraging conversation. From listening carefully, even when what you hear is alien and distasteful. From letting skin show, even baring a breast.

When leaders are frightened, they become brittle and blunted; they lose flexibility, assume messianic demeanors, insist that God is on their side. Subtleties become something for traitors or sissies. It's understandable, but it's not a good thing. There may be moments when dissent has to tone down to a whisper, when freedoms are rightly cauterized or constricted. But if so, such actions must be taken reluctantly, temporarily, with sadness, gravity, self-awareness, and great care. The crowd of witnesses must gather; the grief must be genuine; a lone, mournful bugler needs to play, slowly. And then, into the silent aftermath, let the bereaved unfurl their long, loud wail.

Had the attorney general shed even one tear as his aides hung the curtains, I would have felt our civil liberties safe for now from terrorism's insidious effects. As it is, I say, let the band strike up "Yankee Doodle." Patriots unbutton and present breasts! Apply your sun block! Ready, set, MARCHONS CITOYENNES!

Janna Malamud Smith is a clinical social worker and psychotherapist, and is the daughter of Bernard Malamud. She is the author of Private Matters: In Defense of the Personal Life *(Perseus, 1997) and* A Potent Spell: Mother Love and the Power of Fear *(forthcoming from Houghton Mifflin).*

AN OPEN LETTER TO SENATOR JOSEPH LIEBERMAN AND LYNNE CHENEY
by Martin J. Sherwin

Dear Dr. Cheney and Senator Lieberman,

On November 11, the American Council of Trustees and Alumni (ACTA), an organization you co-founded in 1995, issued a report that listed the names of academics, along with 117 statements they made in public forums or in classes, that questioned aspects of the administration's war on terrorism. Concluding that "College and university faculty have been the weak link in America's response to the attack," the report asked alumni to bring their (presumed) displeasure about these views to the attention of university administrations. While ACTA's report does not have the cachet of President Nixon's "Enemies List," nor the intimidating force (yet?) of Senator Joseph McCarthy's too-numerous-to-list lists, as an American historian I am naturally interested in this project, and I have decided to offer your organization my full cooperation.

Therefore, as an example to my colleagues, I am stepping forward to name a name, my own—Martin J. Sherwin, the Walter S. Dickson Professor of English and American History at Tufts University in Medford, Massachusetts—and to tattle on myself. On December 3, 2001, I remarked to a class at Tufts University studying World War II that there was an ominous resemblance between the sense of panic in 1942 that produced Executive Order 9066, permitting the internment of American citizens of Japanese ancestry, and the post–9/11 atmosphere that supported the Justice Department's arrest of hundreds of Muslims.

Later, on December 6, after hearing Attorney General John Ashcroft assert before the Senate Judiciary Committee that civil liberties critics "aid terrorists . . . erode our national unity, and diminish our resolve," I told my class that Mr. Ashcroft had bolstered my resolve to diminish his effort to remake our public discourse in the image of Pinochet's Chile—even if senators who were equally shocked were too cowed at that moment to challenge such an unAmerican attitude. Surrendering the liberties that define the unique character of our nation will not help us to win the war on terrorism, I noted; on the contrary, it will only erode the constitutional foundation upon which the political strength of our nation rests. The attorney general's defense of military commissions (secret trials) in the United States in 2002—even to try suspected terrorists—is an affront to those who fought and died to protect our freedoms in World War II. I recommended that students read Robert Sherrill's book, *Military Justice Is to Justice As Military Music Is to Music.*

Finally, Dr. Cheney and Senator Lieberman, I implore you as the Founding Mother and Father of ACTA to exert your influence to assure that in the next report Martin J. Sherwin is correctly spelled. Having been too young to be of interest to Senator Joseph McCarthy, and having been embarrassed by my absence from President Nixon's "Enemies List," ACTA's list may be my last opportunity to publicly document my deep love for my country. When my grandchild asks, "What did you do during the 'War on Terrorism,' Grandpa?" I will say, "Harry, I spoke out in order to preserve for you and your friends the best things about America. You can read what I said in the ACTA report of . . ." (date as yet unspecified).

In closing, I call on my colleagues to put political bias aside and assist the organization that Dr. Cheney and Senator Lieberman created; after all, they are one of us: She is a PhD and he claims to be a liberal. You can now tattle on yourself in great company. *The Nation* will post appropriate critical remarks on a new section of its website: "Tattletales for an Open Society" (TAOS). If you are genuinely uncertain whether a specific remark actually crossed the threshold of acceptable criticism, err on the side of caution: Submit the remark to *The Nation*'s tattletale page and give ACTA a chance to determine whether you should be published. Send your submissions to tattletales@thenation.com.

Martin J. Sherwin

p.s. Kai Bird and I are writing a biography of J. Robert Oppenheimer, whose secret security hearing in 1954 is instructive in these matters.

Dr. Martin J. Sherwin is Professor of History and Director of the Nuclear Age History & Humanity Center at Tufts University. He is the author of A World

Destroyed: Hiroshima and the Origins of the Arms Race *(Vintage, 1987), a 1976 runner-up for the Pulitzer Prize. This letter originally appeared as an advertisement in the January 21, 2002, issue of* The Nation.

THE POLITICS OF RETRIBUTION
by Steve Earle

I live with a woman who hates television. She abhors the noise and the unnatural light that pollute the delicious, tranquil environment that she has painstakingly crafted for herself and her family; so I wasn't watching the news on the morning on September 11.

Then the phone rang. It was my dad.

"Have you seen this shit?"

I asked what he was talking about.

"This shit in New York. A plane just crashed into the World Trade Center."

I found the remote and hit the switch. Black, noxious smoke poured from a gaping whole in one of the Twin Towers. CNN was already reporting that witnesses said that the plane appeared to fly directly into the building under its own power. My dad, a retired air traffic controller and licensed pilot, was way ahead of them.

"No way this is an accident."

He meant that it was inconceivable to him that a crew of at least two professional pilots would allow a plane with several hundred passengers aboard to simply careen out of control and strike the tallest structure in the Manhattan skyline.

I wasn't so sure; or maybe I was in denial. Then the second plane hit and we both saw it. Hell, half the country saw it. We all watched in horror as the airliner practically stood on one wing, nearly missing the north tower. My dad said that whoever was flying it must have been "really wracking it" to make that final, fatal turn.

The news only got worse. There were unconfirmed reports of hijackings up and down the East Coast. By the time CNN reported that the Pentagon had been attacked as well, Dad and I weren't talking much. We kept the line open, if only to assure ourselves that the other was still there. When first one tower and then the other collapsed we watched in stunned silence. I can only imagine what was going through my dad's mind. Everything we had witnessed that morning flew in the face of everything he thought he knew about aviation, and for that matter, humanity. I remember vividly what was going through mine.

Thousands of people were dying while millions watched on television. I am certain that, for an instant, we were all connected and focused on the people in those three buildings and four airliners and their families. For me, the moment was fleeting and soon gave way to my own agenda, both personal and political. How will all of this affect me and mine?

I realized, of course, that we were at war. I have a draft-age son. I asked my dad to let me go and rang Justin's phone until he woke up. I told him to turn on the news and to stay in touch.

I have friends in New York. Were they all right? I made several calls, but of course the lines were all busy. It would be days before I knew the answer to that one.

The checklist was long. While I struggled to reconcile my every fundamental belief against a world that would never be the same, public officials began to weigh in on TV. I found their unity and tough talk unnerving somehow and oddly familiar. A vague uneasiness began to settle over me like a pall. I tried to be methodical and stay on task, but my mind was racing and looming ahead was the insistently gnawing realization that the country was in a mood for revenge, and that years of work by death penalty abolitionists all over the world, tough thankless work that was finally starting to bear fruit, had just gone up in smoke.

I oppose the death penalty for anyone, for any crime, regardless of circumstances, on both moral and political grounds. I've attended candlelight vigils outside prisons, gone to rallies on the steps of my state capitol, and camped out on the sidewalk in front of the U.S. Supreme Court. I've corresponded with several death row inmates over the years. I have crisscrossed the country, traveling with murder victims' family members who oppose the death penalty; yeah, you read it right the first time. People who have lost a loved one to violent crime and who actively oppose the death penalty. They reject the idea that retribution is the remedy for their loss and their pain. They say "not in my name" when society at large (in this, and a handful of other countries) suggests that the taking of another life will afford them closure and healing. From these amazing people I learned the greatest lesson of my life as an activist: that no person or group of people will ever bring about fundamental change in the criminal justice system in this country by ignoring the pain and loss of crime victims and their families.

The human components of that system, the prosecutors who aspire to be district attorneys who aspire to be state attorney generals who aspire to be governors and presidents, have been aware of this dynamic for some time. They watch the polls and the polls tell them that the majority of us still support the death penalty. Obviously, victim's rights advocates and death penalty abolitionists, combined, comprise a tiny minority of the electorate. As passionate as activists on both sides of the issue can be, it isn't rhetoric that our leaders are responding to. Rather, it is our empathy. Ask the question, "What if it was your wife, your child, your mother, or father?" and you will elicit a nearly unanimous, emotional response. Thankfully, most of us will never lose a member of our families to violence, but we know that it's not impossible, and we hold a special place in our hearts for those that have been less fortunate than ourselves for we know that there, but for the grace of God, go we.

On September 11, we all became victims' family members. The scope of the tragedy was unprecedented in our history. Nearly three thousand lives were lost. Thousands more were widowed and tens of thousands were orphaned. Entire battalions of firefighters were wiped out, along with scores of police officers, ambulance drivers, and other first responders. Even they were innocent victims, just regular people going about their everyday lives. They all had hopes and dreams and aspirations. When they died their families became our families. Their loss and their pain became our loss and pain. We became them and they became us.

Loss alone is hard enough to process. Dealing with death and loss are at the core of virtually every spiritual system that has evolved on this planet. When death comes suddenly and cruelly, those left behind must deal with anger as well. Anger that, like a fever, is perfectly natural and must be allowed to run its course before any healing can commence. However, that selfsame anger is inherently toxic, and if allowed to smolder unabated, will exact a terrible toll in flesh and spirit.

The very concept of retribution as a healing force is, in my view, inherently faulty. Politicians embrace it only because they have learned that we will respond to it emotionally at the ballot box. My growing fear since September 11 is that they, sensing our anger, may be applying the same principle to the so-called "war on terror."

As we prepared to send American troops into the mountains of Afghanistan, no politician dared to object for fear of impaling his political ambitions on an olive branch in a decidedly warlike political climate. Only one, Congresswoman Barbara Lee of California, voted against an emergency defense spending measure that granted the Bush administration a virtual blank check to cover the costs of a protracted campaign in a theater of war that bankrupted the Soviet Union. Some of our most "liberal" legislators voted for the oddly titled Patriot Act, a sweeping suspension of many of the protections against unlawful search and seizure and invasion of privacy afforded us by our Constitution. They all knew that we were watching them and that we were hurt and frightened and that we would remember what they did and said in the name of the People come Election Day. For fully half of them, that day was a little over a year away and at the party level, the balance of power in both houses of Congress would be at stake. They tell us that extraordinary times call for extraordinary measures. They say that this war with no clear objective except, in the words of our president, "to get 'em," will protect us from violent people who would do us harm. They say the same thing about the death penalty. Never mind that there is no statistical evidence to support any claim that capital punishment deters violent crime. The truth is that when we are hurt and angry, just saying that we are going to go out and "get 'em" feels good. Then we're supposed to move past anger, to mourning, and then on to healing, but these are the more private stages of the grieving process, and a lot less easy to convert into political capital.

As far as the Constitution is concerned, it is my belief that it is crucial at this point in our history to remember that, like me, our attorney general has his own agenda. He's concerned about abortion, gay marriages, and evolution being taught in our schools. Of course, all that will have to wait. We are at war, after all, and that darn Constitution is always getting in the way. But, hey, if this war goes on long enough . . . who knows?

Steve Earle is one of the most respected singer/songwriters of this era. He writes politically profound country music as well as bluegrass, and has been a passionate opponent of the death penalty.

PART 6

DETENTIONS AND RIGHTS

IS THIS A DARK AGE FOR FUNDAMENTAL LEGAL PROTECTION?
by Michael Ratner

INTRODUCTION

I am writing this article in unimaginable times. Since September 11 of last year, I have watched with shock and dismay as rights and legal protections embedded in the U.S. Constitution and in international law have been swept aside by a so-called "war on terrorism." Fundamental legal protections that once limited arbitrary executive and government power to act against individuals have been discarded. Courts, which once stood as a safeguard against governmental lawlessness, have largely surrendered to new "anti-terrorist" measures. The laws of war themselves, fashioned over hundreds of years, have been disregarded. And people's rights, struggled for and embodied in documents such as the Magna Carta, the French Declaration of the Rights of Man and of the Citizen, the Bill of Rights of the Constitution of the United States, and the International Covenant on Civil and Political Rights, are in jeopardy. We are truly entering a dark period.

I live a few blocks from the World Trade Center and saw firsthand the devastation and human suffering caused by the attacks of September 11. Like everyone in New York City, I would like to live once again in a safe city. We want those who attacked us arrested and punished, and we want the network that plotted to harm us eliminated so we will be safe from future attacks. But because safety at home has become such a paramount concern for those living in the United States, there appears to be broad popular support for the new anti-terrorism measures—even those that curtail freedom and constitutional rights.

Unfortunately, as long as people feel unsafe and subject to attack, they will accept severe restrictions upon their liberties and those of others, hoping that limits on their rights will somehow keep them safe. But it is hard to argue that building a Fortress America will really prevent another terrorist attack. The United States has 7,500 miles of border with Canada and Mexico and thousands of miles of coastline, most of it not patrolled. There are more than 10,000 air flights a day in the United States. Eleven million trucks and over two million rail cars cross into the United States each year, as do millions of non-citizen visitors. Terrorists intent on harm can easily slip into the country. This is not to say that good law enforcement has no role, but, rather, that all the laws in the world will not really make the United States safe.

If the U.S. government truly wants its people to be safer and wants terrorist threats to diminish, fundamental changes in its foreign policies will be necessary. Although those changes are not discussed in this article, clearly the current role of the United States in the Middle East and elsewhere is a central issue. As the ancient Arab proverb declares: "He who plunders others always lives in terror." The United States' actions in the Middle East, particularly its unqualified support for Israel, its embargo of Iraq, its bombing of Afghanistan, and its actions in Saudi Arabia, continue to anger people and fertilize the ground where terrorists of the future will take root.

But there is very little room left in the United States for those who question the new anti-terror initiatives, or who identify problems with U.S. policies as central to stopping terror. At this moment, all such criticism is considered the equivalent of support for those who attacked the United States. In December 2001 John Ashcroft, the attorney general of the United States, testified to a congressional committee that "to those who scare peace-loving people with phantoms of lost liberty, my message is this: your tactics only aid terrorists."[1] He went on to say that criticism of the administration "gives ammunition to America's enemies and pause to America's friends."[2] Similarly, White House spokesman Ari Fleisher warned "all Americans . . . to watch what they say [and] watch what they do."[3]

My own experience has borne out the degree to which the government's message is being heard by citizens. Often, in media interviews since September 11, I have raised questions regarding the treatment of the Guantanamo detainees, the detention of non-citizens within the United States, the use of military tribunals, or the questioning by law enforcement officials of thousands of non-citizens. Typical of the hate mail I receive for expressing such sentiments is, "Why don't you go over to Afghanistan and live with the murderers and try to protect them over there? You don't belong in this country."

Without basic alterations in U.S. policies I believe there is little hope of ending the draconian curtailment of liberties in the United States and elsewhere. People will continue to live in fear and accept restrictions on their freedoms in the belief that it will make them safer. The struggle to regain lost liberty and that of creating a more just world abroad is really one struggle—and that is not just rhetoric. We and our children will not be safer and more free until the world is as well.

In the current climate it will obviously not be easy to substantially change the course the United States and its allies have embarked upon. Yet the situation is not utterly hopeless. The U.S. administration has been forced to modify certain of its more draconian proposals, such as its original refusal to apply any part of the Geneva Conventions to combatants captured in Afghanistan. It has lessened although not eliminated the unfairness of trials before military tribunals. Following a great uproar in the press, it has apparently closed the disinformation and propaganda office it had established at the Pentagon.

These changes in policy have come, in part, from dissent within the United States, and even from pragmatic voices within the U.S. Armed Forces. However, more importantly, it has been the countries of Europe, some of which still take the rule of law seriously, that have pressed these modifications upon the United States.

There have also been a number of lawsuits filed regarding the treatment of immigrants in the United States and of captured combatants. Some of these have been successful, although appeals are pending. On March 26, 2002, a judge in New Jersey gave civil rights organizations access to records of those detained in the United States after September 11, saying that secret arrests are "odious to a democracy." On April 4, 2002, a federal judge in Michigan ordered public access to immigration hearings that had been closed in the wake of September 11, saying that government secrecy "only breeds suspicion." And in a decision on March 13, 2002, the Inter American Human Rights Commission of the Organization of American States urged the United States to immediately provide court or tribunal hearings for those detained at Guantanamo Bay, Cuba. Such cases are an indication that there remain those willing to fight back and file suit to protect basic rights, and that there are judges still courageous enough to uphold fundamental rights against a government bent on their elimination.

The sections of this article that follow will discuss some overall themes that characterize the current period, and analyze more closely some of the new "anti-terror" laws and restrictions, particularly those in the United States. I hope that voices around the world, particularly in Europe, can respond to these issues in ways that genuinely help change current U.S. policies into more just ones.

OVERVIEW OF THE PERIOD

A. Permanent War Abroad

The first United States government reaction to September 11 was, and remains, to make war abroad: a war that may well continue without end. In order to fight this war, the U.S. Congress on September 14, 2001, in a resolution entitled "Authorization for Use of United States Military Force," gave the president unbridled power to go to war. He was authorized to attack any nation, organization, or person involved in any way in the September 11 attacks, whether directly or by harboring others involved in those attacks. No nation, organization, or person was named; the decision about who was guilty was left solely up to the president.

The link to the attacks of September 11, however, does not need to be objective or proved: the president could even fabricate it. If he declares war on Iraq, for example, he could justify his actions by claiming that someone *allegedly* from al-Qaida *allegedly* met with an Iraqi official. Congress, basically, gave the president a blank check to make war upon whomever he wants anywhere in the world, even in the United States. The resolution has no time limit; the war may never be over.

This war has been conceptualized as a permanent war abroad. It is a war that the president has repeatedly stated will take many years; it is a war without end. Vice President Cheney said the United States may take military action against "forty to fifty countries" and that the war could last half a century or more.[4]

It can only be imagined what war on that scale means, and the dire consequences for people everywhere. A permanent war abroad means that even more money will go to the military, an expansion of the U.S. military role everywhere, and the likelihood of more bombings and more killings. Within six months of September 11, active United States forces have involved themselves not only in Afghanistan and Pakistan, but also in Colombia, the Philippines, and potentially in Somalia and the Sudan. Future countries targeted include the countries of the so-called "axis of evil": Iraq, Iran, and North Korea. The increase in military spending to pay for this permanent war is gigantic—fifty billion dollars—an amount larger then the military budget of any country in Europe. This will bring United States military spending to the astronomical number of 380 billion dollars.

A permanent war abroad also means permanent anger against the United States by those countries and people that will be devastated by U.S. military actions. Hate will increase, not lessen, and the terrible consequences of that hate will be used as justification for more restrictions on civil liberties in the United States. In the past, when wars ended, there was also an end to the worst deprivations of constitutional rights and civil liberties. In this war without end, we are facing a curtailment of our rights—without end.

B. Permanent War at Home

The second reaction of the U.S. government after September 11 was to launch a permanent war on terror at home by building a fortified surveillance and national security state. However, even on its own terms, the claimed necessity for this war at home is problematic. The legislation and other governmental actions to step up domestic surveillance are premised on the belief that intelligence agencies failed to stop the September 11 attack because they lacked the spying capability to find and arrest the conspirators. Yet recently it has come to light that nine of the hijackers fit profiles used by airport screeners, were asked for identification, and searched on September 11, and none were arrested—although two were on an FBI terrorist watch list. It was also revealed that an instructor at a Minnesota flight school had warned the FBI in August 2001 of his suspicion that a student, later identified as the so-called twentieth hijacker, might be planning to use a commercial airliner as a bomb. And six months after September 11, the U.S. Immigration and Naturalization Service approved the visas of two of the hijackers and sent the approvals to the flight school where they had been trained. These serious lapses in law enforcement strongly suggest that there are serious problems in the system that will not be helped by the curtailment of civil liberties. While the government has been willing to suspend rights in the name of stopping terrorism, it has not been willing to look closely at its own intelligence failures.

Only now is Congress considering a limited, mostly secret investigation of what went wrong, headed by a former CIA official. Thomas Powers, a respected critic of the intelligence agencies, made the point of just how important such an investigation is before any new intelligence powers are granted:

> The bid for increased surveillance and intelligence gathering will become a very big mistake if Congress grants the FBI and CIA more power but fails to investigate what went wrong on September 11 . . . Everybody's afraid. They know they screwed up, and if you have an investigation people will find out how. [5]

But any investigation into intelligence failures must contend with the desires of Attorney General John Ashcroft, a religious fundamentalist with an antediluvian record on civil rights as a senator. Ashcroft clearly sees September 11 as an opportunity to lift restrictions which had been placed on the nation's spy agencies in the 1970s, and as a chance to grant law enforcement agencies the additional powers they have been wanting for years.

The current circumstances that have called forth the U.S. response at home and abroad have rarely, if ever, occurred in the nation's past. Both the war abroad and the response at home have serious consequences for civil liberties and the rule of law. Among the most pernicious tendencies I see at work are the pervasive censorship of information, the silencing of dissent, and widespread ethnic and religious profiling. The war has already created a climate of fear where neighbors live in suspicion of one another and people are afraid to speak out.

Overall, the new anti-terrorist laws represent a tremendous expansion of executive power. The president can now make war on anyone without additional congressional authority, can wiretap attorneys and their clients without a court order, can jail non-citizens permanently on the word of the attorney general—even if they have committed no crimes—and can set up military tribunals which can mete out the death penalty without appeal. The United States' system of checks and balances, made up of the courts, Congress, and the executive branch, and purportedly the pride of the U.S. constitutional system, is in jeopardy.

The new laws and restrictions also mean fundamental changes in the way the United States, historically a nation of immigrants, treats the twenty million non-citizens residing in the country. Since September 11, enforcement of the new laws against non-citizens, mostly from the Middle East, has included incommunicado detentions, the questioning of thousands by FBI agents, and widespread racial, ethnic, and religious profiling. The government's campaign against non-citizens, particularly Muslims, has at times flowered into explicit religious bigotry, as expressed in this remarkable quote from Attorney General Ashcroft:

> Islam is a religion in which God requires you to send your son to die for him. Christianity is a faith in which God sends his son to die for you.[6]

Some important religious leaders have also condemned Islam. Billy Graham's son, Franklin Graham, who gave the benediction at George W. Bush's inauguration, called the Islamic religion "wicked, violent, and not of the same God."[7]

An unprecedented strengthening of the U.S. intelligence and law enforcement apparatus; the erosion of the U.S. system of checks and balances; a new xenophobia and anti-immigrant sentiment—in general, these tendencies are deeply troubling.

Below, I will discuss some of the other consequences of the war on terrorism. Some include challenges to international justice, such as indefinite detention of battlefield detainees outside the standards of the Geneva Convention, the establishment of military tribunals to try suspected terrorists, and the possible use of torture to obtain information.

On the domestic front, I will discuss the creation of a special new cabinet office of Homeland Security, massive arrests and interrogation of immigrants, and the passage of legislation granting intelligence and law enforcement agencies much broader powers to intrude into the private lives of Americans.

Recent new initiatives—such as the wiretapping of attorney-client conversations, or the FBI's new license to spy on domestic, religious, and political groups—add to the undermining of core constitutional protections. The entire situation, when coupled with the ideology of the Republicans currently in control of the executive branch of the government, portends the worst for international human rights and for constitutional rights.

THE NEW "LEGAL" REGIME

The government has established a wide-ranging series of measures in its efforts to eradicate terrorism. Below, I will look more closely at some of the key measures and analyze their implications.

I. THE PRESIDENT'S MILITARY ORDER

A. Military Commissions

On November 13, 2001, President Bush signed a military order establishing military commissions or tribunals to try suspected terrorists.[8] Under this order, noncitizens, whether from the United States or elsewhere, who are accused of aiding international terrorism can be tried before one of these commissions at the discretion of the president. These commissions are not courts-martial, which provide far more protections for the accused.

The divergence from constitutional protections allowed by this executive order is breathtaking, notably Attorney General Ashcroft's explicit statement that terrorists do not deserve constitutional protections. (By "terrorists," Ashcroft means accused or suspected individuals, not those proved to have committed terrorist acts.) Accordingly, what have been set up are essentially "courts" of conviction and not of justice.

These new tribunals represent such a departure from fair and impartial courts that there was a broad outcry against their use both in the United States and Europe. Even conservative U.S. columnists such as William Safire were highly critical. This outcry was probably a factor in the government's decision to have the so-called twentieth hijacker, Moussaoui, tried in a regular federal court in the United States. It certainly contributed to the reasons for the order being modified in March 2002.

Under the provisions of the military order establishing these commissions, the secretary of defense will appoint the judges, most likely military officers, who will decide both questions of law and fact. Unlike federal judges who are appointed for life, these officers will have little independence and every reason to decide in favor of the prosecution. Normal rules of evidence, which provide some assurance of reliability, will not apply. Hearsay and even evidence obtained from torture will apparently be admissible. (This is particularly frightening in light of the intimations from U.S. officials that torture of suspects may be an option.[9])

Under the original order, unanimity among the judges was not required, even to impose the death penalty. That has now been modified, in part, to require a unanimous verdict for a death sentence, but not for the finding of guilt for a crime carrying a potential of a death sentence. The original order did not give suspects a choice of counsel; that too has been modified, but only to the extent a suspect can pay an attorney and that the attorney passes security clearances from the U.S. government. Initially, the only appeal from a conviction was to the president or the secretary of defense; the modified order allows an appeal to a three-person military review panel that then gives a "recommendation" to the secretary of defense or the president as to the disposition of the case. Thus, there is still no review by a civilian court and the final decision remains in the hands of the president or secretary of defense.

Incredibly, the entire process, including execution, can be carried out in secret, although the modified order says the proceeding will be open unless the presiding officer determines otherwise. In other words, they can still be closed in the interests of "national security" and other similar reasons. The trials can be held anywhere the secretary of defense decides. (A trial might occur on an aircraft carrier, for example, with no press allowed, and the body of the executed disposed of at sea.)

Although military tribunals were used during and immediately subsequent to World War II, their use since that time does not comply with important international treaties. The International Covenant on Civil and Political Rights as well as the American Declaration of the Rights and Duties of Man require that persons be tried before courts previously established in accordance with preexisting laws. Clearly, the tribunals are not such courts. In addition, the Third Geneva Conventions of 1949 require that Prisoners of War (POWs) be tried under the same procedures that U.S. soldiers would be tried for similar crimes. U.S. soldiers are tried by courts-martial or civilian courts and not by military tribunals. This is probably one important reason the United States is refusing to classify the Guantanamo detainees as POWs; if they were POWs, the government would not be free to use tribunals.

Surprisingly, a number of prestigious law professors have accepted and even argued in favor of these tribunals, saying that secrecy is necessary for security.[10] The primary argument is that it might be necessary to disclose classified information in order to obtain convictions. But in fact, procedures for safely handling classified information in federal courts have been successfully employed, as in the trial of those convicted in the 1993 bombing of the World Trade Center. The 1993 trials also demonstrated that trials of suspected terrorists do not require special military tribunals, but can safely be held in federal courts.

Trials before military commissions will not be trusted in either the Muslim world or in Europe, where previous terrorism trials have not required the total suspension of the most basic principles of justice. The military commissions will be viewed as what they are: "kangaroo courts." It would be much better to demonstrate to the world that the guilty have been apprehended and fairly convicted in front of impartial and regularly constituted courts. An even better solution would be for the United States to go to the United Nations and have the United Nations establish a special court for the trials, staffed by judges from the United States, Muslim countries, and other countries with civil law systems.

B. Indefinite Detention Under the Military Order and the Guantanamo Prisoners

In addition to authorizing military tribunals, the same military order of November 13 requires the secretary of defense to detain anyone whom the president has reason to believe is an international terrorist, a member of al-Qaida, or anyone who harbored such persons. There is no requirement that a detained individual ever be brought to trial. Detention without any charges and without any court review can last an entire lifetime.

Subsequent to the issuance of the Military Order, U.S. and Northern Alliance forces in Afghanistan captured thousands of prisoners. On or about January 11, 2002, the United States military began transporting prisoners captured in Afghanistan to Camp X-ray at the U.S. Naval Station in Guantanamo Bay, Cuba. As of April 2002, U.S authorities were detaining three hundred male prisoners representing thirty-three nationalities at the Guantanamo compound, and the number was expected to grow. It is these prisoners who may be indefinitely detained or tried by military tribunals to face the death penalty.[11] Remarkably, Secretary Rumsfeld has stated that he reserves the right to continue detaining prisoners even if the tribunals acquit them.

There have been allegations of ill treatment of some prisoners in transit and at Guantanamo, including reports that they were shackled, hooded, and sedated during the twenty-five-hour flight from Afghanistan; that their beards and heads were forcibly shaved, and that upon arrival at Guantanamo they were housed in small cells that failed to protect them against the elements.[12] While such treatment is never acceptable, more serious is the fact that these prisoners exist in a legal limbo, their identities secret and the charges against them unknown.

It is the official position of the United States government that none of these detainees are POWs. Instead, officials have repeatedly described the prisoners as "unlawful combatants." This determination was made without the convening of a competent tribunal as required by Article 5 of the Third Geneva Convention, which mandates such a tribunal "should any doubt arise" as to a combatant's status. In its most recent statement on the status of those detained at Guantanamo, the U.S. government announced that although it would apply the Geneva Conventions to those prisoners it decided were from the Taliban, it would not extend them to prisoners it believed were members of al-Qaida.[13] However, in no case were any of the detained to be considered POWs. The United States has repeatedly refused the entreaties of the international community to treat all the detainees under the procedures established under the Geneva Conventions.[14]

The United States' treatment of the Guantanamo detainees violates virtually every human rights norm relating to preventive detention. The United States has denied the detainees access to counsel, consular representatives, and family members; has failed to notify them of the charges they are facing; has refused to allow for judicial review of the detentions; and has expressed its intent to hold the detainees indefinitely.[15] It continues to do so despite an important ruling from the Inter American Human Rights Commission that it immediately give the detainees some form of judicial process. In its ruling the commission requested that the United States take the urgent measures necessary to have the legal status of the detainees at Guantanamo Bay determined by a competent tribunal.

II. THE OFFICE OF HOMELAND SECURITY

On September 20, 2001, President Bush announced the creation of the Homeland Security Office, charged with gathering intelligence, coordinating anti-terrorism efforts, and taking precautions to prevent and respond to terrorism. It is not yet known how this office will function, but it will most likely try to centralize the powers of existing U.S. intelligence and law enforcement agencies—a difficult, if not impossible, job—and coordinate the work of some forty bickering agencies.

Those concerned with its establishment are worried that the Office of Homeland Security will become a super spy agency and, as its very name implies, that it will encourage the military to play a hitherto unprecedented role in domestic law enforcement. The recent appointment of a general who will be in charge of "defense of the homeland," and the proposed repeal of a federal statute that prohibits the military from playing a domestic law enforcement role, are clear signals of what can be expected in the future.

III. FBI ARRESTS AND INVESTIGATIONS

A. Arrests of Non-Citizens

The FBI has always done more than chase criminals; like the Central Intelligence Agency it has long considered itself the protector of U.S. ideology. Those who have opposed government policies—whether civil rights workers, anti–Vietnam War protesters, opponents of the covert Reagan-era wars, or cultural dissidents—have repeatedly been surveilled and had their legal activities disrupted by the FBI.

In the immediate aftermath of the September 11 attacks, Attorney General John Ashcroft focused FBI efforts on non-citizens, whether permanent residents, students, temporary workers, or tourists. Normally, an alien can only be held for forty-eight hours prior to the filing of charges. Ashcroft's new regulation allowed arrested aliens to be held without any charges for a "reasonable time," presumably months or longer.

The FBI began massive detentions and investigations of individuals suspected of terrorist connections, almost all of them non-citizens of Middle Eastern descent; over 1,300 were arrested. In some cases, people were arrested merely for being from a country such as Pakistan and having expired student visas. Many were held for weeks and months without access to lawyers or knowledge of the charges against them; many are still in detention. None, as yet, have been proven to have a connection with the September 11 attacks; as many as half remain in jail despite having been cleared.[16]

Stories of mistreatment of such detainees are not uncommon. Apparently, some of those arrested are not willing to talk to the FBI, although they have been offered shorter jail sentences, jobs, money, and new identities. Astonishingly, the FBI and the Department of Justice are discussing methods to force them to talk, which include "using drugs or pressure tactics such as those employed by the Israeli interrogators."[17] The accurate term to describe these tactics is *torture*.

There is resistance to this even from law enforcement officials. One former FBI chief of counterterrorism said in an October interview: "Torture goes against every grain in my body. Chances are you are going to get the wrong person and risk damage or killing them."[18] As torture is illegal in the United States and under international law, U.S. officials risk lawsuits by using such practices.

For this reason, they have suggested having another country do their dirty work; they want to extradite the suspects to allied countries where security services regularly threaten family members and/or use torture. It would be difficult to imagine a more ominous signal of the repressive period we are facing.

In fact, with regard to a number of alleged Taliban or al-Qaida members captured or arrested outside the United States, the U.S. has secretly sent them to other countries and not brought them to the U.S. or to Guantanamo. They have been taken to Egypt or Jordan where they can be tortured, in some cases with the involvement of the CIA.

B. Investigations of Middle-Eastern Men and of Dissenters

In late November 2001, Attorney General Ashcroft announced that the FBI or other law enforcement personnel would interview more than five thousand men, mostly from the Middle East, who were in the United States on temporary visas. None of these men were suspected of any crime. The interviews were supposedly voluntary. A number of civil liberties organizations, Muslim, and Arab-American groups objected that the investigations amounted to racial profiling and that interviews of immigrants who might be subject to deportation could hardly be called voluntary. A number of law enforcement officials, including a former head of the FBI, objected as well, saying that such questioning would harm the relationship of police departments with minority communities, that the practice was illegal under some state laws, and that it was a clumsy and ineffective way to go about an investigation. A few local police departments refused to cooperate.

Although Ashcroft claimed the questioning was harmless, the proposed questions themselves made this assertion doubtful. The initial questions concerned the non-citizen's status; if there was even the hint of a technical immigration violation, the person could well find himself in jail and deported. Information was requested regarding all of the friends and family members of the questioned person; in other words, the FBI wanted complete address books. Once the FBI had such information, it would open files and investigations on each of those named, even though no one was suspected of a crime.

Other questions concerned whether the person interviewed had any sympathy with any of the causes supposedly espoused by the attackers on September 11. Media reports in this country and elsewhere have suggested that the attackers were acting in the name of Palestinian rights. Whether or not this is the case, many Arab-Americans are sympathetic with the plight of the Palestinians, and would be put in a bind by FBI questioning about this topic. If the person questioned by the FBI admitted to such sympathy he would immediately become a potential suspect; if he was sympathetic, but denied it, he would be lying to the FBI, which is a federal crime.

The FBI was also instructed to make informants of the persons it questioned, and to have them continue to report on and monitor the people they are in contact with. Oliver "Buck" Revel, a former FBI assistant executive director, has criticized this practice as "not effective" and as "really gut[ting] the values of our society, which you cannot allow the terrorists to do."[19]

In March 2002, Ashcroft announced that the Justice Department was launching a new investigation of three thousand more non-citizens, mostly young Arab men. This is despite the fact that only just over half of the initial group of five thousand could even be found for the interviews and that little, if any, information was learned. The American-Arab Anti-Discrimination Committee was sharply critical of this new effort and said it was an "ineffective method of law enforcement and constituted an unacceptable form of racial profiling."[20]

The FBI is also currently investigating political dissident groups it claims are linked to terrorism—among them pacifist groups such as the U.S. chapter of Women in Black, which holds peaceful vigils to protest violence in Israel and the Palestinian territories. The FBI has threatened to force members of Women in Black to either talk about their group or go to jail. As one of the group's members said, "If the FBI cannot or will not distinguish between groups who collude in hatred and terrorism, and peace activists who struggle in the full light of day against all forms of terrorism, we are in serious trouble."[21]

Unfortunately, the FBI does not make that distinction. We are facing not only the roundup of thousands on flimsy suspicions, but also an all-out investigation of dissent in the United States.

C. Renewed FBI Spying on Religious and Political Groups

According to a front page December 2001 *New York Times* story, Attorney General John Ashcroft is considering a plan that would authorize the FBI to spy upon and disrupt political groups.[22] This spying and disruption would take place even without evidence that a group was involved in anything illegal. A person or group could become a target solely by expressing views different from those of the government or taking a position in support of, for example, Palestinian rights.

Ashcroft would authorize this by lifting FBI guidelines that were put into place in the 1970s after abuses of the agency, including the spying upon and efforts to disrupt the activities of such nonviolent leaders as Dr. Martin Luther King, were exposed. That earlier spying and disruption were done under a program called COINTELPRO, which stands for "Counterintelligence Program." It was a program to "misdirect, discredit, disrupt, and otherwise neutralize" specific individuals and groups. Probably the most notorious goal of COINTELPRO was the FBI's effort to prevent the rise of what it called a "Black Messiah." At one point, the FBI tried to induce Dr. King to commit suicide by threatening to expose his extramarital affairs to his wife. It is not known whether this proposed new version of COINTELPRO has been adopted.

IV. VIOLATION OF THE ATTORNEY-CLIENT RELATIONSHIP

A. Wiretapping of Attorney-Client Communications

At the heart of the effective assistance of counsel is the right of a criminal defendant to a lawyer with whom he or she can communicate candidly and freely without fear that the government is overhearing confidential communications. This right is fundamental to the adversary system of justice in the Untied States. When the government overhears these conversations, a defendant's right to a defense is compromised. On October 30, 2001, with the stroke of a pen, Attorney General Ashcroft eliminated the attorney-client privilege and said he will wiretap communications when he thinks there is "reasonable suspicion to believe" that a detainee "may use communications with attorneys or their agents to further facilitate an act or acts of violence or terrorism."[23] Ashcroft says that approximately one hundred such suspects and their attorneys may be subject to the order. He claims the legal authority to do so without court order; in other words, without the approval and finding by a neutral magistrate that attorney-client communications are facilitating criminal conduct. This is utter lawlessness by our country's top law enforcement officer and is flatly unconstitutional.

B. The Wiretapping and Indictment of a Lawyer: The Lynne Stewart Case

On April 9, 2002, Ashcroft flew to New York to announce the indictment of a well-known defense attorney, Lynne Stewart. Stewart had represented Sheik Omar Abdel Rahman in his 1995 trial for conspiracy to bomb the World Trade Center for which he had been convicted and sentenced to life plus sixty-five years. She had continued to represent him in prison.

Stewart was arrested by the FBI and freed the same day on $500,000 bond. That same day the FBI raided her office, removed her hard drives from her computers, and took many of her legal files. Many of Stewart's clients are facing trials in federal courts; now the FBI and the Justice Department have possession of those confidential legal files. The damage that can be done to the constitutional rights of her clients is incalculable.

The indictment, for which she faces forty years in prison, primarily accuses Stewart of having given material support to a terrorist organization. It charges that she "facilitated and concealed communications" between the Sheik and members of an Egyptian terrorist organization, the Islamic Group. The essence of the claim is that on an occasion when Stewart visited her client in prison, the Arabic translator that accompanied her spoke to the Sheik regarding messages that the Sheik wanted transmitted to the terrorist group. In other words, the translator allegedly did not just translate for Stewart, but had his own agenda with the Sheik. It is claimed that Stewart permitted and even facilitated those conversations. These communications, if they occurred, resulted in no terrorist incidents.

It seems highly improbable that Ashcroft will have sufficient evidence to support the charges against Stewart. As she does not speak or understand Arabic, she could not have known the content of the conversations that allegedly occurred between the translator and the Sheik. If she was unaware of the supposed illegal nature of the conversations, it is difficult to see how she could be accused of giving material aid to a terrorist organization. Moreover, the conversations occurred prior to Aschroft's tenure, when Janet Reno was the attorney general. Apparently Reno did not believe that there was sufficient evidence to indict Steward.

That is by no means the only problem with the indictment. The claimed "evidence" was gathered through a wiretap; a wiretap obtained by Janet Reno that has been in effect for almost two years. This wiretap was not authorized by a warrant, nor did it meet the "probable cause" standard of the Fourth Amendment that is normally required in criminal investigations. Rather, a special secret court, the Foreign Intelligence Surveillance Court, authorized the wiretap without any showing of "probable cause." (The functioning of this court is explained below.) Such a wiretap raises serious legal questions, particularly as attorney-client conversations were monitored.

Interestingly, Ashcroft is now using this indictment of Stewart to justify his claim that there is a need to wiretap attorney-client conversations in terrorism cases. In addition, as has been explained, he claims the authority to do so without any court approval, even that of the Foreign Intelligence Surveillance Court. Immediately after the indictment he announced that his first use of this claimed power would be aimed at attorneys meeting or speaking with the Sheik. There is no reason for this bypassing of the Constitution; courts are the appropriate place to approve, or disapprove, any such requests for wiretapping. Hopefully, the court test of and rejection of this new reach for power will come swiftly and decisively.

It is difficult to divorce Stewart's indictment from the politics of John Ashcroft. This is the man who states that critics of claimed deprivations of constitutional rights are aiding terrorists and that "foreign terrorists who commit war crimes against the United States are not entitled to and do not deserve the protections of the American Constitution . . ."[24] In this context, his indictment of Stewart must be viewed with extreme skepticism. It seems more then likely that it was contrived, and that one of its main purposes was the intimidation of those who believe all persons, even those accused of terrorism, are entitled to constitutional protections, most importantly the right to a lawyer. Because of Ashcroft's action, it will be increasingly difficult to find defense lawyers willing to take these unpopular cases.

V. The New Anti-Terrorist Legislation

On October 26, 2001, Congress passed and President Bush signed sweeping new anti-terrorist legislation, the U.S.A.-Patriot Act ("Uniting and Strengthening America by Providing Appropriate Tools Required to Intercept and Obstruct Terrorism"), aimed at both aliens and citizens. The legislation met more opposition than one might expect in these difficult times. A National Coalition to Protect Political Freedom of over 120 groups ranging from the right to the left opposed the worst aspects of the proposed new law. They succeeded in making minor modifications, but the most troubling provisions remain, and are described below:

A. "Rights" of Aliens

Prior to this legislation, anti-terrorist laws passed in the wake of the 1996 bombing of the federal building in Oklahoma had already given the government wide powers to arrest, detain, and deport aliens based upon secret evidence—evidence that neither the alien nor his attorney could view or refute.[25] The new legislation makes it even worse for aliens. First, the law would permit "mandatory detention" of aliens certified by the attorney general as "suspected terrorists." These could include aliens involved in barroom brawls or those who have provided only humanitarian assistance to organizations disfavored by the United States. Once certified in this way, an alien could be imprisoned indefinitely with no real opportunity for court challenge. Until now, such "preventive detention" was believed to be flatly unconstitutional.

Secondly, current law permits deportation of aliens who support terrorist activity; the proposed law would make aliens deportable for almost any association with a "terrorist organization." Although this change seems to have a certain surface plausibility, it represents a dangerous erosion of the constitutionally protected rights of association. "Terrorist organization" is a broad and open-ended term that could, depending on the political climate or the inclinations of the attorney general, include liberation groups such as the Irish Republican Army, the African National Congress, or NGOs that have ever engaged in any destruction of property, such as Greenpeace. An alien who gives only medical or humanitarian aid to similar groups, or simply supports their political message in a material way, could also be jailed indefinitely.

B. More Powers to the FBI and CIA

A key element in the U.S.A.-Patriot Act is the wide expansion of wiretapping. In the United States wiretapping is permitted, but generally only when there is probable cause to believe a crime has been committed and a judge has signed a special wiretapping order that specifies limited time periods, the numbers of the telephones wiretapped, and the type of conversations that can be overheard.

In 1978 an exception was made to these strict requirements, permitting wire-tapping to be carried out to gather intelligence information about foreign governments and foreign terrorist organizations.[26] A secret court, the Foreign Intelligence Surveillance Court, was established that could approve such wiretaps without requiring the government to show evidence of criminal conduct. In doing so the constitutional protections necessary when investigating crimes could be bypassed.

The secret court has been little more than a rubber stamp for wiretapping requests by the spy agencies. It has authorized over 13,000 wiretaps in its twenty-two-year existence, about one thousand last year alone, and has apparently never denied a request for a wiretap. Under the new law, the same secret court will have the power to authorize wiretaps and secret searches of homes in criminal cases—not just to gather foreign intelligence. The FBI will be able to wiretap individuals or organizations without meeting the stringent requirements of the U.S. Constitution, which requires a court order based upon probable cause that a person is planning or has committed a crime. The new law will authorize the secret court to permit roving wiretaps of any phones, computers, or cell phones that might possibly be used by a suspect. Widespread reading of email will be allowed, even before the recipient opens it. Thousands of conversations will be listened to or read that have nothing to do with any suspect or any crime.

The new legislation is filled with many other expansions of investigative and prosecutorial power, including wider use of undercover agents to infiltrate organizations, longer jail sentences, lifetime supervision for some who have served their sentences, more crimes that can receive the death penalty, and longer statutes of limitations for prosecuting crimes. Another provision of the new bill makes it a crime for a person to fail to notify the FBI if he or she has "reasonable grounds to believe" that someone is about to commit a terrorist offense. The language of this provision is so vague that anyone, however innocent, with any connection to someone even suspected of being a terrorist can be prosecuted.

C. The New Crime of Domestic Terrorism

The U.S.A.-Patriot Act creates a number of new crimes. One of the most threatening to dissent and to those who oppose government policies is the crime of "domestic terrorism." It is loosely defined as acts that are dangerous to human life, violate criminal law, and "appear to be intended" to intimidate or coerce a civilian population" or "influence the policy of a government by intimidation of coercion." Under this definition, a protest demonstration that blocked a street and prevented an ambulance from getting by could be deemed domestic terrorism. Likewise, the demonstrations in Seattle against the World Trade Organization in 2000 could fit within the definition. This was an unnecessary addition to the criminal code; there are already plenty of laws making such civil disobedience criminal without labeling protest as "terrorist" in order to impose harsh prison sentences.

Overall, the severe curtailment of legal rights, the disregard of established law, and the new repressive legislation represents one of the most sweeping assaults on liberties in the last fifty years. It is unlikely to make us more secure; it is certain to make us less free. It is common for governments to reach for draconian law enforcement solutions in times of war or national crisis. It has happened often in the United States and elsewhere. We should learn from historical example. Times of hysteria, of war, and of instability are not the times to rush to enact new laws that curtail our freedoms and grant more authority to the government and its intelligence and law enforcement agencies.

The U.S. government has conceptualized the war against terrorism as a permanent war, a war without boundaries. Terrorism is frightening to all of us, but it's equally chilling to think that in the name of anti-terrorism our government is willing to permanently suspend constitutional freedoms as well.

Michael Ratner, one of the most prominent international human rights lawyers, works with the Center for Constitutional Rights and has supported liberation struggles in Puerto Rico, Grenada, El Salvador, Nicaragua, Guatemala, Cuba, and Haiti.

ENDNOTES:

1. Neil A. Lewis, "Ashcroft Defends Anti-terror Plan; Says Criticism May Aid U.S. Foes," *New York Times*, Dec. 7, 2001, A-1.

2. *Ibid.*

3. Editorial, "Say What You Will," *Oregonian*, Oct. 2, 2001, B-10.

4. John Pilger, "The Colder War," at: www.counterpunch.org/pilgercold.html

5. Tim Weiner, "Look Who's Listening: The CIA Widens Its Domestic Reach," *New York Times*, Jan. 20, 2001, 4-1.

6. American-Arab Anti-Discrimination Committee, "Action Alert, Protest Ashcroft's Anti-Islamic Statements," Feb. 11, 2002.

7. Jim Avila, "Christian Leader Condemns Islam," NBC News, Nov. 16, 2001, at: www.msnbc.com/news/659057.asp.

8. "Detention, Treatment, and Trial of Certain Non-Citizens in the War Against Terrorism," at: http://www.whitehouse.gov/news/releases/2001/11/20011113-27.html.

9. Walter Pincus, "Silence of Four Terror Probe Suspects Poses Dilemma," *Washington Post*, Oct. 21, 2001, A-6.

10. See, e.g., Remarks of Yale Professor Ruth Wedgewood, at: http://www.justicetalking.org/shows/show195.asp.

11. See, e.g., Richard Sisk, "Airport Gun Battle Firefight Erupts as Prisoners Are Flown to Cuba," *New York Daily News*, Jan. 11, 2002, 27.

12. See, e.g., Amnesty International, U.S.A.: "AI Calls on the U.S.A to End Legal Limbo of Guantanamo Prisoners," AI Index: AMR 51/009/2002, issued 15/01/2002, at: http://web.amnesty.org/ai.nsf/Index/AMR510092002.

13. White House Press Release, at: http://www.whitehouse.gov/news/release/2002-/02/20020207-13.html.

14. On February 8, the day after announcement of the United States' position, Darcy Christen, a spokesperson for the ICRC, said of the detainees: "They were captured in combat [and] we consider them prisoners of war." Richard Waddington, "Guantanamo Inmates Are POWs Despite Bush View—ICRC," *Reuters*, Feb. 9, 2002.

15. These detentions are currently under challenge in United States courts and the author of this article is one of the attorneys in those cases. The court papers can be obtained at: http://www.campxray.net.

16. Homeland Security Director Tom Ridge said that there was no evidence yet than any of the more than one thousand people detained were terrorists. "U.S. Draws Up List of Over 5,000 Men it Wants Interviewed in Terrorism Probe," *Wall Street Journal*, Nov. 14, 2001, A-6.

17. Walter Pincus, "Silence of Four Terror Probe Suspects Poses Dilemma," *Washington Post*, Oct. 21, 2001, A-6.

18. *Ibid.*

19. Jim McGee, "Ex-FBI Officials Criticize Tactics on Terrorism," *Washington Post*, Nov. 28, 2001, A-1.

20. "A.D.C. Reiterates Objections to Government Investigations Based on Racial Profiles," Mar. 20, 2002, at: "http://www.adc.org/press/2002/20March2002.html."

21. Report by Ronnie Gilbert, "FBI Investigation of Women in Black," October 4, 2001, at: http:/www.labournet.net/world/0110/wmnblk1.html.

22. David Johnston and Don Van Natta Jr., "Ashcroft Seeking to Free FBI to Spy on Groups," *New York Times*, Dec. 1, 2001, A-1.

23. National Security; Prevention of Terrorist Acts of Violence, 28 Code of Federal Regulations, Parts 500 and 501.

24. Tom Wicker, "Response to Terror Threatens Constitutional Rights," *Earth Times News Service*, Nov. 24, 2001, at: http://www.earthtimes.org/nov/worldinchallengeresponsenov25_01.htm.

25. This 1996 legislation was aimed at aliens, although U.S. citizens living in the United States carried out the bombing of the federal building.

26. Foreign Intelligence Surveillance Act (1978).

HUMAN RIGHTS AND THE CAMPAIGN AGAINST TERRORISM
by Kenneth Roth

The U.S. government's single overriding goal since September 11 has been to defeat terrorism. Determined as this campaign has been, it remains to be seen whether it is merely a fight against a particularly ruthless set of criminals or also an effort to defeat the logic of terrorism. Is it a struggle against only Osama Bin Laden, his al-Qaida network, and a few like-minded groups? Or is it also an effort to undermine the view that anything goes in the name of a cause, the belief that even the slaughter of civilians is an acceptable political act?

The answer to these questions will, in the long run, determine the success of the campaign. If conceived broadly, as it should be, the fight against terrorism must be understood as a campaign for human rights. That is because it is the Geneva Conventions and the body of international human rights and humanitarian law, with their limits on permissible conduct, that explain why terrorism is not a legitimate act of war or politics. These rules codify the principle that civilians should never be deliberately killed or abused, regardless of the cause.

Yet the urgency of the effort to defeat particular terrorists has tempted governments to compromise human rights. Many of the governments joining the fight against terrorism have yet to decide whether this battle provides an opportunity to reaffirm the principles of human rights or a new reason to ignore them, whether this is a moment to embrace values governing means and ends or an excuse to subordinate means to ends. Their choices will not determine whether any particular perpetrator is captured or killed. But over the long-term they will affect the strength of the ends-justify-the-means rationalization that underlies terrorism. Unless the global anti-terror coalition firmly rejects this amorality, unless the rules of international human rights and humanitarian law clearly govern all anti-terror actions, the battle against particular terrorists risks reaffirming the warped instrumentalism of terrorism.

The fight against terrorism thus should be seen only in part as a matter of security. It is also a matter of values. Police, intelligence units, even armies all have a role to play in meeting particular terrorist threats. But terrorism emanates as well from the realm of public morality. It may never be possible to understand the pathology that led a group of men to attack thousands of civilians on September 11. But it is essential to understand the mores that would countenance such mass murder as a legitimate political tool. Sympathy for such crimes is the breeding ground for terrorism, and sympathizers are the potential recruits. Building a stronger human rights culture—a culture in which any disregard for civilian life is condemned rather than condoned—is essential in the long run for defeating terrorism.

THE MIDDLE EAST

A human rights culture as an antidote to terrorism is especially needed in the Middle East and North Africa, where al-Qaida seems to have attracted many of its adherents.

Unfortunately, the willingness of most Western governments to tolerate abuses in the region has tended to undermine a human rights culture.

Most prominent has been the West's failure to rein in Israeli abuses against Palestinians and its refusal to restructure sanctions against Iraq to minimize civilian suffering. This neglect has incited intense regional anger as the death toll mounts in the Israeli-Palestinian conflict, and as Iraqi sanctions drag on with no indication that Saddam Hussein will acquiesce to the United Nations' demands. The United States has proposed rendering Iraqi sanctions moot by invading Iraq and toppling Saddam, but the Arab world in particular has greeted this proposal coolly, in part because of Washington's weak response to Israeli abuses. The Bush administration has repeatedly called for a stop to the "violence," but its reluctance to insist more specifically on an end to abuses has made it easier for Israel to respond to suicide bombers with its own indiscriminate or disproportionate violence.

The West's commitment to human rights in places such as Saudi Arabia and Egypt has also been feeble. In Saudi Arabia, the native land of Osama Bin Laden and fifteen of the nineteen presumed hijackers of September 11, the government imposes strict limits on civil society, severely discriminates against women, and systematically suppresses dissent. But the West has contented itself with purchasing Saudi oil and soliciting Saudi contracts while maintaining silence toward Saudi abuses. Egypt, the native land of the alleged September 11 ringleader and other al-Qaida leaders, features a narrowly circumscribed political realm and a government that does all it can to suffocate peaceful opposition. Yet as a "partner" for Middle East peace, the government has secured massive U.S. aid and tacit Western acceptance of its human rights violations.

In societies where basic freedoms flourish, citizens can press their governments to respond to grievances. But in Egypt, Saudi Arabia, and many of the other countries where Osama Bin Laden strikes a chord of resentment, governments restrict debate about how to address society's ills. As the option of peaceful political change is closed off, the voices of nonviolent dissent are frequently upstaged by a politics of radical opposition.

In a cycle of self-fulfilling prophecy, the West has quietly accepted this pattern of repression because it fears the instability of the democratic alternative. Regional governments have played on this fear brilliantly. By silencing mainstream political opponents, they have created an environment in which they can credibly portray themselves to be the only bulwark against extremism. They can claim, credibly if paradoxically, that human rights must be suppressed to be protected, that democratization would lead to its own demise. The stark choice, they posit, has been reduced to blocking political liberalization, as the Algerian military did in 1992 to head off an Islamist victory at the polls, or repeating the Iranian experience of 1979, in which the West's backing away from the authoritarian Shah led to a repressive theocratic state.

The challenge for the campaign against terrorism is to recognize the role that governmental repression plays in creating this dilemma. An immediate democratic transition may not be possible in such a warped political environment, but steps can and should be taken to begin to provide a meaningful array of electoral choices. Of course in a democracy there is no guarantee of any particular political result. But if pressure is put on authoritarian governments to allow a spectrum of political options, the likelihood increases that democracy will lead to governments that respect human rights.

A number of Middle Eastern and North African governments have begun the process of liberalization without empowering extremists. In recent years, Morocco and Jordan have become more open societies, Qatar and Bahrain have begun to loosen political restraints and promised to hold elections, and Kuwait has allowed an elected parliament (though with limited powers, and no vote for women and many other native-born residents). Even in Iran, a gradual and partial political opening has corresponded with the emergence of a movement demanding respect for civil liberties.

Although the correlation is not always neat, these experiences suggest that the appeal of violent and intolerant movements diminishes as people are given the chance to participate meaningfully in politics and to select from a range of political parties and perspectives. Promoting this range of options should thus be a central part of any anti-terrorism strategy for the region. But if the West continues to accept repression as the best defense against radicalism, it will undermine the human rights culture that is needed to defeat terrorism.

THE GLOBAL COALITION

In the days following September 11, various governments tried to take advantage of the tragedy by touting their own internal struggles as battles against terrorism. Most prominently, Russian President Vladimir Putin embraced this rhetoric to defend his government's brutal campaign in Chechnya, while Chinese Foreign Minister Tang Jiaxuan did the same to justify his government's response to political agitation in Xinjiang province.

Russia's experience shows that this cynical strategy could work. Shortly after September 11, German Chancellor Gerhard Schröder and Italian Prime Minister Silvio Berlusconi said that Russia's actions in Chechnya must be reassessed. The U.S. government, which just six months earlier had supported a resolution at the U.N. Human Rights Commission condemning Russian atrocities in Chechnya, began to play down its concerns over human rights and play up alleged links between Chechen rebels and the al-Qaida network. As this essay goes to press, the European Union is proposing to temper criticism of Russia at this year's session of the U.N. Human Rights Commission even though Russia has done little to improve its conduct in Chechnya.

Uzbekistan had a similar experience. The U.S. State Department is required each year to name "countries of particular concern" for their repression of religious freedom. With its torture and long prison sentences for Muslims who seek to pray peacefully outside the state-controlled mosque, Uzbekistan is an obvious candidate for this list. But as a frontline state for the war in Afghanistan, the country avoided being named when the State Department issued the latest list in October. (Nor, for that matter, did the State Department list Saudi Arabia, despite admitting that there is "no religious freedom" there.)

The Bush administration did better in March when Uzbekistan president Islam Karimov visited Washington. Under U.S. pressure, Karimov made several limited concessions, including registering the first independent Uzbekistan human rights organization, declaring an amnesty for certain political and religious prisoners, convicting four police officers for physical abuse that led to the death of a Muslim detainee, and agreeing to prison inspections by the International Committee of the Red Cross (ICRC). But other independent human rights groups (as well as other would-be members of civil society) remain in legal limbo; the amnesty, part of a semi-annual ritual throughout Central Asia designed to address the problem of overcrowding in prisons, excluded most of the estimated seven thousand independent Muslims in prison on religious grounds because their sentences were longer than six years; those included in the amnesty were forced to renounce their religious beliefs or face severe retaliation; torture remained rampant and largely unpunished; and the promise of ICRC inspections simply repeated a vow that had been made and broken the previous year. Yet these half-measures enabled Karimov to embrace the American president and greatly bolster his legitimacy. Given that Karimov has faced his own Afghanistan-based insurgency and thus welcomes U.S. military assistance, Washington's failure to use its leverage to insist on more systematic respect for human rights sent at best a mixed signal.

This inconsistent attention to violence against civilians can be found elsewhere as well. In Colombia, the U.S. government has declared both the FARC rebel group and the AUC paramilitary organization to be terrorists. Washington has been eager to send military aid to Colombia to fight the FARC, but seems ready to settle for token implementation of U.S. law requiring the Columbian military to break its ties with the AUC as a condition of the aid going forward. Similarly, the U.S. government continues to shelter Emmanuel "Toto" Constant, the ruthless former Haitian paramilitary leader, from Haiti's efforts to secure him for trial. During the military dictatorship of 1991–94, Constant oversaw the killing and torture of many Haitian civilians who were perceived as opponents of military rule. Meanwhile, NATO troops in Bosnia still have not arrested former Bosnian Serb political leader Radovan Karadzic from his French-protected sanctuary, and the international community has tended to close its eyes to Belgrade's continued harboring of former Bosnian Serb military leader Ratko Mladic; both men have been indicted for genocide. And when Nigerian President Olusegun Obasanjo visited Washington in November, no mention was made of soldiers' recent massacre of civilians in central Nigeria, but Obasanjo was praised for his support of the fight against terrorism.

The message sent by this inconsistency is that violence becomes intolerable based not on whether civilians are attacked but on whose civilians are attacked and who is doing the attacking. To build a coalition on these terms hardly promotes broad public support for the human rights culture needed to defeat terrorism.

THE FUTURE OF AFGHANISTAN

Human rights will be especially put to the test as the international community works to construct a post-Taliban Afghanistan. The Taliban had an abysmal human rights record, most notably its systematic discrimination against women, its ready use of violence against those who failed to abide by its harsh vision of Islam, and its periodic resort to massacres of those perceived to sympathize with its military adversaries. The U.S.-led overthrow of this regime creates an opportunity for positive change in Afghanistan. But many of the forces vying to replace the Taliban, including elements of the Northern Alliance, have their own records of abuse, ranging from ethnic massacres to the destruction of vast swathes of Kabul. Violent attacks on ethnic Pashtuns in northern Afghanistan since the fall of the Taliban suggest that this ugly record is not simply historical.

The test of the anti-terror coalition's commitment to human rights will come in the pressure it exerts on the Afghan parties to end these atrocities. Unfortunately, the Bush administration has rejected pleas by U.N. officials and the Afghan interim government to deploy international peacekeeping troops outside of Kabul, the capital. Washington says it prefers to train Afghans to take care of their own security—a fair long-term goal, but one that holds no prospect of stopping ethnic violence anytime in the near future.

The international community has also resisted steps to establish the rule of law in Afghanistan. U.N. High Commissioner for Human Rights Mary Robinson has begun the process of collecting evidence of abuses, which later might be delivered to an international tribunal or a reinforced Afghan court. But she has received no endorsement from the U.N. Security Council or even from U.N. administrators in Afghanistan. A formal or de facto amnesty would risk condemning Afghanistan to substitute one set of persecutors for another—hardly a recipe for undermining terrorism.

U.S. RESISTANCE TO INTERNATIONAL STANDARDS

Another impediment to building a global human rights culture is Washington's resistance to enforceable human rights standards. That is not to say that the U.S. government ignores human rights; most U.S. citizens enjoy a wide range of rights. But Washington has never been willing to subject itself to binding international human rights scrutiny. Even after September 11, when the Bush administration suddenly needed global cooperation to fight terrorism, its resistance to international human rights law remained strong.

The Bush administration follows on a long tradition of U.S. hostility to international human rights treaties. Often Washington simply refuses to ratify major treaties, such as those on women's rights, children's rights, and economic, social, and cultural rights. The U.S. government also has not ratified the First Additional Protocol of 1977 to the Geneva Conventions of 1949 (the leading set of standards on the use of air power, Washington's primary warfare tool).

Moreover, when periodically the U.S. government does ratify a human rights treaty, whether under a Republican or Democratic administration, it always does so in a way designed to ensure that there will be no right of enforcement, that no one can base a legal claim on the treaty in any court of law. The result is that ratification imposes no practical constraint on official U.S. action. It becomes an act for purely external consumption (an empty declaration that the United States is part of the international human rights system, not a good-faith effort to grant or even solidify rights in the United States).

The Bush administration has gone a step further in its hostility toward international human rights law, as illustrated in its response to the International Criminal Court (ICC). The ICC is a potential forum for prosecuting future cases of genocide, war crimes, and crimes against humanity committed anywhere in the world. Faster than anyone expected, over sixty governments have ratified the court's treaty, allowing it to come into force on July 1. President Clinton had signed the treaty but expressed reservations about the court's possible scrutiny of U.S. Armed Forces. Just two weeks before the bombing began in Afghanistan, the Bush administration took the added step of endorsing proposed legislation that would permit sanctions against many governments that ratify the ICC treaty and would even authorize invasion of The Hague, where the court will be based, to liberate any U.S. citizen who might find himself in the dock. The legislation is stillborn, but the administration is seriously considering the unprecedented act of "unsigning" the ICC treaty. The administration is thus in the uncomfortable position of seeking global law enforcement cooperation to protect its own citizens from terrorism, while trying to undermine a global law enforcement institution that many governments rightfully see as essential for protecting others from comparably severe crimes.

This resistance to accountability, replicated over the last year in international negotiations on climate change, nuclear weapons, biological weapons, small arms, and racism, contributes to global unease about Washington's use of force. The U.S. government seems to assume that if its declared policy is to respect international humanitarian law, its military conduct should be beyond reproach. Few elsewhere share that view. Moreover, Washington's refusal to submit to any independent enforcement machinery handicaps efforts to encourage others to respect international human rights and humanitarian law, including those who might be drawn to terrorism.

THE WEST'S INDIFFERENCE

In the West, the magnitude of the September 11 crimes has led many to accept a scaling back of certain rights in the name of enhancing security. If everyone faced heightened scrutiny, the odds are that an appropriate balance would be struck between freedom and security. But because anti-terrorism efforts have focused largely on a minority—young men from the Middle East and North Africa—rights are in far greater jeopardy. Most members of the public perceive that the balance is not between their own security and freedom, but between their own security and other peoples' freedom. Governments have been quick to take advantage of the resulting greater public willingness to countenance rights restrictions.

For example, emergency legislation rushed through the U.S. Congress in October, the so-called U.S.A.-Patriot Act, permits the indefinite detention of certain non-deportable non-citizens once the attorney general certifies that he has "reasonable grounds to believe" that the individual endangers national security or is engaged in terrorist activities. These activities are defined expansively to include activities that are remotely if at all connected to actual violence. Similarly, the U.S. government detained over one thousand suspects following the September 11 attacks, but threw a shroud of secrecy over the cases that made it impossible to determine whether detention powers were being used appropriately. As best as can be determined, only one suspect has been charged in connection with the September 11 attacks—Zacarias Moussaoui, the alleged "twentieth hijacker" who was already in custody on September 11. Most of the detainees are charged with minor crimes or immigration offenses yet are denied the usual bail and often held in maximum-security jails for little apparent reason other than that they are young males of a certain religion and national origin.

Perhaps most egregious has been President Bush's refusal to apply the Geneva Conventions to the detainees held at the U.S. naval base in Guantanamo, Cuba. After intensive criticism the administration announced with great fanfare in February that it would apply the Geneva Conventions to Taliban but not al-Qaida detainees in Guantanamo. The decision appeared to reverse earlier administration statements that the detainees did not merit protection under the laws of war. But by refusing to recognize at least the Taliban detainees as prisoners of war, the administration continues to breach the Geneva Conventions.

Under Article 4 of the Third Geneva Convention, the regular armed forces of a government, if captured by enemy forces, must be recognized without condition as POWs, whether or not the government is recognized. Taliban troops, as the regular armed forces of the deposed government of Afghanistan, thus merit automatic POW status. In the case of irregular troops—militia unattached to a government's regular armed forces—detainees qualify for POW status only if they meet a four-part test, involving bearing arms openly, wearing distinctive uniforms, having a responsible chain of command, and generally respecting the laws of war. Al-Qaida troops probably fail one or more parts of this test.

However, the Bush administration has sought unilaterally to rewrite the Geneva Conventions by applying this four-part test to the Taliban detainees as well. They point to a Red Cross commentary saying that a government's regular armed forces are assumed to meet this test. But this assumption cannot override the plain language of the conventions which, in contrast to their treatment of irregular militia, do not impose this test on government troops.

Such flouting of the laws of war not only violates the detainees' rights, it also endangers U.S. and allied soldiers who might someday find themselves captured in combat. By manufacturing this new test for government troops, President Bush hands enemy forces a ready excuse for denying POW status to captured American and allied troops. One can easily imagine Saddam Hussein, for example, using the administration's argument to deny POW status to a captured pilot by asserting that his bombing violated the laws of war, or to deny POW status to captured special forces who were operating undercover, without distinctive insignia.

Contrary to the administration's claims, granting POW status to Taliban fighters would not disrupt legitimate U.S. efforts to interrogate and prosecute terrorist suspects. The convention does preclude punishing POWs for refusing to reveal more than their name, rank, serial number, and date of birth. But it does not prohibit broader interrogation, including the use of incentives, such as plea bargaining, to secure additional information. (Torture is prohibited regardless of the detainees' status.)

Similarly, POW status prohibits prosecution only for lawful attacks on opposing military forces. It still permits prosecutions for war crimes or attacks on civilians, whether before or during the conflict. And if a POW is prosecuted for such offenses, the ordinary duty to repatriate POWs at the end of hostilities would take effect only after any sentence had been served.

So why is the administration stubbornly refusing to apply the Geneva Conventions' straightforward rules? Probably to ensure that the Taliban detainees can be tried by President Bush's controversial military tribunals. The conventions entitle POWs to the same trial procedures that the detaining power would give its own troops facing similar charges—that is, a court martial. Under U.S. law, any defendant convicted before a court martial is entitled to an appeal to the United States Court of Appeals for the Armed Forces—a civilian court outside the military chain of command. But in refusing to recognize the Taliban detainees as POWs, the Bush administration proposes to try them before military tribunals. Even after the regulations issued in March which remedied many of the most serious defects in the president's November order establishing the military tribunals, the only "appeal" permitted from the tribunals is to President Bush or Defense Secretary Rumsfeld. That allows the executive branch to serve as both prosecutor and judge—hardly a model of due process.

Apart from protecting POWs, the Geneva Conventions also contain the most broadly accepted international prohibitions against waging war by attacking civilians. They are thus a critical legal bulwark against terrorism. To suggest that certain causes, however laudable, justify ignoring the conventions sets a dangerous precedent, since even terrorists tend to see their cause as worthy.

The military tribunals are also troubling due to the breadth of their jurisdiction. Because they are authorized to try anyone accused of international terrorism, their scope could extend far beyond the traditional use of military tribunals to address offenses by combatants on the battlefield. Suspects arrested far from Afghanistan or any other battlefield who ordinarily would be entitled to the full protections of a civilian trial can instead be thrown before a substandard military tribunal on the mere say-so of the president or the defense secretary.

Other governments have shown a similar tendency to subordinate human rights to the fight against terrorism. Australian Prime Minister John Howard, stoking post–September 11 fears of foreigners, built his candidacy for reelection in November around his summary expulsion, in blatant violation of international refugee law, of asylum-seekers who had reached outlying Australian territory. A new British law permits the prolonged arbitrary detention of foreigners suspected of terrorist activity. At the United Nations, Western governments have proposed an anti-terrorism treaty that threatens to codify an overly broad definition of terrorism without adequate guarantees that the fight against terrorism would be circumscribed by human rights concerns. Ironically, the major obstacle to adopting the treaty has been not states defending human rights but states arguing that terrorist means should be tolerated if used as part of a war for "national liberation."

These steps matter because it is profoundly more difficult to promote the values of human rights if some of the most visible and powerful proponents seek to exempt themselves from the same standards. Such exceptionalism has grown since September 11, as governments seek to justify extraordinary constraints on rights in the name of combating extraordinary threats.

Yet in the long-term, this trend will prove counterproductive. If the ends-justify-the-means logic of terrorism is ultimately to be defeated, governments must redouble their commitment to international standards, not indulge in a new round of excuses to ignore them.

Kenneth Roth is the Executive Director of Human Rights Watch.

LEGALIZED COINTELPRO
by Kit Gage

The date September 11 is still a chasm for many people. It is a before and after in many ways. Obviously the attacks that occurred on that unfortunate date were traumatic for millions, not just in New York or Pennsylvania or the Washington, D.C. area. I think of the impact on those not directly affected as an expanded post-traumatic stress disorder. Like with PTSD, people have long-term reactions and strong urges and some dysfunction. So does the government.

People wanted to help, desperately. All over the country people gave blood, when it was in surplus. Congress wanted to help—so it desired legislation, and right away. The White House had it ready. There was the three-hundred-page off-the-shelf bill that became the U.S.A.-Patriot act.

A number of civil liberties veterans who had been through previous terrorism crises and government responses knew approximately what was coming. There would be enormous pressure to pass an immediate bill. So we organized a statement and a loose collection of groups. We knew a bill would be introduced soon, and wanted to give the Congress some breathing time to read the legislation and consider it. There was no question among us that a bill would be passed. The pressure would be too great to resist. So our task was to try and help Congress pass a focused response.

In Defense of Freedom—this odd-fellows collection—issued a statement. It did not take a position on the legislation. Rather, it asked that any legislative effort not be rushed through, that it be focused on particular needs and not target First Amendment activity or people because of their ethnicity, race, or religion. IDOF was an extraordinary assembly as it included people from all political stripes, left, right, and center. And its efforts did help give some space to the House of Representatives in its consideration of a terrorism bill.

LEGISLATION

The anti-terrorism bill that became the U.S.A.-Patriot Act, P.L. 107-56, came over from the Department of Justice (DOJ) as a diverse collection of measures, many of which had been introduced previously and rejected. This, however, was the best opportunity DOJ would ever have to get its dream legislation of increased law enforcement authority.

From at least 1984, the government had begun to introduce anti-terrorism provisions. A number were passed in the 1996 Anti-terrorism and Effective Death Penalty Act. Many of the rest which previously had been rejected were loaded onto this legislation.

One of the saddest things about the legislative process is that no one looked at the terrorist attacks and carefully assessed the gaps in law enforcement, security, and intelligence. The legislation continued the trend of criminalizing whole organizations and donations, and expanding the collection of data on a massive scale, not at all limited to terrorist activity. In the Senate, besides some closed-door negotiations, the bill passed almost as introduced, with no hearings or mark-up. Senator Leahy, who as chair of Senate Judiciary had charge of the bill, reportedly was essentially threatened that if he didn't pass the bill soon, any subsequent terrorist attack would be deemed his fault. Parenthetically, it is difficult to imagine any legislation for which its immediate mere passage would stop any criminal act. This pressure came both from the Bush administration and from the Democratic leadership of the Senate.

In the House, a full mark-up was held in the Judiciary Committee. After about eight hours and about thirty amendments, the modified and more focused bill was passed unanimously—a rare event. The House committee took some time to do its job—to read and consider the provisions and craft them more carefully. Then the House Republican leadership decided this amended version was too lenient and introduced instead virtually the original bill, forcing it through the House as the final bill. The vote on this replacement was close and very contentious. Many in the House Judiciary Committee expressed outrage at this circumvention of care, particularly as the bill contained so many provisions that raised constitutional concerns. As expected, the final bill passed overwhelmingly in both houses.

REGULATIONS, ORDERS, MEMOS

While the U.S.A.-Patriot Act was extraordinary in scope, the executive orders, regulations, and even just government memoranda which continue to be issued through today are in some ways more troubling. They are created apart from the oversight of Congress and the courts, which can only years after the fact correct abuses. Many of these provisions have enacted major changes in government practice with no debate before their enactment. Among them:

> 1) Regulations issued October 31 expanded temporary automatic stays by which people can be kept in detention solely at the attorney general's discretion, without case-by-case assessment of a person's danger to society. In practice people are being kept in detention much longer than this regulation implies.

> 2) A 9/21 memo from Immigration Judge Michael Creppy authorizes use of hearings closed to everyone but the government, the immigrant, and his/her lawyer.

> 3) Previously, a judge could authorize surveillance of lawyer-client communication. Now, without judicial authorization the government can notify a person that their communication with their lawyer is being monitored—rendering legal communication virtually useless.

> 4) The presumptions of the Freedom of Information Act have been upended. Former Attorney General Janet Reno had directed that government information should be made public unless there was some compelling reason to keep it secret. Now the government is to change the way it looks at this information—if there's some reason that can be articulated to keep it secret, then that's the priority.

> 5) Military commissions: This is an essay in itself. Rather than go into depth on the content of the original presidential Military Order, and the recently released regulations, I'll summarize each and talk about how they became different.

The core question is, how does the U.S. choose to prosecute people captured abroad who have committed crimes against humanity (as opposed to soldiers), and anyone left alive who was also culpable in part for the September 11 attacks? There are three obvious choices: A) international tribunals or the soon-to-be-authorized international criminal courts—these are the kinds of crimes they were designed for; B) U.S. criminal courts, which handle mass murderers, terrorists, and spies; C) some hybrid model which allows the U.S. to keep control over the process and use the death penalty, that is separate from a U.S. criminal court and tries to separate itself from constitutional rights. The U.S. said it might want to try people abroad and didn't want to confer rights not offered in the defendants' home countries.

President Bush issued a military order. This first document was a marvel. It capsized in one stroke many pivotal historical constitutional rights. Any non-citizen would theoretically be subject to the court. The individual would be in a titularly military court, before military judges and with a military attorney, not necessarily an attorney of their choosing. The person could face the death penalty with a low level of proof for conviction and only two-thirds of the judges voting for death (not a jury trial). No appeals would be allowed. The proceeding would not necessarily be open and could include secret evidence.

The reaction was immediate and widespread. Not only constitutional scholars, civil liberties experts, and military law experts expressed strong objections. Many military people were quite public about their concerns, mostly that if the U.S. didn't conform with the Geneva Conventions in this proceeding, our military and intelligence personnel would then have no grounds to demand such rights if they faced legal proceedings in other countries. The weight of the opposition created pressure for significant change.

While regulations often just flesh out an initial law or executive order, in this case the regulations were used to help fix the order. The Geneva Conventions were to be generally followed; a unanimous vote was required for the death penalty; a civilian lawyer could be hired; proof beyond a reasonable doubt would be required for a conviction; an oddly cobbled military-style appeals body could be invoked to challenge convictions; the proceedings would be open to the press, though secret evidence and other protections for witnesses could be used. Many consider the regulations a halfway fix, but they represent substantial backpedaling from the initial order. The vocal and organized opposition to the original order also represents the first successful amendment of an overreaching plan, out of the vast array of legislative and administrative changes put in place following the September 11 attacks.

DETENTIONS

Quickly after September 11, the government began rounding up Arabs and Muslims across the country and jailing them; estimates of about two thousand people nationally are credible. They didn't charge them with crimes initially. They didn't acknowledge who had been detained. It was as if we were living in Chile during the Pinochet takeover. The U.S. was "disappearing" people.

Legal organizations and national ethnic-rights groups started organizing to find out who was detained, see if they were being charged with crimes, try to find them legal counsel. While initially the government gave numbers about who was currently detained, it quickly stopped the practice. Just as quickly, the Center for National Security Studies, on behalf of several dozen groups, sued under the Freedom of Information Act for the names or sufficient identifying information to determine if people had legal counsel and with what they were being charged.

Soon it became evident to the National Lawyers Guild, the ACLU, the American Friends Service Committee, and several Arab-American rights groups in New Jersey that people from all over the country had been brought to New Jersey lock-ups if they were being put into deportation proceedings. The U.S. finally admitted this to be the case, and said that none of the five hundred or so people were suspected of any criminal activity besides being in the U.S. with visa violations. Yet initially they were all held in jail, denied access to lawyers, to family visits, to the standard know-your-rights presentations. And the U.S. refused for "privacy" reasons to confirm to family and to these groups the basic information about people being held.

The ACLU of New Jersey sued for this information, and on March 26 won the case in court. Calling the secret arrests "odious to a democracy," New Jersey Superior Court Judge Arthur D'Italia granted the ACLU access to records of the detainees. The federal government is expected to appeal, and got an immediate stay of the release until appeals are exhausted. Nonetheless, this is an important step in the process of readjusting the balance of due process.

At the same time the ACLU was suing, the coalition of groups was organizing to provide legal assistance and know-your-rights training to those detained on immigration charges. At every step, the INS resisted these efforts, but persistence and public attention to the issues have opened many of the doors. The challenge to provide mostly pro bono legal help is complex. The ongoing challenge to identify new legal needs will require the best legal talent in the country. In some of the cases, the hearings are being closed to all but lawyer and client. It is expected that secret evidence may form part of some proceedings. Who knows what's next? Comprehensive cooperation among local support organizations and national legal organizations will be essential.

ORGANIZING FOR RATIONALITY

It's clear there are going to be long-term consequences to the new government authorization. One way it can be characterized, somewhat over the top, is as COINTELPRO legalized. The trend to legitimize expanded investigative authority does give this credibility. What was embarrassing in Hoover's day when exposed—the "black bag jobs"—is now legal in some circumstances under the U.S.A.-Patriot Act. The FBI is no longer put in the position of having to apologize for investigating whole movements. They can spy on entire organizations for long periods for allegations of limited crimes by a small number. Now this core First Amendment investigative tactic is arguably authorized.

The organizations I direct have particular experience with defending dissent. The National Coalition Against Repressive Legislation (NCARL) and its sister nonprofit, the First Amendment Foundation, exposed a decades-long FBI investigation of NCARL. The FBI spent millions of dollars and collected 136,000 pages of files from its minute-to-minute surveillance, intimidation, and neutralization efforts against Frank Wilkinson, NCARL's director. His crime? Following the House Un-American Activities Committee around the country to organize resistance to its destruction of peoples' lives for their associations and beliefs. Frank was a threat only for his speech, which never advocated violence. He spent a year in jail for refusing on principle to tell the government his memberships and associations. That jailing hinged up to the Supreme Court on the testimony of a witness the Justice Department privately called unreliable (early use of secret evidence). The only crime the government ever uncovered was a planned assassination against Wilkinson. What did the FBI do? Watched to see if it would take place—the FBI never sought to catch the perpetrators. These priorities were upside down, and they are critical lessons today.

The National Coalition to Protect Political Freedom (NCPPF) was organized following the passage of the 1996 anti-terrorism act. Its concerns have included the use of secret evidence in deportation proceedings. A couple dozen Arab and/or Muslim men spent years in jail, unable to see or rebut information that was kept secret from them. After significant national organizing and pressure, we helped declassify most of the evidence. It was then easily disproved, or shown to be news clippings, hearsay, etc. With strong legal and political efforts, almost all the men won their cases and were released, often with accompanying strong condemnation of secret evidence by the judges. The lessons were two-fold: As long as due process is denied, people will not be able to defend themselves; and when the government is allowed the opportunity to use evidence of dubious quality free from challenge, it will do so. NCPPF helped organize legal support, launched a massive education and press effort, and member organizations worked with Congress to try to prohibit the use of secret evidence. It almost succeeded. Now we have more comprehensive due process and First Amendment efforts to wage.

Activist responses to the post–9/11 government changes must be modified as we proceed and as the changes evolve. When the government adds new regulations, memoranda, and laws to its capacity, those concerned with government overreaching need to be prepared to educate people about the implications of these changes, and respond to change and any new legal needs. The broad effort involves legal, political, media, and educational fields across lines of ethnicity, religion, and politics, and it is nationwide. The organizing should not be defensive. We are raising fundamental issues of governance and constitutional rights. We are participating in shaping the direction this country takes, domestically and abroad. There is no greater responsibility and challenge as Americans.

Citizens bear particular responsibility. We are not at risk of deportation for speaking out, as many immigrants are. We tend to be targeted less frequently than immigrants. Also, those of us who understand the history of government abuses know that the government often confuses dissent with crime. Lacking an understanding of those "strange" foreigners, the government has frequently attributed dangerous purposes to activities and speeches with which it's unfamiliar or doesn't bother to translate. Citizens can translate, literally and figuratively. We have organized over and again, demanding that the government act responsibly, and succeeded. And today we must continue to succeed.

We dare not repeat the mistakes of McCarthyism, of COINTELPRO. The closer international connections in the world today make it imperative that the U.S. allow political dissent to exist, and continue to bring about gradual change to our government and in the world. The alternatives to that change we can imagine better today than ever.

Kit Gage (kgage@igc.org) is the Director of the First Amendment Foundation, and the National Coordinator of the National Coalition to Protect Political Freedom. Rights reserved to reprint for personal use.

MILITARY TRIBUNALS

by Arthur N. Eisenberg

May 6, 2002

"It is not only unconstitutional," President Woodrow Wilson observed, "but . . . in character it would put us nearly upon the level of the very people we are fighting and affecting to despise." Wilson was responding to a congressional proposal, put forward during World War I, that would have allowed individuals accused of committing acts of espionage in this country to be tried and punished by military tribunals. Because of Wilson's opposition, the proposal died in committee.

Ignoring Wilson's wisdom, President George W. Bush issued an order, on November 13, 2001, authorizing military trials in circumstances that extend, in many respects, beyond the World War I proposal. Indeed, the president's order is extraordinary in its breadth, unconstitutional in at least some of its potential applications, and ill-conceived as a matter of public policy and international relations.

The order authorizes military trials for persons who are not citizens of the United States and who the president, in his sole discretion, has "reason to believe" are or were "member[s] of al-Qaida" or have assisted or engaged in acts of "international terrorism . . . or acts that threaten to cause injury . . . to the United States, its citizens, national security, foreign policy, or economy." Moreover, under the order such military trials need not comport with even the most basic constitutional, procedural, and evidentiary requirements traditionally designed to ensure fundamental fairness within our legal system. It dispenses with trial by jury and, instead, allows trials before military commissions. It also allows the tribunals to disregard the usual rules of evidence; allows such trials to proceed in secret; permits conviction upon a two-thirds vote of the tribunal; authorizes the imposition of the death penalty; and purports to deny any judicial review of the tribunals' decisions. In addition, the order is not limited by any temporal or geographic restraints. It applies to acts that may have occurred years ago. And it applies to conduct that takes place, and to individuals that are detained, anywhere in the world.

Reaction to the president's order has been decidedly mixed. Supporters have defended the order as well within the president's power as Commander in Chief. Critics have contended that our constitutional system contemplates civilian control of the military, and that, even as Commander in Chief, the president is a civilian officer subject to the constraints of constitutional principles respecting separation of powers and due process of law.

Debates between supporters and opponents of the president's order regarding its constitutionality have seemed rarely to join issue. This is, in part, because supporters of the order have generally focused upon persons arrested and detained within the theater of active military operations, namely Afghanistan. By contrast, opponents of the order properly express constitutional concern about its application to individuals accused of engaging in proscribed conduct in the United States. But because the order is global in its reach, any evaluation of its constitutionality must distinguish between four categories of persons to whom the order might extend: first, persons who commit acts injurious to the United States within the theater of an active military operation; second, persons who commit acts injurious to the United States and do so outside the theater of active military operation but also outside of the United States; third, persons who are members of the al-Qaida organization who are found and arrested in the United States; fourth, persons who are not members of al-Qaida but are aliens lawfully within this country who are detained or arrested and accused of committing acts within this country that are injurious to the United States. It is with respect to this fourth category that the presidential order is almost certainly unconstitutional.

Two principal Supreme Court decisions bear upon the constitutionality of imposing military trials upon persons living in this country who are accused of conduct injurious to the United States. The first is the *Milligan* case. During the Civil War, Milligan was a Southern sympathizer living in Indiana. He was accused of participating in a secret organization that planned to engage in various acts designed to disrupt the Northern war effort. The organization's plans included releasing prisoners of war from an Indiana facility, and its activities included counseling individuals to avoid the draft. Although he was a civilian, and not a member of either the Confederate or Union armed forces, Milligan was arrested at his home in Indiana by military officials, tried before a military tribunal, found guilty, and sentenced to death pursuant to a presidential order. Prior to his execution, Milligan challenged the authority of the military tribunal in a petition for a writ of habeas corpus filed in federal court.

His claim was ultimately certified to the Supreme Court, which rendered a decision after the Civil War ended and, therefore, in an environment free from the pressure of wartime decision-making. In ordering Milligan's release, the court held that only Congress could authorize the substitution of military tribunals for judicial proceedings, and that Congress could only do so in circumstances where the civilian courts were not open and functioning. Under the facts of *Milligan*, the court concluded that Congress had not, in fact, authorized the use of military tribunals for individuals who were not members of any military units, and that Congress could not do so in Indiana, where the state and federal courts remained open and available.

Defenders of the president's November 2001 order insist that the *Milligan* decision has been modified by a World War II decision of the Supreme Court in the *Quirin* case. And it is true that the *Quirin* case narrowed somewhat the general principles articulated in *Milligan;* but not to the degree urged by the president's supporters. The *Quirin* case arose when, in 1942, eight German marines arrived at two American beaches via Nazi submarines. A group of four went ashore on Long Island. A second group of four landed in Florida. Upon reaching the beaches, the marines removed their uniforms and buried them in the sand as they changed into civilian clothes for the pursuit of their mission. The eight marines had been sent by the Germans to engage in acts of sabotage directed at war industries and facilities. But they were arrested within days and by order of the president were tried before a military tribunal and convicted of violating the Law of War.

In *Quirin*, the German marines filed petitions for habeas corpus in the federal courts challenging the jurisdiction of the military tribunal and arguing that they were entitled to be tried in the federal courts. The government responded to these petitions by asserting, first, that the federal courts did not even have the authority to review the president's determination that these individuals should be tried before a military tribunal. Second, the government contended that even if the decision to subject these individuals to military tribunals was susceptible to federal court review the decision should, nonetheless, be sustained because it was authorized by Congress and consistent with the Law of War.

The *Quirin* case ultimately reached the Supreme Court, which held, in the first instance, that the presidential directive did not preclude the federal courts from entertaining the habeas corpus petitions and from adjudicating whether the president had the authority to direct that the eight German marines were to be subjected to military trials. But in addressing the merits of the controversy, the *Quirin* court sustained the president's directive. In so doing, the court reasoned that Congress had authorized the president to use military tribunals in the prosecution of certain individuals who engaged in conduct in violation of the Law of War by incorporating the Articles of War into the federal statutes. In this regard, the court further recognized that under the Law of War there is a distinction between "lawful combatants" and "unlawful combatants." By way of example, the court suggested that "lawful combatants" are uniformed members of a military force who "are subject to capture and detention and entitled to be treated as prisoners of war." By contrast, the court identified as "unlawful combatants" members of an enemy military force "who during war pass surreptitiously from enemy territory into our own, discarding their uniforms upon entry, for the commission of hostile acts involving destruction of life or property." Under the Law of War, these "unlawful combatants"—also described as "unprivileged combatants"—are not entitled to be treated as prisoners of war but may, instead, be subjected to military tribunals and punished for engaging in belligerent behavior surreptitiously and out of uniform.

But the central feature of both "lawful" and "unlawful combatants" is that both groups are members of the armed forces of a country with whom we are at war. This was the basis upon which the *Quirin* court distinguished the *Milligan* case. The German marines before the court in *Quirin* were all members of the German Armed Forces. But *Milligan*, the court observed, "not being a part of or associated with the armed forces of the enemy, was a non-belligerent [and] not subject to the Law of War."

When read together, *Milligan* and *Quirin* establish the following principles: First, the substitution of military tribunals for civilian courts, with respect to persons who are captured outside the theater of military operations, can only be undertaken pursuant to congressional authorization. Second, such authorization would itself be unconstitutional at least as applied generally to persons in this country where the civil government is functioning and the courts are open. Third, notwithstanding the general prohibition of military trials when civilian courts are open in this country, *Quirin* allows a narrow exception where Congress authorizes and the president directs military tribunals to try and punish individuals who are in this country as "unlawful combatants," and who, as military personnel from a country with whom we are at war, can be tried for violating the Law of War.

When measured against these principles, several questions arise with respect to the president's November 2001 order. The first is whether the order was authorized by Congress. Certainly, no express congressional authorization has been identified. And, indeed, the recent enactment by Congress of the U.S.A.-Patriot Act—which creates new federal crimes and new criminal procedures to prosecute terrorism in federal courts—would seem to support the claim that Congress intended that terrorism and conduct in support of terrorism committed in this country should be prosecuted under federal law, in federal courts, and not before military tribunals. On the other hand, in *Quirin*, the court found congressional authorization to try and punish the German marines under the Law of War by virtue of Congress' enactment of legislation that incorporated the Articles of War into the United States Code and that allowed military tribunals to punish offenses against the Law of War. Much of that legislation, which is now called the Law of Armed Conflict, remains incorporated within the United States Code. But in this respect, *Quirin* must again be understood as a very narrow case. For, as noted, the individuals who were subjected to military tribunals in *Quirin* were members of the German Armed Forces against whom the Law of War could have been applied appropriately. *Quirin* provides no basis for concluding that Congress has authorized military tribunals for individuals who are not members of an enemy military force.

It might be argued, however, that al-Qaida should be treated as an enemy military force and that members of al-Qaida who came into this country surreptitiously to commit acts of violence should be regarded as "unlawful combatants" and, as such, subject to prosecution in military courts for violating the Law of War. There is much force to this argument.

Even assuming that members of al-Qaida who are arrested in this country could be tried before military tribunals, *if* such tribunals were authorized by Congress, it seems reasonably clear that persons who are not members of any military or paramilitary organization with whom we are at war cannot be tried by military tribunals for acts committed in this country, if the civilian courts in this country are open and functioning—which they clearly are.

Consider, in this regard, Mazen al-Najjar, a Palestinian who had lived in Florida for many years and, indeed, had been employed as an adjunct professor at a Florida university. The *New York Times* reported that the government was seeking to deport this individual and that the deportation order rested upon a technical violation of the immigration law. Mr. al-Najjar, it seems, had over-stayed a student visa in the early 1980s. But, the real reason for the deportation appeared to be that the Palestinian was associated with two organizations—the World and Islam Studies Enterprises (WISE) and the Islamic Concern Project (ICP)—that, according to the Justice Department, were "front organizations" that supported Palestinian terrorist activities. Mr. al-Najjar maintained that WISE was an academic research organization and that ICP was a charitable organization; that neither of these organizations supported Palestinian terrorism; that, in any event, he was unaware of any support for terrorism in which these organizations may have engaged; and that he, as an individual, had not know-ingly supported any acts of terrorism. But, suppose that Mr. al-Najjar had not violated the immigration laws in the 1980s and had, therefore, not provided the government with the opportunity to deport him. In that circumstance, the Justice Department might well have been tempted to prosecute Mr. al-Najjar criminally and President Bush's November 2001 order is broad enough to invite such a prosecution before a military tribunal.

This situation exposes the serious threat to civil liberties posed by the presi-dential order. An individual who has lived here for many years but is not a United States citizen may associate with, or contribute money to an ideological or religious or academic organization and may do so without knowing that the organization, in addition to its lawful activities, is also providing assistance to other organizations that commit acts of terrorism. Under the November 2001 order such an individual is subject to prosecution by military tribunals because the order does not require, as a condition of prosecution or conviction, that the individual has knowingly supported acts of terrorism. Accordingly, such an individual can be whisked off the streets, detained and tried with secret evi-dence before a secret tribunal consisting of military officials whose decision is unreviewable by an independent federal court.

It seems clear, however, that the government would violate the constitutional principles of *Milligan* and *Quirin* were it to prosecute such an individual in a military tribunal. But, how would such an individual raise an objection to the jurisdiction of the military tribunal? The presidential order does not, by its terms, provide a mechanism to allow federal courts to decide, at the outset, whether an individual can appropriately be remanded for prosecution before a military tribunal or whether such individual can be prosecuted, if at all, only by a civilian court. Indeed, the order seems intentionally ambiguous on this point. It provides that "military tribunals shall have exclusive jurisdiction with respect to individuals subject to the order." And it provides that "any individual subject to this order shall not be privileged to seek any remedy" in any federal or state court or in any foreign or international tribunal.

It is likely, however, that the federal courts would hold, as did the Supreme Court in *Quirin*, that habeas corpus review is available at least to determine the authority and jurisdiction of the military tribunal to hear a particular case. This conclusion rests not only upon a fair reading of *Quirin;* it also rests upon the general understanding that the president does not possess the power to suspend habeas corpus without congressional authorization and that Congress must articulate its intent in specific and unambiguous language.

But suppose the president directs that an individual is to be remanded for trial before a military tribunal and suppose further that, prior to any military trial, the individual seeks and secures habeas corpus review in a federal district court to test the jurisdictional authority of the military tribunal. A question remains as to how the district court should proceed in evaluating the jurisdictional issue. Consider, in this regard, an individual who is accused by the government of being an active member of al-Qaida with knowledge of al-Qaida's violent activities. And suppose that the individual disputes the allegations and insists that he is not a member of al-Qaida and is unsupportive of its aims. It would appear that, in order to determine the jurisdictional authority of the military tribunal, the federal court would need to conduct a hearing to evaluate, in some preliminary fashion, the sufficiency of the government's allegations. The precise contours of such a hearing and the standard of proof that might be required are matters that will need to be developed by the federal judiciary should such a situation arise. Alternatively, such procedures might have been developed under the regulations that were promulgated in March 2002 by the Department of Defense to amplify and implement the president's order. Unfortunately, the regulations fail to address this matter.

The regulations do, however, address some matters left unresolved by the presidential order. And, in certain respects, the regulations adopt procedures that embrace traditional notions of fair criminal processes in filling in the details left unaddressed by the order. For example, the regulations provide that an accused shall be entitled to a presumption of innocence and that the prosecution must establish guilt beyond a reasonable doubt. Moreover, while the regulations provide—as did the presidential order—that a conviction may be secured by a two-thirds vote of a tribunal, the regulations further require that the imposition of a death penalty can only occur if there is a unanimous vote of a tribunal consisting of seven members.

In other respects, the regulations promise what may amount only to illusory rights. These are rights that look good on paper but are likely easily to disappear in the heat of a contested litigation. Again, by way of example, the regulations permit the accused to retain a civilian counsel of choice to assist the military attorney in presenting a defense to the charges. But at the same time, the regulations also provide that the civilian defense counsel will not necessarily be permitted to attend closed hearings. Similarly, the regulations provide for open proceedings *unless* the secretary of defense or the presiding officer of the tribunal decides to close the hearings to protect "the physical safety of participants in [the] proceeding . . . ; intelligence and law enforcement sources, methods or activities; and other national security interests." Inasmuch as a principal reason for employing military tribunals rather than federal courts turns upon the capacity to close the military proceedings more easily than federal court proceedings, hearings before the military tribunals may often be closed. Furthermore, under the regulations, proceedings may not only be closed but they may involve *ex parte* communication between the prosecution and the presiding officer from which defense counsel are excluded.

The most serious failings of the regulations are three-fold: First, although disputes over the jurisdiction of the military tribunals can reasonably be anticipated, as noted, the regulations provide no mechanism for the resolution of such jurisdictional matters by an independent federal judiciary. Second, the regulations perpetuate the suggestion advanced by the presidential order that, at the conclusion of the military proceedings, judicial review of convictions by independent federal courts will not be available. Third, the regulations do not cure the unconstitutional reach of the presidential order. The regulations perpetuate the possibility that persons who are living in this country but are not citizens might be accused of supporting or engaging in acts injurious to the United States and tried before military tribunals—even though such persons are not accused of being members of al-Qaida, and even though the federal courts remain open and available.

The regulations leave other questions unresolved, as well. Beyond persons who are arrested in the United States for acts committed in this country, there remain two categories of individuals to whom the November 13 order might extend. The first pertains to persons who are captured within the theater of active military operations and accused of violating the Law of War. Under previously existing law, military tribunals in these circumstances were legitimate, and a more narrowly crafted military order from the president could have appropriately amplified and supplemented such authority. In this regard, however, it is important to distinguish between "prisoners of war" and "unlawful" or "unprivileged combatants." Prisoners of War are simply captured belligerents who have not violated the Law of War and have otherwise engaged in no conduct-warranting trial before a military tribunal. By contrast, as noted, "unlawful combatants" can be tried by military courts for violation of the Law of War.

The final category involves individuals who commit or support violent acts injurious to the United States and do so both outside of the United States and outside any active theater of military operations. The application of the November 13 order to such individuals raises questions regarding the wisdom and efficacy of the president's approach from the standpoint of our relations with other countries. Spain has already expressed reservations about extraditing individuals to the United States because of the potential that such individuals will be subjected to military trials and possible death sentences. Other Western democracies are likely to respond in a similar fashion.

In the face of these constitutional, international-law, and policy objections to important aspects of the president's order, what possible justifications could be advanced in support of the president's directive? Two justifications are commonly advanced. The first involves the assertion that classified information will be compromised if members of al-Qaida or other accused terrorists are tried in public proceedings in federal court. But there is a federal statute, the Classified Information Procedures Act, that protects classified information that might be introduced in criminal trials and establishes special procedures to ensure that the introduction of such evidence does not compromise intelligence-gathering operations. Such procedures allow for hearings held in judges' chambers rather than in open courtrooms, authorize court orders deleting classified information, and confer judicial authority to seal transcripts of the proceedings held in chambers. In addition, the administration's decision to try, in federal district court, an alleged coconspirator connected to the September 11 events, Zacarias

Moussaoui, weakens considerably the claim that to protect intelligence information such individuals can only be tried before military tribunals. The second justification relates to the need to protect judges and jurors against retaliation. But again, procedures have been used for years in connection with the prosecution of members of organized crime to protect against jury tampering or retaliation. Such procedures involve protective orders ensuring the anonymity of jurors, and using federal marshals to protect judges and other trial participants.

At bottom, peace and security are not incompatible with respect for our constitutional traditions and with the rule of law. Indeed, the goals of peace and security that we all share cannot be achieved successfully without adherence to democratic and constitutional values. That is the lesson that we must understand for ourselves. That is the lesson that we must try to convey to the world at large. We must teach by example. We fail in that exemplary responsibility when expediency driven by fear impels us to ignore our own constitutional tradition and our basic commitment to fair and open trials. We simply appear hypocritical before the world when we repeatedly urge other countries to respect principles of fair and open judicial processes while we very quickly abandon those principles on the first occasion of deep national anxiety. President Wilson understood this.

Arthur N. Eisenberg is the Legal Director of the New York Civil Liberties Union.

DEHUMANIZATION VIA INDEFINITE DETENTION
by Judith Butler

On March 21, 2002, the Department of Defense, in conjunction with the Department of Justice, issued new guidelines for the military tribunals in which some of the detained suspected terrorists and captured prisoners, domestically and in Guantanamo Bay, would be tried by the U.S. What has been striking about these detentions from the start, and what continues to be alarming, is that the right to legal counsel and, indeed, the right to a trial, have not been granted to most of these detainees. The new military tribunals are, in fact, not courts of law to which the detainees are entitled. Some will be tried and others will not, and at the time of this writing, none have been tried at all. The Geneva Convention's right to counsel, to means of appeal, and to expatriation have not been granted to any of the detainees in Guantanamo, and although the U.S. has announced its recognition of the Taliban as "covered" by the Geneva Accord, it has made clear that even the Taliban do not have POW status; indeed, no prisoner in Guantanamo does.

In the name of a security alert and national emergency, the law is effectively suspended in both its national and international forms. And with the suspension of law comes a new exercise of state sovereignty, one that not only takes place outside the law, but through an elaboration of administrative bureaucracies in which officials now decide not only who will be tried and who will be detained, but hold ultimate power over how long someone may be detained. With the publication of the new regulations, the U.S. government holds that a number of detainees at Guantanamo will not be given trials at all, but detained indefinitely. On the one hand, it is crucial to ask, under what conditions do human lives cease to become eligible for basic, if not universal, human rights? How does the U.S. government construe these conditions? And to what extent is there a racial and ethnic frame through which these imprisoned lives are viewed and judged such that they are judged as less than human, or as having departed from the recognizable human community? On the other hand, in maintaining that some prisoners will be detained indefinitely, the state allocates to itself a power, an indefinitely prolonged power, to exercise judgments on who is dangerous and without entitlement to basic legal rights.

In detaining some prisoners indefinitely, the state appropriates for itself a sovereign power that is defined over and against existing legal frameworks, civil, military, and international. The military tribunals may well acquit someone of a crime, but that acquittal is not only subject to mandatory executive review, but the Department of Defense has also made clear that acquittal will not necessarily end detention. Moreover, according to the new tribunal regulations, those tried in such a venue will have no rights of appeal to U.S. civil courts. Here we can see that the law itself is either suspended or regarded as an instrument that the state may use in the service of constraining and monitoring a given population; the state is not subject to the rule of law, but law can be suspended or deployed tactically and partially to suit the requirements of a sovereign state that acts in the name of its own self-preservation; but also, in that name, extends its own power to imprison some group of people indefinitely without trial. In the very act by which state sovereignty suspends law, or contorts law to its own uses, it extends its own domain, its own necessity, and develops the means by which the justification of its own power takes place.

The state augments its own power in at least two ways. In the context of the military tribunals, the trials are effectively advisory to the executive branch, since the executive branch will not only decide whether or not a "detainee" will stand trial, but will appoint the tribunal, review the process, and have final say over matters of guilt and innocence as well as on the punishment, if any, to be received. Because detainees are not entitled to these trials, but may be offered them at the will of executive power, there is no semblance of separation of powers in these circumstances. For those who are detained indefinitely, their cases will be reviewed by officials—not by courts—on a periodic basis. These acts are themselves not grounded in law, but in another form of judgment. In this sense, they are already outside the sphere of law, since the determination of when and where, for instance, a trial might be waived and detention deemed indefinite does not take place within a legal process; it is not a decision made by a judge, for which evidence must be submitted, or a case that must be made that meets certain established criteria or conforms to certain protocols of evidence and argument. It is a unilateral judgment made by officials, government officials, who simply deem that a given individual or, indeed, a group poses a danger to the state. This act of "deeming" takes place in the context of a state of emergency that is understood to warrant the suspension of law, including due process for these individuals.

But if detention may be indefinite, and such detentions are presumably justified on the basis of a state of emergence, then the government is imagining a protracted, if not indefinite, state of emergency. Indeed, whereas it makes sense that the U.S. government would take immediate steps to detain those with whom there is evidence that they intend to wage violence against the U.S., it seems important to question whether the government extends conditions of national emergency such that the state will now have recourse to extra-legal detention and the suspension of established law, both domestic and international, for the foreseeable future. Indeed, the "indefinite" detention of the untried prisoner—or the prisoner tried by military tribunal and detained, regardless of the outcome—is a practice that presupposes the indefinite extension of the war on terrorism. And if this "war" becomes a permanent part of the state apparatus, a condition which justifies and extends the use of military tribunals, then the executive branch has set up its own judiciary function, one that overrides the separation of power, the writ of habeas corpus (for the Guantanamo Bay prisoners), and the entitlement to due process.

These men are detained indefinitely; they are not really called "prisoners" since the rights pertaining to prisoners would then come into play. They are "detainees," those who are held in waiting, those for whom waiting may well be without end. To the extent that the state arranges for this pre-legal state as an "indefinite" one, it maintains that there will be those held by the government for whom the law does not apply, not only in the present, but for the indefinite future.

The military tribunals are understood to apply not only to those arrested within the U.S., but for "high-ranking" officials currently detained in Guantanamo Bay. The *Washington Post* reported that "there may be little use for the tribunals because the great majority of the three hundred prisoners being held at the U.S. naval base at Guantanamo Bay, Cuba, are low-ranking foot soldiers. Administration officials have other plans for many of the relatively junior captives now at Guantanamo Bay: indefinite detention without trial. U.S. officials would take this action with prisoners they fear could pose a danger of terrorism even if they have little evidence of past crimes."

"Could pose a danger of terrorism." This means that conjecture is the basis of detention, but also that conjecture is the basis of an indefinite detention without trial. One could simply respond to these events by saying that everyone detained deserves a trial, and I do believe that is the right thing to say. But saying that is not enough, since we have to look at what constitutes a trial in the cases where a detainee would be tried in these new military tribunals. What kind of trial does everyone deserve? In these new tribunals, evidentiary standards are very lax. In fact, hearsay and secondhand reports will constitute relevant evidence, whereas in regular trials, either in the civil court system or the established military court system, they would be dismissed out of hand.

The Department of Defense says explicitly that these trials are planned "only for relatively high-ranking al-Qaida and Taliban operatives against whom there is persuasive evidence of terrorism or war crimes" (March 21, 2002). If the trials are saved for high-ranking officials against whom there is persuasive evidence, then this suggests that either the relatively low-ranking detainees are those against whom there is no persuasive evidence, or that even if there is persuasive evidence against them, these members have no entitlement to hear the charge, to prepare a case for themselves, or to obtain release or final judgment through a tribunal procedure. Given that the notion of "persuasive evidence" has become effectively rewritten to include conventionally non-persuasive evidence, such as hearsay and secondhand reports, and there is a chance that the U.S. means that there is no evidence that would be found to be persuasive by a new military tribunal, the U.S. is effectively admitting that neither hearsay nor secondhand reports would work as evidence to convict these low-ranking members. Given as well that the Northern Alliance is credited with turning over the al-Qaida and Taliban detainees to U.S. authorities, it would be important to know whether that organization had good grounds for identifying the individuals detained, before the U.S. decides to detain them indefinitely. If there is no such evidence, one might well wonder, why they are being detained at all? And if there is evidence, but such individuals are not given a trial, one might well wonder, how is the worth of these lives regarded such that they are not eligible for legal entitlements guaranteed by existing U.S. law and international human rights law?

To be fair, there are international precedents for indefinite detention without trial. The U.S. cites European human rights courts that allowed British authorities to detain Irish Catholic and Protestant militants for long periods of time, if they were, "deemed dangerous, but not necessarily convicted of a crime." But the "deeming" is not, as I've mentioned, a judgment that needs to be supported by evidence, or for which there are rules of evidence. The "danger" has to be understood quite clearly in the context of a national emergency. In those cases cited by the Bush administration, the detentions lasted indefinitely, as long as "British officials"—notably not courts—reviewed the cases from time to time. The appeal process is automatic, but the final say in matters of guilt and punishment resides with the executive branch, and the office of the president himself. This means that whatever conclusions these trials come up with can be potentially reversed or revised by the executive branch, a procedure which effectively overrides the separation-of-powers doctrine, suspending once again the binding power of the Constitution in favor of an unchecked enhancement of executive power.

The Department of Defense published pictures of prisoners shackled and kneeling, with mouths covered by surgical masks and eyes blinded by blackened goggles. They were reportedly given sedatives, their heads were shaved, and the cells where they were brought measure 8 feet by 8 feet and 7-1/2 feet high, and which, Amnesty International reported in April 2002, are appreciably smaller than international law allows. There is a question of whether the metal sheet called a "roof" offers any of the protective functions against wind and rain associated with that architectural function.

The photographs of these conditions produced an international outcry, because the degradation—and the publicizing of the degradation—contravened the Geneva Convention, as the International Red Cross pointed out, and because these individuals were rendered faceless and abject, likened to caged and restrained animals. Indeed, Secretary Rumsfeld's own language at press conferences seems to corroborate this view that the detainees are not like other humans who enter into war, and that they are, in this respect, not "punishable" by law but deserving of immediate and sustained forcible incarceration. When Secretary Rumsfeld was asked why these prisoners were being forcibly restrained and held without trial, he explained that if they were not restrained, they would kill again. He implied that restraint is the only thing that keeps them from killing, that they are beings whose very propensity it is to kill—that is what they would do as a matter of course. Are they pure killing machines? If so, then they are not humans in need of restraint, entitled to trials, to due process, to knowing and understanding a charge against them. They are something less than human, and yet they assume a human form. They represent, as it were, an equivocation of the human, which forms the basis for some of the skepticism about the applicability of legal entitlements and protections.

In the news conference on March 21, Department of Defense General Counsel Haynes answered a reporter's question in a way that confirmed that this equivocation is at work in their thinking. The danger that these prisoners are said to pose is unlike dangers that might be substantiated in a court of law and redressed through punishment. A reporter, unnamed in the news conference, concerned about the military tribunal, asked whether, if someone is acquitted of a crime under this tribunal, they would be set free. Haynes replied, "If we had a trial right this minute, it is conceivable that somebody could be tried and acquitted of that charge, but might not automatically be released. The people we are detaining, for example, in Guantanamo Bay, Cuba, are enemy combatants that we captured on the battlefield seeking to harm U.S. soldiers or allies, and they're dangerous people. At the moment, we're not about to release any of them unless we find that they don't meet those criteria. At some point in the future . . ." The reporter then interrupted, saying, "But if you [can't] convict them, if you can't find them guilty, you would still paint them with that brush that we find you dangerous even though we can't convict you, and continue to incarcerate them?" After some to and fro, Haynes stepped up to the microphone and explained that "the people that we now hold at Guantanamo are held for a specific reason that is not tied specifically to any particular crime. They're not held—they're not being held on the basis that they are necessarily criminals."

Therefore, they will not be released unless the U.S. finds that "they don't meet those criteria," but it is unclear what criteria is at work in Haynes's remark. On the one hand, if it is the new military tribunal that sets the criteria, those tribunals do not guarantee the release of the prisoner, even if the prisoner is acquitted of a crime in the course of a tribunal. The reason for this is that the prisoner may well be "deemed dangerous," but we are given no criteria by which to understand how that deeming takes place, or on what basis. Establishing dangerousness is not the same as establishing guilt and, in Haynes's view, subsequently repeated by administrative spokespersons, the executive branch's power to deem a detainee dangerous preempts any determination of guilt or innocence established by a military tribunal.

At every step of the way, the executive branch decides the form of the tribunal, appoints its members, determines the eligibility of those to be tried, and assumes power over the final judgment; it imposes the trial selectively; it dispenses with conventional evidentiary procedure. And it justifies all this through recourse to a determination of "dangerousness" which it alone is in the position to decide. A certain level of dangerousness takes a human outside the bounds of law, and even outside the bounds of the military tribunal itself, making that human into the state's possession, infinitely detainable. What counts as "dangerous" is what is deemed dangerous by the state, so that, once again, the state posits what is dangerous, and in so positing it, establishes the conditions for its own preemption and usurpation of the law, a notion of law that has already been usurped by a tragic facsimile of a trial.

We have already seen this process at work in racial profiling; in the detention of hundreds of Arab residents or Arab-American citizens, sometimes on the basis of last names alone; in the attacks on individuals of Middle Eastern descent on U.S. streets; and in the targeting of Arab-American professors on campuses. A population of Islamic peoples, or those taken to be Islamic, becomes targeted by this government mandate to be on heightened alert, with the effect that the Arab population in the U.S. becomes visually rounded up, stared down, watched, hounded, and monitored by a group of citizens who understand themselves as foot soldiers in the war against terrorism. What kind of public culture is being created when a certain "indefinite containment" takes place outside the prison walls, on the subway, in the airplanes, on the street, in the workplace? A falafel restaurant run by Lebanese Christians that does not exhibit the American flag becomes immediately suspect, as if the failure to fly the flag becomes read as a sign of sympathy with al-Qaida, a deduction that has no justification but which nevertheless rules public culture—and business interests—at this time.

We saw evidence for this de-realization of the human in the photos released by the Department of Defense of the shackled bodies in Guantanamo. The DOD did not hide these photos, but published them openly. My speculation is that they understood the publishing of these photographs as a certain vanquishing, the reversal of national humiliation, a sign of a successful vindication. These were not photographs leaked to the press by some human rights agency or concerned media enterprise. So the international response was no doubt disconcerting, since instead of moral triumph, many people, many British parliamentarians and European human rights activists among them, saw moral failure. Instead of vindication, many saw instead revenge, cruelty, and a nationalist and self-satisfied flouting of international convention. Several countries asked that their citizens be returned home for trial.

But there is something more in this degradation that calls out to be interpreted. There is a reduction of these human beings to animal status, where the animal is figured as out of control, in need of total restraint. Indeed, it is important to remember that the bestialization of the human in this way has little, if anything, to do with actual animals, since it is a figure of the animal against which the human is defined. Indeed, even if, as seems most probable, some or all of these people have violent intentions, have been engaged in violent, murderous acts, there are ways with which murderers have been dealt with under criminal law and under international law. The language by which they are described by the U.S., however, suggests that these individuals are exceptional, that they may not be individuals at all, that they must be constrained in order not to kill, that they are effectively reducible to a desire to kill, and that regular criminal and international codes cannot apply to them.

The treatment of these prisoners is considered as an extension of war itself, not as a post-war question of appropriate trial and punishment. Their detention stops their killing. If they were not detained, and forcibly so, they would apparently start killing on the spot; they are beings who are in a permanent and perpetual war. Now it may be that al-Qaida representatives speak this way—Moussaoui certainly does—but that does not mean that every individual detained embodies that position, or that those detained are centrally concerned with the continuation of war. Indeed, recent reports, even from the investigative team in Guantanamo, suggest that some of the detainees were only tangentially or transiently involved in the war effort ("Some Detainees Held on Guantanamo are Young Foot Soldiers Caught Up in the Afghan War, U.S. Officials Say," *Associated Press*, March 29, 2002). But even General Dunlavey, who makes this admission, claims that the risk is still too high to release such detainees. And Rumsfeld cites in support of forcible detention the uprisings in Afghanistan in which prisoners managed to get hold of weapons and stage a battle inside the prison. In this sense, the war is not, and cannot be, over; there is a chance of battle in the prison, and there is a warrant for physical restraint, such that the post-war prison becomes the continuing site of war. It would seem that the rules that govern combat are in place, but not the rules that govern the proper treatment of prisoners separated from the war itself. Indeed, if it is a war against terrorism, how can it end? Is it therefore a war without end, given the liability of the terms "terrorism" and "war"? Although the pictures were published as a sign of U.S. triumph, and so apparently indicated a conclusion to the war effort, it is clear that bombing and armed conflict continue in Afghanistan. Thus the war was not over, and even the photographs, and the degradation, and the indefinite detention, are continuing acts of war. Indeed, war seems to have established a more or less permanent condition of national emergency, and the sovereign right to self-protection outflanks any and all recourse to law.

When General Counsel Haynes was asked, "So you could in fact hold these people for years without charging them, simply to keep them off the street, even if you don't charge them?" he replied, "We are within our rights, and I don't think anyone disputes it that we may hold enemy combatants for the duration of the conflict. And the conflict is still going and *we don't see an end in sight right now*" (my emphasis).

The exercise of sovereign power is bound up with the extra-legal status of these official acts of speech. These acts become the means by which sovereign power extends itself; the more it can produce equivocation, the more effectively it can augment its power in the apparent service of justice. These official statements are also media performances, a form of state speech that establishes a domain of official utterance distinct from legal discourse. When many organizations and countries questioned whether the U.S. was honoring the Geneva Convention protocols on the treatment of prisoners of war, the administration waffled in its response. Administration officials maintained that the prisoners at Guantanamo were being treated in a manner *"consistent with"* the Geneva convention. They did not say that they understood the U.S. to be obligated to honor that law, or that this law has a binding power over the U.S.

Indeed, the power of the Geneva Convention has been established by the U.S. as unbinding in several instances over the last month. The first example was the claim that appears to honor the Convention, namely, that the U.S. is acting in a manner consistent with the convention, or, alternatively, that the U.S. is acting *in the spirit of* the Geneva Accord. To say that the U.S. acts consistently with the accords is to say that the U.S. acts in such a way that does not contradict the accords, but this does not mean that the U.S., as a signatory to the accords, understands itself as *bound to* the accords. To acknowledge the latter would be to acknowledge the limits that international accords impose upon claims of sovereignty. To act consistently with the accord is to determine one's own action, and to regard that action as in some unspecified way compatible with the accords. Matters get worse, however, when we see that certain rights laid out in the Geneva Accords, Article 3, such as the right to counsel, the right to know the charge against a prisoner, the consideration by a regularly constituted court, rights of appeal, and a timely repatriation, are not being honored and are not in the planning.

Matters become even more vexed, but perhaps finally more clear, when we hear, as we have, that, well, none of the detainees in Guantanamo are to be regarded as prisoners of war according to the Geneva Convention, since none of them belong to "regular armies." Under pressure, the Bush administration conceded that the Taliban were covered by the Geneva Convention, because they were the representatives of the Afghan government, but that they still are not entitled to prisoner of war status under that accord. Indeed, the administration finally said quite clearly that the Geneva Accord was not designed to handle this kind of war, and so its stipulations about who is and is not regarded as a prisoner of war, who is entitled to the rights pertaining to such a status, are anachronistic. The administration thus dismisses the accord as out-dated, but claims to be acting consistent with it.

When relatively widespread outrage emerged in response to the publication of the shackled bodies in Guantanamo, the U.S. asserted it was treating these prisoners humanely. The word "humanely" was used time and again, and in conjunction with the claim that the U.S. was acting consistently with the Geneva Convention. It seems important to recognize that one of the tasks of the Geneva Convention was to establish what does and does not qualify as the humane treatment of prisoners of war. In other words, one of the tasks was to seek to establish an international understanding of "humane treatment" and to stipulate what conditions must first be met before we can say that humane treatment has been offered. The term "humane treatment" thus received a legal consideration, and the result was a set of conditions, explicitly formulated, which, if satisfied, would constitute this treatment.

When the U.S. says, then, that it is treating these prisoners humanely, it uses the word in its own way and for its own purpose, but it does not accept that the Geneva Accord stipulates how the term might legitimately be applied. In effect, it takes the word back from the accord at the very moment that it claims to be acting consistently with the accord. In the moment that it claims to be acting consistently with the accord, it effectively maintains that the accord has no power over it. Similarly, if the U.S. says that it recognizes that the Taliban are to be considered under the Geneva Convention, but then says that even Taliban soldiers are not entitled to prisoner of war status, the U.S. effectively disputes the binding power of the agreement. Given that the agreement maintains that a competent tribunal must be set up to determine prisoner of war status, and that all prisoners are to be treated as POWs until such time as a competent tribunal makes a different determination, and given that the U.S. has arranged for no such tribunal and has made this determination unilaterally, the U.S. disregards the very terms of the agreement again. As a result, the "recognition" of the Taliban as being covered by an accord that the U.S. treats as nonbinding is effectively worthless, especially when it continues to deny POW status to those it ostensibly recognizes.

So these prisoners, who are not prisoners, will be tried at all, if they will be tried at all, according to rules that are not those of a constitutionally defined U.S. law. Under the Geneva Convention, they would be entitled to trials under the same procedures as U.S. soldiers—through court-martial or civilian courts—not through military tribunals as the Bush administration has proposed. The current regulations for military tribunals provide for the death penalty if all members of the tribunal agree to it. But the president will be able to decide on that punishment unilaterally if he decides so at the final stage of deliberations in which an executive judgment is made. And there are no rights of appeal. Is there a timeframe set forth in which this particular judicial operation will cease to be in effect? In response to a reporter who asked whether the government was creating procedures that would be in place indefinitely, "as an ongoing additional judicial system created by the executive branch," General Counsel Haynes pointed out that the "the rules [for the tribunals] . . . do not have a sunset provision in them . . . I'd only observe that the war, we think, will last for a while."

To the extent that the Geneva Convention gives grounds for a distinction between legal and illegal combatants, it distinguished between legitimate violence and illegitimate violence. Legitimate violence is waged by recognizable states or "countries," as Rumsfeld puts it, and illegitimate violence is precisely that which is committed by those who are landless, stateless. In the present climate, we see the intensification of this formulation as various acts of political violence are called "terrorism," not because there are valences of violence that might be distinguished from one another, but as a way of characterizing violence waged by, or in the name of, authorities deemed illegitimate by established states. As a result, we have the wholescale and sweeping dismissal of the Palestinian Intifada as "terrorism" by Ariel Sharon, whose use of state violence to destroy homes and lives is surely extreme.

The use of the term "terrorism" thus works to delegitimize certain forms of violence committed by non-state-centered political entities at the same time that it sanctions a violent response by established states. Obviously, this has been a tactic for a long time as colonial states deal with the Palestinians and with the Irish Catholics, and it was as well a case made against the A.N.C. in South Africa. But the new form that this kind of argument is taking in Israel, and the naturalized status it assumes, will only intensify the enormously damaging consequences for the struggle for Palestinian self-determination. Israel takes advantage of this formulation by holding itself accountable to no state of law at the very same time that it understands itself as engaged in legitimate self-defense. In this sense, the framework for conceptualizing global violence is such that terrorism becomes the name to describe the violence of the illegitimate, whereas legal war becomes the prerogative of those who can assume international recognition as legitimate states.

The fact that these prisoners are seen as pure vessels of violence, as Rumsfeld claimed, suggests that they do not become violent for the same kinds of reason that other politicized beings do, that their violence is somehow constitutive, groundless, and infinite. If this is terrorism rather than violence, it is action that has no political goal, or cannot be read politically. It emerges, as they say, from fanatics, extremists who do not espouse a logical point of view, exist outside of "reason," and do not have a part in the human community. That it is Islamic terrorism simply means that the dehumanization that Orientalism already performs is heightened to an extreme, so that the uniqueness and exceptionalism of this kind of war makes it exempt from the presumptions and protections of universality and civilization. When the very human status of those who are imprisoned is called into question, it is a sign that we have made use of a certain parochial frame and have failed to expand our conception of human rights to include those whose values may well test the limits of our own.

The figure of Islamic extremism is a very reductive one at this point in time, belying an extreme ignorance about the various social and political forms that Islam takes—the tensions, for instance, between Sunni and Shiite Muslims, and the wide range of religious practices that have little, if any, political implications, or whose political implications are explicitly pacifistic. If we assume that everyone who is human goes to war like us, or that the violence we commit is violence that falls within the realm of the recognizably human, we make use of a limited and limiting cultural frame to understand what it is to be human. But to be human implies many things, one of which is that we are the kinds of beings who must live in a world where clashes of value do occur, and that these clashes are a sign of what a human community is. *Whether we continue to enforce a universal conception of human rights at moments of outrage and incomprehension, precisely when we think that others have taken themselves out of the human community as we know it, is a test of our very humanity.*

We make a mistake, therefore, if we take a single definition of the human, or a single model of rationality, to be the defining feature of the human, and then extrapolate from that pre-given understanding of the human to all of its various cultural forms. That direction will lead us to wonder whether some humans who do not exemplify reason and violence by our definition are still human, or whether they are "exceptional" (Haynes), or "unique" (Hastert), or "really bad people" (Cheney). To come up against what functions, for some, as a limit case of the human is a challenge to rethink the human. And the task to rethink the human is part of the democratic trajectory of an evolving human rights jurisprudence. It should not be surprising to find that there are racial and ethnic frames by which the recognizably human is currently constituted. One critical operation of any democratic culture is to contest these frames, to allow a set of dissonant and overlapping frames to come into view, to encounter the challenges of cultural translation, especially those that emerge when we find ourselves living in proximity with those whose beliefs and values challenge our own at very basic levels.

More fundamentally, it is not that "we" have a common idea of what is human, for Americans are constituted by many traditions, including Islam in various forms, so any radically democratic self-understanding will have to come to terms with the heterogeneity of human values. This is not a relativism that undermines universal claims; it is the condition by which a concrete and expansive conception of the human will be articulated, the way in which parochial and implicitly racially and religiously bound conceptions of human will be made to yield to a wider notion of how we consider who we are as a global community. In this sense, human rights law has yet to understand the full meaning of the human. It is, we might say, an ongoing task of human rights to reconceive the human when it finds that its putative universality does not have universal reach.

The question of who will be treated humanely presupposes that we have first settled the question of who does and does not count as a human. And this is where the debate about Western civilization and Islam is not merely an academic debate, a misbegotten pursuit of Orientalism by the likes of Bernard Lewis and Samuel Huntington, who regularly produce monolithic accounts of the "East," contrasting the values of Islam with the values of Western "civilization." "Civilization" is thereby a term that works against an expansive conception of the human, one that has no place in an internationalism that takes the universality of rights seriously. The term, and the practice, of "civilization" works to produce the human differentially by offering a culturally limited norm for what the human is supposed to be. It is not just that some humans are treated as humans and others are dehumanized; it is rather that dehumanization becomes the condition for the production of the human to the extent that a "Western" civilization defines itself over and against a population understood as definitionally illegitimate, if not dubiously human.

The question is, rather, how a spurious notion of civilization provides the measure by which the human is defined at the same time that a field of would-be humans, the spectrally human, the deconstituted, are maintained and detained, made to live and die within that extra-human and extra-juridical sphere of life. It is not just the inhumane treatment of the Guantanamo prisoners that attests to this field of beings apprehended, politically, as unworthy of basic human entitlements. It is also found in some of the legal frameworks through which we might seek accountability for such human treatment, such that the brutality is continued—revised and displaced—in, for instance, the extra-legal procedural antidote to the crime. We see the operation of a capricious proceduralism outside of law, and the production of the prison as a site for the intensification of managerial tactics untethered to law, bearing no relation to trial, to punishment, and to the rights of prisoners. We see, in fact, an effort to produce a secondary judicial system and a sphere of non-legal detention that effectively produces the prison itself as an extra-legal sphere maintained by the extra-judicial power of the state.

It may seem that the normative implication of my analysis is that I wish the state were bound to law in a way that does not treat the law merely as instrumental or dispensable. This is true. I am not interested in the rule of law *per se,* but in the place of law in the articulation of an international conception of rights and obligations that limit and condition claims of state sovereignty. I am well aware that international models can be exploited by those who exercise the power to use them to their advantage, but I think that a new internationalism must nevertheless strive for the rights of the stateless, and for forms of self-determination that do not resolve into capricious and cynical forms of state sovereignty. A mode of self-determination for any given people, regardless of current state status, is not the same as the extra-legal exercise of sovereignty for the purposes of suspending rights at random. As a result, there can be no legitimate exercise of self-determination that is not conditioned and limited by an international conception of human rights that provides the obligatory framework for state action.

My fear is that the indefinite detainment of prisoners on Guantanamo, where no rights of appeal will be possible within federal courts, will become a model for the branding and management of so-called terrorists in various global sites where no rights of appeal to international law and to international courts will be presumed, and that we will see the resurgence of a violent and self-aggrandizing state sovereignty at the expense of any commitment to global cooperation that might support and radically redistribute rights of recognition for who is human. We have yet to become human, it seems, and now that prospect is even more radically imperiled, if not, for the time being, indefinitely foreclosed.

Judith Butler is Maxine Elliot Professor of Rhetoric and Comparative Literature at the University of California at Berkeley. She is the author of several books and articles on feminist theory, social and political philosophy, and contemporary social criticism.

THE ASHCROFT RAIDS
by David Cole

In 1919, a series of politically motivated bombing attempts culminated in an explosion at the Washington home of Attorney General A. Mitchell Palmer. The federal government responded by rounding up thousands of suspected subversive immigrants across the country over the next several months. They were held in unconscionable conditions, interrogated incommunicado, and in some cases tortured. In the end, more than five hundred were deported, not for the bombing, but for their political associations. The "Palmer Raids," led in part by a young J. Edgar Hoover, then head of the Justice Department's "Alien Radical" division, were roundly criticized, and brought the nation's first Red Scare to what appeared to be an end.

We have undoubtedly learned from the Palmer Raids, but it's still not clear what precisely we have learned. On the one hand, the government's investigation of the terrorist attacks of September 11, 2001, does not yet appear to have matched the excesses of the Palmer Raids. But on the other hand, the government has been so secretive about the detentions this time around that it is difficult to know. We don't even know how many people have been detained. In early November, less than two months into the investigation, the Justice Department said the number was 1147. But as criticism mounted over the numbers detained, the Justice Department responded by simply stopping its practice of announcing the running tally. Thus, there has been no public accounting of the total number detained since November 5, 2001. And since the total number was about all the information the Justice Department was willing to share, to this day the detentions remain shrouded in unprecedented secrecy.

What we do know, however, suggests that we may be repeating some of the mistakes of the past. As in the Palmer Raids, the government seems to have dispensed with developing probable cause before arresting individuals, and instead has used pretexts—usually of routine immigration violations—as its justification for the detention of hundreds of persons for whom it has only the faintest suspicion. As in 1919, the government seems to be proceeding not on grounds of individual culpability, but of guilt by association. And as in the Palmer Raids, the government has targeted its efforts almost exclusively at immigrants, a group that by definition has no voice in the political process.

As of April, despite the arrest of 1200 to 2000 people, only one person had been charged with involvement in the 9/11 violence—Zacarias Moussaoui. And he was picked up three weeks *before* the attacks. Justice Department officials have claimed (in the newspapers, but not in any legal forum where they might actually have to prove it) that ten or twelve detainees may be linked to al-Qaida, but that leaves hundreds unaccounted for. They fall into four categories: More than 725 have been held for alleged immigration status violations; about 120 for federal crimes unrelated to September 11; an undisclosed number for state criminal charges; and a similarly undisclosed but assertedly small number as federal material witnesses, purportedly to preserve their testimony for a criminal proceeding.

The Justice Department has been especially close-mouthed about the largest group of detainees, the more than 725 people held on immigration charges. It refuses even to name them and has ordered them tried in secret, with proceedings closed to the public, the press, legal observers, and even family members. On orders from Attorney General Ashcroft, Chief Immigration Judge Michael Creppy has instructed immigration judges not to list the cases on the public docket, and to refuse to confirm or deny that they even exist. In April 2002, a federal judge in Detroit ruled the closure order unconstitutional, citing the fundamental importance of open proceedings in our legal culture and criticizing the government's sweeping closure of proceedings whether or not sensitive information would be disclosed. Not even during the Palmer Raids did the U.S. engage in such a wholesale practice of secret detentions and trials. But what we do know, in part from a Freedom of Information Act (FOIA) lawsuit filed by the Center for National Security Studies and from enterprising investigative journalists, indicates that nearly all the detainees are from Arab countries, and that most have little or no connection to the events of September 11.

The fact that the government has cast its net so widely—when it admits that only a handful are even thought to be connected to al-Qaida—is a reflection of how lacking the government's intelligence was. Indeed, it seems fair to say that the breadth of the government's sweep is inversely proportional to the shallowness of its intelligence. It is swinging in the dark.

GUILTY UNTIL PROVEN INNOCENT

With the exception of Zacarias Moussaoui and perhaps the material witnesses, all the detainees are being held on "pretextual" charges. The real reason for their incarceration is *not* that they worked without authorization or took too few academic credits, for example. Rather, the government has used these excuses to detain them because it thinks they just might have valuable information, because it suspects them but lacks sufficient evidence to make a charge, or simply because the FBI is not yet convinced that they are innocent.

Consider, for example, Ali Maqtari. A Yemeni citizen, Maqtari was picked up on September 15 when he accompanied his U.S. citizen wife to Fort Campbell, Kentucky, where she was reporting for Army basic training. Agents interrogated him for more than twelve hours and accused him of being involved with terrorists. Maqtari took and passed a lie detector test, but was detained on the highly technical charge that he had been in the country illegally for ten days while changing his status from tourist to permanent resident. The government never offered any evidence linking him to terrorism or crime of any kind. It merely submitted a boilerplate affidavit from an FBI agent arguing that Maqtari should be detained because the investigation of terrorism is a "mosaic," and therefore, seemingly innocent facts might at some future time turn out to indicate culpability. Two months later, Maqtari was released without charges.

Another man, Osama Elfar, was detained on September 24, 2001, apparently because he was Egyptian, attended a Florida flight school, and worked as a mechanic for a small airline in St. Louis. He agreed to leave the country, but as of November 2001, he was still detained. Hady Hassan Omar, also an Egyptian, spent two months in jail because he made plane reservations on a Kinko's computer around the same time as one of the hijackers. He was released without charges on November 23, 2001.

These and other cases suggest that the Justice Department policy has been to lock up first, ask questions later, and presume that an alien is dangerous until the FBI has a chance to assure itself. Thus, government documents disclosed in the FOIA lawsuit in December showed that of 725 people held on immigration charges, over 300 had been determined to be of no interest to the investigation.

Yet until individuals are "cleared," they are detained, even when the government has no legitimate basis for detention. The *New York Times* reported that as of February 18, 2002, for example, the Justice Department was blocking the departures of eighty-seven foreign citizens who had either agreed to leave or had been ordered deported. The government was continuing to hold them simply because it had not yet satisfied itself that they were innocent, even though they were charged with no crimes. At that stage, there is no legitimate immigration purpose for the detention, yet non-citizens have been held for months without any further legal justification.

CHANGING LAW TO FIT FEARS

Many of those detained were initially held without charges for several weeks. Shortly after September 11, the Immigration and Naturalization Service (INS) unilaterally amended a regulation governing detention without charges. The preexisting regulation had required the INS to file charges within twenty-four hours of detaining an alien. Under the new regulation, detention without charges is permissible for forty-eight hours, and for an unspecified "reasonable" period beyond that in times of emergency. Documents disclosed in the FOIA lawsuit show that many of the detainees were held for more than two weeks without any charges whatsoever.

Defenders of the administration often respond that the detainees violated immigration laws, and therefore deserve to be thrown in jail. But while an allegation of an immigration violation, if proven, may justify deportation, it does not in itself justify *detention*. Before September 11, the INS could detain an alien charged with a deportable offense as a preventive matter, but *only* if it could show an immigration judge that the alien posed a threat to national security or a risk of flight. Under a new regulation issued October 29, 2001, however, even if the immigration judge rules that there is no basis for detention, INS prosecutors can keep the alien locked up simply by filing an appeal of the release order. Appeals of immigration custody decisions routinely take months and often more than a year to decide. And the prosecutor need not make any showing that the INS's appeal is likely to succeed.

None of these measures would pass muster if applied to citizens. Citizens are entitled to a public trial. They may be subjected to "preventive detention," but only if charged in a public proceeding and brought before an independent judge within forty-eight hours for a probable cause hearing. The requirement for a "speedy trial" means that unless a citizen agrees to an extension, preventive detention is limited to a matter of weeks. And if a judge rules that a citizen should be released on bail pending trial, the prosecutor cannot keep him in jail simply by filing an appeal. In other words, we have imposed on foreign citizens widespread human rights deprivations that we would not tolerate if imposed on ourselves. Yet the Supreme Court has repeatedly stated that the due process clause applies to all persons, aliens and citizens alike, in this country.

The Last Refuge of Scoundrels

It is likely to get still worse. An as-yet-unused provision in the U.S.A.-Patriot Act, passed within six weeks of September 11, gives the attorney general unilateral authority to detain aliens on his say-so, without a hearing and without any opportunity for the alien to respond to the charges. The attorney general may detain any immigrant whom he certifies as a "suspected terrorist." While "suspected terrorist" might sound like a class that ought to be locked up, the Patriot Act defines that class so broadly that it includes persons who have never engaged in or supported a violent act in their life, but are merely "associated" with disfavored groups, as well as virtually every immigrant who has used or threatened to use a weapon, even in barroom brawls, domestic disputes, or other settings having nothing whatsoever to do with terrorism as it is commonly understood. Such aliens can be held *without charges* for seven days, and in some circumstances can be held indefinitely, even if they cannot be deported because they have a legal right to remain in the U.S.

One reason the Patriot Act provision has not yet been invoked may be that it raises a multitude of serious constitutional concerns. The Supreme Court has never permitted preventive detention absent a finding of dangerousness or flight risk, yet this provision would authorize just that. It was only last year that the Supreme Court interpreted another immigration law *not* to authorize indefinite detention because to do so would violate due process. In the criminal setting, the court has limited detention without charges to forty-eight hours. And the INS is likely to argue that the Patriot Act standard for detention is less than probable cause, yet the court has always required at least probable cause to arrest a human being.

The unspeakable horror of September 11 has undoubtedly affected us all. Few things are more important than bringing the surviving perpetrators to justice and ensuring that such an attack never happens again. But precisely because the terrorists violated every rule of human decency, it is critical that in responding to the terrorist threat, we hold fast to the rule of law. Dragnet sweeps and secret detentions fail that test. They did under the Palmer raids and still do today.

David Cole, a professor at Georgetown University Law Center and attorney with the Center for Constitutional Rights, is co-author of Terrorism and the Constitution: Sacrificing Civil Liberties in the Name of National Security *(New Press, 2002). This article appeared in an earlier form in* Amnesty Now, *Spring 2002, and reflects the views of the author, not Amnesty policy. Amnesty International is investigating the INS detentions.*

NATIONAL AND INTERNATIONAL COURT SYSTEMS TO FIGHT TERROR
by Anne-Marie Slaughter

The debate over military tribunals has been conducted largely in terms of the trade-offs between national security and civil liberties. But this debate has tended to obscure an equally important issue: How does the question of where to try accused terrorists fit into the larger goals of fighting terrorism? The Bush administration has tried to prepare the public for a protracted new Cold War, punctuated by occasional hot wars. New hot phases of the war on terrorism could take place in any state deemed to be supporting global terrorism—a list that might include Somalia, Sudan, Iraq, Iran, North Korea, Yemen, and Syria. Yet because of the nature of terrorist acts, a war on terrorism must be fought not simply against states but also against individuals.

So a protracted war against terror must combine military force with the resources of the criminal justice system. And this exercise must be multilateral in two complementary senses: Military campaigns and their aftermath require the assembly of coalitions, the cooperation of allies, and the use of international peacekeeping forces and relief efforts under the aegis of international agencies. Furthermore, a war against terror necessarily requires the cooperation of many nations in hunting down and bringing to justice individual suspects. Simply to try all suspected terrorists before U.S. military tribunals intended for emergency battlefield conditions would put America at odds not only with its own domestic constitutional safeguards but with international conventions on the treatment of prisoners of war. In the long run, this would jeopardize alliances, put Americans overseas at risk, and set back our own values as well as the war effort.

In some respects, international terror is analogous to international organized crime. Fighting more traditional organized crime poses many of the same difficulties: the tension between securing convictions and jeopardizing informants, security risks, and the difficulty of collecting sufficient evidence to convict. But we have developed laws and procedures that make it possible to hunt down and prosecute drug lords, traffickers in women and children, illicit arms traders, and money launderers—all operating through global networks. We can fight global terrorist networks the same way, by relying on greater international collaboration.

Developing a global criminal justice response to terrorism first requires building networks of law enforcement officials to match global criminal networks. Here the Bush administration has a good start. Networks of police officers, intelligence operatives, immigration officials, and financial regulators have already yielded important dividends. Indeed, Tom Ridge's job as Office of Homeland Security director is to coordinate these networks, not only across the nation but across the world. The European Union is moving to institutionalize its law enforcement networks even further by creating a European warrant.

Yet cooperation between the United States and its allies is still uneven. Several European countries initially hesitated when the United States asked them to freeze financial assets of organizations suspected of funneling funds to al-Qaida. Recently, however, Interpol and U.S. officials reached agreement on a common database to which all 179 Interpol members will contribute and have access. Thus, the United States is now reaching out to the world's principal international law enforcement agency.

A related challenge is to develop a mature global court system. The "where will the terrorists be tried" debate has been miscast, because it inevitably assumes that there is one answer. The media have constructed an artificial trichotomy among military tribunals, national courts, and an international tribunal. In fact, all of these forums are likely to be necessary, at different times and for different purposes.

THE ROLE OF MILITARY TRIBUNALS

Military tribunals have been used historically to try spies and saboteurs. They have provided rough battlefield justice when no other form was practically available. Trial by military tribunal is certainly fairer than summary execution.

In Afghanistan we're actually on a battlefield. Al-Qaida members captured under such circumstances can be tried by military tribunals if they are "unlawful combatants" under the 1949 Geneva Conventions. The convention governing prisoners of war defines unlawful combatants as participants in an armed conflict who abuse their civilian status to gain military advantage: those who do not carry arms openly and do not carry a "fixed distinctive sign" such as a uniform or other insignia that would identify them as soldiers. Terrorists appear to fall into this category almost by definition, as they depend on concealing their identity before their attacks.

If a prisoner is deemed an unlawful combatant, he or she is entitled only to a conviction pronounced by an impartial and regularly constituted court respecting the generally accepted principles of regular judicial procedures. This is a relatively low standard of due process, which military tribunals would almost certainly meet. But out of respect for our own values and traditions as well as public diplomacy, we should at least ensure that the rules governing such proceedings bring them up to minimum international standards of due process: a presumption of innocence, the right to choose counsel (although it may be from a list provided by the tribunal), a speedy trial, the right to confront and rebut adverse evidence publicly, and the right of appeal (which could be to a higher military tribunal).

Ordinary prisoners of war, by contrast, may also be tried for war crimes but are entitled to the same standard of process that would be applied to our own soldiers: that is, a full court martial under the Uniform Code of Military Justice. But here's the catch: How do we distinguish between lawful and unlawful combatants in the first place? Until such a determination is made, all prisoners are presumptively entitled to POW status. Membership in al-Qaida, per se, suggests unlawful combatant status, since a lawful combatant must be a member of an organization capable of complying with the laws of war. But it's not clear who gets to make this determination—a military tribunal or a full court martial?

* * * *

In addition to these legal complexities, military tribunals are likely to present a number of unforeseen political headaches. Dozens of al-Qaida members are being detained in Afghanistan; hundreds more could follow in Pakistan as well. Once we establish tribunals, do we have to try them all? It is one thing to detain combatants until after hostilities are over, but once tribunals are in place and in use against some defendants, where do we stop? The Bush administration emphatically does not want to conduct mass trials; the logistical difficulties are enormous and there would be no faster way to turn many of our new Afghan allies into enemies. Identifying a few notable leaders and shipping them back to the United States for trial in ordinary federal court may begin to look better and better.

Finally, other nations will be watching how we interpret and apply the Geneva Conventions. As the world's leading military power, the United States has been a strong supporter of the 1949 Conventions, on the grounds that widespread adherence to their provisions is more likely to benefit our soldiers captured abroad than to burden us in treating those we have captured. Deviations from those provisions now, when our soldiers are in the field in substantial numbers, are likely to come back to haunt us.

NATIONAL COURTS

National courts, both in the United States and abroad, form the backbone of a global criminal justice system. Considering the issue of military versus civilian justice during the Civil War, the U.S. Supreme Court ruled in *ex parte Milligan* that military tribunals cannot operate when civil courts are open and functioning in the normal exercise of their jurisdiction. The military's need "to furnish a substitute for the civil authority" is limited to extraordinary situations, the justices found, as "in foreign invasion or civil war, [when] the courts are actually closed, and it is impossible to administer criminal justice according to law [amid] active military operations."

The court modified the starkness of this holding in *ex parte Quirin*, the Nazi-saboteur case that the Bush administration has relied on so heavily in promulgating and defending the president's executive order authorizing military tribunals. It allowed the trial of eight saboteurs by military tribunal, even when the ordinary courts were open. But in reciting the facts of the case, the court began by noting that the defendants were "admittedly citizens of the German Reich, with which the United States is at war." It then added that when the saboteurs landed, "they wore German Marine Infantry uniforms," which they quickly buried on the beach before proceeding in civilian clothes.

The difference today is not the existence of a formal declaration of war but the relative ease of identifying the enemy. In a war against terrorism, citizenship tells nothing and uniforms don't exist. Instead of trying foreign saboteurs, we may be trying permanent-resident aliens allegedly involved in financing terrorist activities through purported charitable organizations. The difficulty of even identifying the proper defendant makes this a job for the federal courts. Those who want to substitute military tribunals, citing fears that defendants will become martyrs or that intelligence sources and methods will be compromised, overlook how well the federal courts work to try and convict terrorists. The government obtained convictions both in the 1993 World Trade Center attack and in the U.S. embassy bombings in Africa, and no secret intelligence was compromised.

U.S. courts should try any suspect found within the United States, unless the U.S. government chooses to extradite the accused to another country or to an international tribunal with jurisdiction. Similarly, suspects apprehended in any other country outside the theater of actual military operations should be tried in the national courts of that country or else extradited to the United States or another country that is willing to prosecute. The indictment of Zacarias Moussaoui in federal court in Virginia, the indictment in early December of eight suspected terrorists in Spain, and indictments likely to follow soon in Germany, France, and other European countries establish unequivocally the ability of national courts—and national criminal justice systems, more generally—to tackle the problem. Indeed, if the Moussaoui case is any guide, the chief obstacle to national courts working together most effectively is a lack of clear guidelines for cooperation. In 1994, the British government denied a French investigating judge a warrant to search Moussaoui's apartment in London for lack of sufficient evidence.

The victory for those in the administration who wanted to try Moussaoui in federal court rather than before a military tribunal is enormous. Practically speaking, this choice suggests that issues of protecting sensitive sources, preventing a public circus and a propaganda opportunity for the defendants, and assuring the safety of U.S. jurors can be resolved within our existing system. But much more fundamentally, this choice recognizes that ordinary courts are open. In a fight purportedly pitting the values of democracy, the rule of law, liberty, tolerance, and justice against fanaticism (whether religious, ethnic, or cultural), supplanting civilian justice with martial justice in any but the most extreme circumstances should be unthinkable.

INTERNATIONAL TRIBUNALS

To many Americans, the international adjudication option seems naïvely utopian. But the 1990s witnessed enormous strides for international criminal justice— strides unthinkable even a decade previous. First came the establishment of the International Criminal Tribunals for the former Yugoslavia and Rwanda. Widely regarded as little more than political window-dressing at first, they have earned the respect of domestic and international lawyers and judges around the world. They have also handed down an increasingly important body of uniform rules interpreting international treaties and customary law governing war crimes, crimes against humanity, and genocide.

Then came the successful conclusion to the treaty establishing an International Criminal Court (ICC). As disfavored as it may now be in Washington, President Clinton did sign it. And all of our NATO allies will be helping to bring it into existence as early as next summer. As presently constituted, the ICC will not have jurisdiction over terrorism. But a United Nations Security Council resolution, necessarily with U.S. consent, could designate a chamber of the ICC or indeed the entire ICC as an ad hoc tribunal charged with hearing selected cases related to the terrorist attacks of September 11, with the addition of at least one U.S. judge. This option would be consistent with the U.S. position throughout the ICC negotiations, which was to establish a permanent criminal court whose jurisdiction would be triggered only if the Security Council referred a case or set of cases. At the same time, it would not establish a new ad hoc tribunal that could undercut the ICC, a change the Europeans and many other nations would oppose.

* * * *

Many other international options are also possible. To bring any one into existence will require a livelier appreciation of both the practical and symbolic advantages of having an international alternative to military tribunals and national courts, as one, albeit only one, dimension of a fully effective global criminal justice system. From a practical perspective, the existence of such a tribunal will facilitate extradition of suspects found in moderate Islamic countries such as Egypt, Jordan, or even Pakistan. These are nations whose governments are unlikely to want to stage terrorist trials at home but will face strong political opposition against extradition to the United States or Western Europe. Symbolically, as President Bush said in his very first major address to the nation after September 11, this is not just America's fight. It is the world's fight. Not only did victims from more than eighty nations die in the attacks, but the hideous visions of those attacks that replay in all our minds also remind us daily of a deeper violation of values, the values that define our common humanity.

WAR AND LAW

It is possible to see September 11 as an act of war and still claim a useful role for the system of criminal justice. The most terrifying lesson of September 11 and of the ensuing anthrax scare is that it is possible to threaten the security of a nation and the liberty of its citizens without ever attacking an army. The enemy can leapfrog perimeter defenses and target civilians directly. Other countries have long known this; the United States required September 11 to drive it home.

Yet a purely military approach tends to create its own self-perpetuating logic. The distinguished military historian Michael Howard identified this problem, based in part on the long experience of the British in Northern Ireland. In a speech to the Royal United Services Institute, he worried that declaring "war on terrorists immediately creates a war psychosis that may be totally counterproductive to the objective." It creates "inevitable and irresistible pressure to use military force as soon, and as decisively, as possible," which then puts the terrorists "in a win-win situation. Either they will escape to fight another day, or they will be defeated and celebrated as martyrs." These arguments may seem unduly pessimistic as al-Qaida fighters flee through the Afghan mountains. But the long and painful experiences of countries from Britain to Sri Lanka to Israel suggest that many will rise to fight again, with renewed fervor.

Rather than fighting them wherever they stand, we should keep them on the run. Members of al-Qaida are not military combatants except in their own understanding of their cause. They are criminals, a threat to every society in which they move. Their acts are prohibited under all national legal systems. And under international law, the attacks of September 11 qualify as crimes against humanity, rendering their perpetrators global outlaws, like pirates, slave traders, and torturers.

Focusing on criminal justice also regains our edge in public diplomacy. By defining a limited role for the use of military force as part of a larger strategy for fighting a global criminal network, we unequivocally reject the al-Qaida vision of an Islamic war against America. And by trying suspects in national and possibly international courts in addition to military tribunals, we can shift the focus of attention from war crimes to crimes such as mass murder, hijacking, kidnapping, and destruction of property.

Furthermore, framing the fight against terrorism primarily in criminal justice terms will make it easier to marshal the continued support of our coalition members, who are unlikely to wage war at our side, or even in less visible supporting roles, in perpetuity. But they will fight crime, in increasingly cooperative ways. And with their cooperation, we will be able to obtain and make public evidence of terrorist criminal activity over years and even decades, cementing public condemnation of attacks against civilians by any actor, state, or nonstate, for any cause. If terrorists are seen as a global criminal conspiracy, subject to a criminal justice system, we will have an easier time persuading other nations to extradite suspects.

Finally, thinking about fighting a global criminal network through a global criminal justice system helps us begin to answer questions that currently seem unanswerable. If we're fighting a military war, when will it be "won"? How do we operate during lulls? According to the *Financial Times* (which relied on outside sources as well as Western intelligence agencies), al-Qaida has operations in forty to sixty countries, with as many as seventy thousand operatives who have been trained in al-Qaida camps spread throughout the world. Bombs and even ground troops cannot target and destroy this kind of decentralized, dispersed enemy. Intelligence operations and criminal prosecutions must be part of a prolonged struggle.

Western Europe has lived with intermittent acts of terror for a quarter century. Europe has minimized them by tightening security and by relying on better police and intelligence work—and courts. War in the usual sense is not a practical option. For Americans, the rhetoric and psychology of war, as well as the necessary military operations against al-Qaida, are a more satisfying response to the enormity and horror of September 11. But as we move into a phase of protracted struggle with intermittent incidents, a purely military response, or psychology, is no solution.

Critics of the criminal justice approach argue that it trivializes the gravity and magnitude of the attacks—essentially equating Osama Bin Laden with Al Capone. We are not fighting organized crime but, rather, a religious war. The better comparison, in this view, is the struggle against Nazism in World War II. Would we have sent law enforcement agents after Hitler? Clearly not, or not only. He waged aggressive war against all of Europe and had to be stopped. Over the ensuing decades, however, we have come to see his evil through a different lens. He is universally reviled not only for aggression but also, and more intensely, for what have come to be understood as his crimes against humanity. A Nuremberg prosecution today would try him for precisely those crimes.

The growth of the international criminal justice system has been an important achievement. The international tribunal for Yugoslavia has tried thirty-eight high-ranking generals and commanders; these trials have been widely seen as fair, and they have cemented international support for the basic justice of the military campaign to protect civilian Bosnians and ethnic Albanians, and for its legal aftermath. Although the United States took the lead in the Yugoslavia campaign, these international trials have made the process of bringing Yugoslavian war criminals to justice less of an American show and more of an effort on behalf of humanity.

The new realities of war, with undeclared terrorist attacks by stateless attackers, call for refinements in how we think about war and criminal justice. Paradoxically, a stronger system of criminal justice will help us prosecute this new form of war. And it vindicates one of our greatest political and military assets: the rule of law.

Anne-Marie Slaughter is the J. Sinclair Armstrong Professor of International, Foreign and Comparative Law at Harvard Law School, and the President-elect of the American Society of International Law.

HUMAN RIGHTS VIOLATIONS AND DISCRIMINATION IN SAN FRANCISCO IN THE WAKE OF SEPTEMBER 11

by The San Francisco Human Rights Commission

The September 11 attacks have affected many San Francisco residents, especially Arab-Americans, Muslims, people of Middle Eastern descent, and those perceived as Middle Eastern. Several incidents of discrimination have been reported to local officials. The San Francisco Human Rights Commission (HRC) is the city department established in 1964 to help resolve intergroup tensions and now enforces the city's anti-discrimination ordinances. The HRC immediately held a hearing to address the backlash many of the city's residents were experiencing. The following accounts are examples of the discrimination the above groups have been facing.

The first account involved a Yemeni man of Muslim faith who became a U.S. citizen in 1996. The following information comes from his testimony at the hearing as well as an interview with an HRC employment-discrimination compliance officer. He alleged that he suffered discrimination and retaliation by his former employer. At the hearing, he testified that he had worked as a janitor for a building maintenance company for over a year. Before September 11, 2001, he was harassed and threatened because of his Muslim beliefs and practices. The harassment caused him such severe stress that by mid-summer he felt he had no alternative but to quit his job. He then filed a police report because of the threats. He also filed discrimination complaints with the Department of Fair Employment and Housing, the Labor Relations Board, and the Equal Employment Opportunity Commission.

On October 1, 2001, the Muslim Yemeni-American received a visit from an FBI agent who questioned him about his religion and Osama Bin Laden. The agent showed him a list that contained three names and asked if he recognized any of the names. They were people who worked for his former employer. The agent stated that the three had contacted the FBI and said that the former Yemeni employee was a "terrorist." He told the agent that he was being retaliated against because he filed the discrimination complaints. The Yemeni man showed the agent copies of his complaints. The whole ordeal had made him more afraid and he started having difficulty breathing. The agent asked him to step outside for some fresh air, but he was too scared. He refused to leave his apartment for two days. This man is the sole provider for his wife and five children, who still reside in Yemen. He has been afraid to tell his family of the harassment because he knows it will upset them. He later filed a complaint of retaliation with the HRC.

Another account of discrimination and harassment reported at the hearing involved an Arab-American man of Palestinian descent who alleged that he suffered retail discrimination and police harassment. The following comes from his testimony at the hearing and information he provided to the HRC. He testified that on September 29, 2001, he went to a well-known coffeehouse to get a cup of coffee. He was the sixth person in line and when it was his turn to be served, a white male employee turned his back on him and walked away. He asked for a cup of coffee several times. Instead of assisting him, the employee gave him a disgusted facial expression. He asked the employee about the expression, but the employee failed to respond. Another employee turned to the Palestinian man and said, "You can't talk to my partner like that, we are not going to serve you coffee." This employee asked him to leave three times.

At this point, the Palestinian man demanded to speak to the manager. The manager was a white female and told him that he should leave the store because he was not speaking appropriately to her employees. She refused to hear his side of the story, and he asked her if there was a video camera in the store so that she could see for herself what happened. She refused this request as well. Again, he stated that all he wanted was a cup of coffee. She told him that he was not getting a cup of coffee and that he had to leave.

Frustrated, the Palestinian man asked her to call the police or give him a cup of coffee. Within minutes, two white male police officers arrived at the coffeehouse and immediately grabbed him, took him outside, and searched him. The first officer asked him where his gun and knife were located. The same officer also asked him why he had large sums of money in his pockets. He explained that he was a taxicab driver. The officer then asked for his identification and ran a check on him. He told the officer he was very upset about the treatment he was receiving and that the officer should have heard both sides of the story before dragging him outside and treating him like a criminal. He asked if he could make a report of discrimination against the coffeehouse and the police department. He also asked for the officers' badge numbers. The first officer told the second officer to write him a ticket for double-parking. The second officer tried to calm the Palestinian man and stated that his partner was just mad. He told the second officer that that all he wanted was a cup of coffee, that he was the one who requested police assistance, and that he should not have been dragged around like an animal.

Aside from harassment in employment and public accommodations, some of the most widely publicized discrimination in San Francisco targeted Arab-American-owned businesses. One Arab-American merchant in a middle-class neighborhood had a brick thrown through his window and shortly thereafter was forced out of business entirely. This shopkeeper, who has been a citizen since 1996, was so traumatized that he is contemplating leaving the country.

Another store-owner reported ongoing harassment that started on the morning of September 11. A person came into his store and yelled at him, his wife, and his two-year-old daughter, "Arab terrorists, look what you have done. You all have to die." Later, the family received threatening phone calls and the store was vandalized with garbage, eggs, and graffiti such as "Arab terrorists go home." Of course, the store-owner was already home. He told us he came here in search of the American dream of liberty.

While the store-owner poignantly referred to America as "the land that has seen my two daughter[s] being born," he reported that all the harassment was nothing compared to hearing his five-year-old daughter recount that she had been called a terrorist on the school playground. Barely able to contain tears, the storekeeper simply said, "I was devastated." Many of us were prepared to hear about harassment in schools but were dismayed that it occurred as early as kindergarten.

A counselor at the Arab Cultural Center in San Francisco offered testimony on the abuses suffered by Arab-American and Muslim students in the San Francisco School District. On September 12, a Palestinian student was beaten and school officials did not punish the responsible student. According to the counselor, many students reported that they were taunted in school corridors, spat on, and accosted with epithets such as "terrorist" and "Bin Laden." Several girls and young women wearing the hijab or head scarves reported that their scarves were yanked from their heads. The counselor reported that students in one school made and circulated flyers listing Arab and Muslim students and substituting the last name Bin Laden for the correct surname of each student.

Perhaps most disturbing to those who expect more of teachers, the counselor reported that in an ESL class discussing the events of 9/11, an Iraqi boy offered that "America not deserve this." The teacher heard "America deserves this." The counselor testified: "So great was the teacher's counter-transference that she made no attempt at verification but went immediately to the principal. The student was interrogated, but fortunately a written diary entry confirmed his version of the comment and saved him from further harassment."

The counselor recommended that the school district and Department of Education collaborate with Arab and Muslim organizations to: 1) rapidly implement counseling services to help students and teachers deal with bigotry in the aftermath of 9/11; 2) plan in-service cultural competency training for teachers and students at all levels; and 3) plan assemblies for students to teach tolerance.

Amidst grim reports of student harassment, there was also some encouraging testimony about student cooperation. A South Asian Sikh woman who coordinates a school program for a local agency dedicated to preventing hate violence reported that much of the proactive work that has occurred in response to the backlash against targeted communities has been youth led and organized. The program coordinator testified that student groups and youth programs have taken the lead in ensuring safety and protection for one another.

The HRC is dedicated to providing the necessary resources to help reduce the harassment and discrimination faced by Arab-Americans, Muslims, people of Middle Eastern descent, and those perceived as Middle Eastern. We are in the process of generating a report that will include recommendations made by San Francisco residents and community organizations who testified at the hearing. Also, a task force is being set up to do follow-up work from the hearing. The HRC remains committed to the preservation of community diversity, as well as preventing and responding to discrimination in all forms.

PART 7

PERSONAL TESTIMONY

TALE OF THE MUSTAFAS
by Dan B. Gerson

On September 15, 2001, two Middle Eastern men, sixty-seven-year-old Fahti Mustafa and his son, twenty-four-year-old Nacer Mustafa, traveled by air from Leon, Mexico to Bush Intercontinental Airport in Houston, Texas, en route to their home in Florida. They had gone to Mexico on September 9 in order to purchase leather and other dry goods to be resold in Fahti Mustafa's dry goods store located in their hometown of Labelle, Florida, a small agricultural town. Fahti Mustafa, a Palestinian-American who became a United States citizen in 1972, took Nacer, who is also a United States citizen, having been born in Puerto Rico, along with him to help because Fahti is very hard of hearing and suffers from other medical problems, including diabetes and heart disease.

The father and son were originally scheduled to return to Florida on September 13, but due to the emergency shutdown of air travel following the terrorist attacks of September 11 were unable to travel until the 15th. The Mustafas landed in Houston and presented their United States passports to immigration authorities. An INS officer thought that he saw something suspicious about the passports and called in an FBI agent, who, after detaining the Mustafas, summoned an agent of the State Department Diplomatic Service, which is in charge of passport matters. The State Department agent, who also happened to be part of the Gulf Coast Terrorist Task Force, concluded that each passport, although issued at separate locations and dates, had been altered by the placing of an extra layer of laminate over the existing laminate. Both Mustafas, after being taken to separate rooms and questioned, denied any knowledge of improprieties regarding their passports. The agent, Christopher Culver, tried to get Nacer to admit that he had altered his passport and asked to which country he would like to go if deported. Nacer told the agent that he was a United States citizen, but that information did not seem to make an impression on the agent. A criminal complaint was filed against both Mustafas alleging that they were in possession of altered passports.

In the complaint, Agent Culver swore that the passports "had obviously been altered with the introduction of an additional clear sheet on top of the genuine laminate." He explained how altered passports can be used to aid terrorist activity and drug-smuggling organizations. The agent attempted to cast the Mustafas in the worst light, stating that, when questioned, "The Mustafas declined to offer any explanation," when in fact they denied knowledge of any alterations. He suggested that no records were available regarding Fahti's naturalization, and characterized Nacer's nickname and family name as "aliases."

Both Mustafas were placed in the Federal Detention Center in Houston, Texas. The assistant United States attorney handling the case requested that both Mustafas be detained without bail as flight risks because of "national security." The pre-trial services officer, in this relatively minor case that would ordinarily result in a sentence of approximately six months incarceration or probation, recommended detention. At the detention hearing, Agent Culver, although admitting that he had no evidence linking either Mustafa to terrorism, expanded his earlier allegations and showed the magistrate judge where the passport had been taken apart and resewn. He also repeated to the court how altered passports can be used to aid terrorism and drug smuggling. In court the Mustafas presented records and witnesses that showed that they were stable citizens of their county. The judge considered everything about the Mustafas suspicious: the fact that both father and son had traveled to the Middle East; the year that Nacer graduated high school; whether or not Fahti was retired or operated a business. The whole process was skewed against the Mustafas in light of the events of September 11. They were definitely not being afforded the presumption of innocence even though none of the September 11 hijackers were Palestinian and none were United States citizens. Following the hearing, and after eleven days in jail, Fahti was released (just barely). He was required to wear an electronic leg monitor and to remain under a curfew that amounted to a virtual home arrest, allowing him to go to work during the day. The next day, Fahti, in ill health, hard of hearing, and speaking poor English, afraid to get on an airplane, took a bus home to Florida.

The magistrate, in a scathing detention order, denied Nacer bond and detained him as a flight risk and a possible threat to national security. This is a man that lives in the same small town as his parents, operates his own filling station, has a wife and two small children, and whose only conviction was a misdemeanor probation for assault that he lived out. Nacer immediately appealed the magistrate's detention order. The district judge wrote an even more harsh opinion upholding the detention. In it he questioned how a small store-owner could afford to travel to the Middle East and cited the aliases and false birth dates and social security numbers that Nacer had allegedly used in the past. Apparently some law enforcement officer had written down his date of birth and social security number with one digit off or transposed; and as stated before, his "aliases" were his nickname "Victor" and his mother's last name.

Nacer sat in the Federal Detention Center for sixty-seven days, far from home, missing his family, locked up in his own country, and charged with an offense for which he was totally innocent. Shortly before the case was set for trial, the assistant United States attorney received a scientific report from the INS lab that showed that there was no evidence that the two passports had been tampered with or altered. The cases were dismissed and Nacer Mustafa was let out of the Federal Detention Center. He received no explanation and no apology, he just walked out. Both Nacer and Fahti filed petitions under the Hyde Amendment, requesting that the government reimburse them for reasonable attorney's fees because they had been wrongfully prosecuted. In order to collect money from the government under the Hyde Amendment, the prevailing defendant must show that the government's actions were " frivolous, vexatious, or in bad faith." We claimed that Agent Culver's assertions that the passports had obviously been resewn and altered were, in fact, frivolous, vexatious, and in bad faith. The same district judge who denied Nacer bail wrote the opinion denying the Hyde Amendment claim, stating that in this time of dire national emergency all parties working for the government acted "in the utmost good faith."

That is the end of the legal saga of Fahti and Nacer Mustafa, but their lives have been altered by what they have gone through. Nacer wonders what his customers and neighbors are thinking when he speaks to them, feeling that perhaps he is under suspicion even though everyone knows that the charges were dropped. He keeps the dismissal papers handy to show people if they are interested or curious. Nacer maintains a lower profile than before and is a little more guarded, refraining from loud conversations and debates with his friends and family when out in public. Fahti has gone through a heart bypass operation since his release, and, according to Nacer, sometimes just sits and stares into space. The hardest thing, says Nacer, was hearing his father in the next cell, crying. "This man has never even had a parking ticket, and he loves this country, but we were innocent, and look what they did to us."

Unlike the hundreds of Middle Eastern men who were detained indefinitely after September 11, held in secret without criminal charges or due process of law, the Mustafas were given due process. However, due process did them little good when all parties involved, including the arresting agent, the pre-trial services officer, the federal prosecutor, the magistrates, and the district judges took the worst view of the Mustafas and concluded that they were a risk to national security. Both men were incarcerated, humiliated, prosecuted, and forced to spend a large amount of money to defend themselves . . . collateral damage in the war against terrorism.

Dan Gerson is an attorney at law in Houston, Texas.

THE WEIGHT OF A NATION
by Andrew Kirkland

The attacks on September 11 were tragic events and will shape this nation for years to come. As a law enforcement officer I was inspired by the heroic efforts of all those police and firefighters who put their lives on the line and in some cases gave their lives to save the victims on that day.

As the events unfolded over the next several weeks, we in law enforcement across this country tried to figure out what to do to keep our communities safe. As those of us who have been strong proponents of community policing over the years can tell you, it is very important to not only deal with crime, but to address the fear of crime. The attack upon this country placed the collective *us* in fear of things and people who most Americans did not fear before.

Consequently, given the fact that we in law enforcement were incredibly busy trying to work within our communities to make things safe, I could not imagine that I would feel as if the weight of a nation would somehow be upon me.

The immense pressure began after a *New York Times* article appeared quoting me as symbolically saying "No" to John Ashcroft's request to have interviews done with individuals who were not suspected of a crime. That, in and of itself, was not the only issue—some questions focused on immigration issues. Our city attorney staff advised us that within our state we would violate state law if we participated in the interviews as they were.

If this were the only issue to consider or debate I think this would have been a simple discussion, but it is not. The questions out there were many. For example, should you do the interviews or not, is this racial profiling or not, do you forget the Constitution or not in times of war? All of these came up from several individuals and organizations. I still contend there is a way to effectively deal with terrorists while maintaining the civil rights of individuals.

Something I found interesting about this entire incident is that there was very little if any debate about how we as a country should or should not respond to war preparation or efforts. It seemed as if there was an almost quiet acceptance of everything as fact without debate, which is unusual in our country. It appeared that no one wanted to be viewed in a negative light by taking a different view. Even television news stations had flags in the background of the newsrooms as the reporters were talking about stories. It was not my intent to make the issue a national debate, nor did I expect what would happen next. My step into this debate at the national level on this issue seemed to give others some reason or cover to come out and say later that they also had questions or doubts about some aspects of where the federal government might be headed, but might have been reluctant to say publicly.

As I sat at home late in the evening working, I got a call from the public information officer who said a local reporter and one from the Associated Press wanted to interview me regarding the *Times* article. After doing those interviews and clarifying points but not changing the position on interviewing, I went to bed thinking things were over. I was awakened the next morning by the public information officer who said he had local and national radio shows waiting to interview me.

I will forever remember this: As I walked into the Justice Center, taking the elevator up to my office, the receptionist said to me, "WHAT DID YOU DO?" saying the phones had been ringing nonstop. What precipitated the calls was an interview I granted to a *New York Times* reporter.

The following is part of that conversation:

When a reporter called me on November 20, 2001, and asked if my law enforcement agency was going to interview Middle Eastern men as had been requested by the Justice Department, I explained that based on research of our state laws by our city attorney, we could and would not, as it was structured, do the interviews. I reinforced that this was a legal decision.

The reporter told me that other law enforcement agencies might have problems with it because of the racial profiling aspect. I explained our problem was a legal one at this point. I can see how law enforcement agencies that have touted community policing and anti–racial profiling positions with their citizens would struggle with turning their backs on it now.

I explained to those who asked that my input on decisions was based on the legal advice we received, but that I was sensitive to the issue of racial profiling because as a law enforcement officer I was a victim of it and thus could understand how communities would be upset with local law enforcement for going back on their promise not to use action against them based simply on their race. I was referring to one specific example for me when traveling cross country on a train. I was changing trains in Chicago, walking across the station, when two officers stopped me and asked if they could talk to me. Talking to me was fine— I had nothing to hide. When I asked why, they said I met a profile—young black males traveling across the country with one bag. I met the profile of a drug runner. When you are in that situation you seem only to hear the words "profile" and "drug dealer." When I told them I was a law enforcement officer they quickly walked away, but that experience was not soon forgotten.

After my interview with the *New York Times,* hundreds and hundreds of phone calls and emails poured in from across the nation and around the world, some of them threatening economic sanctions, and worse. The majority of the phone calls and emails I received from out of state were negative: This issue sparked a passion in people. Some said I should be ashamed and in times of war we needed to ignore our state law.

I was not the only one receiving email. The Chamber of Commerce was getting emails as a result of the articles. Most of what they got were threats to take some type of economic action against the city and the state because of our stance. Additional pressure was felt when a copy of a letter that was sent to me from the United States House of Representatives Committee on the Judiciary was published. The following is just one quote from the letter: "I would appreciate your providing the subcommittee with an accounting of all federal monies paid or directed to Oregon law enforcement or anti-crime programs, including specifically the Portland police department, which is administered by the Department of Justice."

Imagine getting this letter and reading references to your state law enforcement, and specifically *my* organization, knowing that everyone who could be affected by this would be angry now. Each day that went by, I looked for some support for my decision. The thing that helped were some of the supportive emails and letters I was beginning to receive. On the other hand, the immense pressure was just beginning, both internally and externally.

I had the opportunity to address, as part of a group, the press. As they began to ask questions, the thing that struck me about all this was not the majority of the questions they asked that seemed reasonable, but the one that stuck out.

The question was, if we were refusing to do interviews based on state law, why couldn't we? Because of the magnitude of the situation nationally, couldn't we just not abide by the law this time, under these circumstances?

I explained to this reporter that I didn't think anyone would want any police department doing that, ever. If you ignored this law because of national pressure, what message would you send your police officers? That it's OK to blur the line if the majority says so, or it's popular, and you want us to do it now? Where do we stop? Do we begin to make these calls ourselves in law enforcement as to when to abide by the law and when not to? I told the reporter that as police officers we have to uphold both the U.S. Constitution and the Constitution of our state. This too caused many emails from citizens saying in a time of war, you need to ignore your laws, telling me to "do my job," and calling me a "traitor." I saved most of those emails as a reminder of the mind-set of some people.

It seemed that each day another state or city agency or organization would come out against our decision, trying to distance themselves from the heat. As I took that walk back from the meeting with the press to the Justice Center, I looked up at a pillar on the wall where a quote from Martin Luther King, Jr., is etched. It reads, "An injustice anywhere is a threat to justice everywhere." As I read this and remembered that question, it helped prepare me for the onslaught of pressure I was about to face.

Andrew Kirkland is the Assistant Police Chief in Portland, Oregon.

HORROR AT HOME: AN INNOCENT VICTIM'S STORY
by Michel Shehadeh

On January 26, 1987, in the wee hours just before dawn, the INS/FBI swat teams swooped down on my home and the homes of seven other members of my community. We were arrested at gunpoint, shackled, and held in solitary confinement at Terminal Island, a maximum-security state prison, for twenty-three days. This was done in the name of "fighting terrorism."

"War on Terrorism Hits L.A.," screamed the next day's headline banner of the now-defunct *Los Angeles Herald Examiner.* President Reagan had declared his "war on terrorism." He needed a pretext to push his anti–civil rights legislation, so he created the Los Angeles Eight, as we became known. The charges against us evoked never-before-used provisions from the 1952 McCarthy-era law, the McCarran-Walter Act: "You have been a member of or affiliated with an organization that advocated the economic, international, and governmental doctrines of world Communism through written and/or printed publications."

It wasn't that we had done anything against the law, but that we had distributed literature, and that literature advocated ideas deemed undesirable by the government.

The most incredible part about all of this is that the case still persists even after fifteen years of the government's failure to produce a shred of evidence of any wrongdoing on our part.

The Los Angeles Eight case, the mother of all cases, as it is being called by Arab-Americans because of the many political cases against our community that came after it, changed the legal climate for immigrants. In the 1990s the ideological grounds of exclusion and deportation that had been incorporated into immigration law in the early 1950s at the height of the McCarthy hysteria changed to reflect new global realities. The Soviet Union collapsed suddenly, and Soviet Communism no longer presented an immediate challenge. So Communism was replaced by terrorism as the great enemy. And U.S. laws started to develop accordingly.

As a result of litigation in the Los Angeles case, Congress acted to repeal the infamous McCarran-Walter Act provisions, and enacted in their place the Immigration and Nationality Act of 1990. In this act the anti-Communist provisions in the McCarran-Walter Act were merely replaced with new anti-terrorism provisions. One could no longer be deported for advocating "world Communism," but one could still be deported for membership or affiliation with a designated terrorist organization. The Los Angeles Eight were again charged retroactively under this new law. There is no end in sight, because the pertaining laws are still changing.

After the first World Trade Center and the Oklahoma City bombings occurred, Congress swiftly passed the Anti-terrorism and Effective Death Penalty Act of 1996 (AEDPA). This act curtailed our civil liberties tremendously by authorizing the use of secret evidence in courts in violation of our basic right to due process.

Since then, the secret evidence cases around the country have all involved immigrants of Muslim or Arab descent, all of whom have been imprisoned by the Immigration and Naturalization Service with the intention of deporting them.

All of the secret evidence cases monitored by civil rights groups have unraveled as soon as the targeted individuals either got a glimpse of the government's evidence or were granted a re-trial in which the government was legally forced not to use secret witnesses or documents.

The government's evidence has always crumbled when the principles of due process, on which the American legal system was founded, are applied. The rights to rebut evidence, confront one's accusers, and meaningfully cross-examine witnesses are all principles that lie at the heart of the liberties the Constitution seeks to protect. Yet these principles have been sacrificed in the name of national security without any proven benefits to security, and have resulted in a chilling effect on the constitutionally protected activities of various American groups.

But nothing in our recent history curtails our civil liberties more than the Patriot Act that was enacted after the tragic events of September 11. The horrific murder of innocent civilians in the Twin Towers, and the attacks on the Pentagon and in Pennsylvania by terrorists, were politicized by the administration to produce the Patriot Act. This act provides a perfect example of legislation made under the guise of national security that sacrifices constitutional rights and protections. It has terrible implications for U.S. immigrants, but virtually no implications for right-wing militia groups and terrorists on American soil.

After the terrorist acts of September 11, the whole American mosaic, including Arab-Americans, felt the need for greater security. But to pit security against civil liberty is false and dangerous. We can enhance our security while at the same time preserving and protecting our civil liberties; it is never either/or. Our civil rights and liberties were achieved through many generations of struggles and sacrifice. There is a major threat to these rights today. We faced a similar situation right after the attack on Pearl Harbor when our government detained 120,000 innocent Japanese-Americans in concentration camps. Everyone today admits, sixty years later, that that was an awful mistake. We must work hard and diligently to reverse this threat today, so we'll never face the same situation again.

We must not fall into the trap of those who are dividing the world into two sections, one for the rebels and the other for the officers of the law, one for absolute good and the other for absolute evil, or one for the believers and another for the infidels. All of these "clash-of-civilizations" arguments have the same logic. The Bush administration started this war on terrorism in Afghanistan, but no one knows where it will end, and what it will produce. Simple solutions and military solutions will not stop the terrorists. The best weapon to eradicate terrorism lies in the cooperation of the international community in respecting the rights of all peoples. It lies in the reduction of the ever-increasing gap between the rich north and the poor south. And the most effective way to defend freedom is through fully realizing the meaning of justice for all.

The president asked, "Why do they hate us?" but that question is deceitful and precarious. It assumes a general "they," which lumps all Arabs and Muslims together. It does not distinguish between the terrorists and the vast majority of people who condemn violence and injustice. It also presupposes that Arabs and Muslims do not appreciate the great ideals and values of justice, peace, security, and freedom. But many have been denied these rights, often as a direct result of American influence or intervention. The problem lies in the fact that whenever anyone tries to explain this reality, to provide a context, to fill the vacuum left by the analysis paralysis in the U.S. mainstream media about events and conflicts taking place in the Arab and Muslim regions, they are accused of condoning or justifying terrorism and are eventually silenced.

Therefore, when our country searches for reasons to explain the animosity toward its foreign policies (an animosity not held toward us, the American people, or our globally popular culture), our country must distance itself from the concept of the "conflict of cultures." It should also give up this need to always have an ever-present enemy to justify the government's domestic and foreign policies. Instead, it should move into a political arena, where the United States can ponder the honesty of its foreign policy. In particular, it should reexamine its failures in the Middle East, where the American values of freedom, democracy, and human rights have been crushed—especially in Palestine, where the Israeli occupation is blatantly violating international law, and where the U.S. provides full diplomatic, economic, and military support for this brutal occupation.

Those who preach "clash of civilizations" are looking backward to the dark ages of history, while peace-loving people everywhere are working in an opposite direction: the direction of a universal value system which doesn't differentiate between one people and another; the direction of tolerance and mutual respect. We struggle toward asserting our common humanity because human civilization is the result of world societies contributing together toward a global heritage of justice and peace.

When the rights of any of us are threatened by the authorities we must remember the wisdom in the words of Pastor Martin Niemoeller, spoken during the time of Nazi Germany: "First they came for the Communists and I didn't speak up because I wasn't a Communist. Then they came for the Jews, and I didn't speak up because I wasn't a Jew. Then they came for the trade unionists, and I didn't speak up because I wasn't a trade unionist. Then they came for the Catholics, and I didn't speak up because I was a Protestant. Then they came for me, but by that time, no one was left to speak up."

Michel Shehadeh works in the West Coast regional office of the American Arab Anti-Discrimination Committee (ADC).

ACADEMIC FREEDOM AND FREE SPEECH IN THE WAKE OF SEPTEMBER 11
by Dr. Sami Al-Arian

> *The only thing necessary for the triumph of evil is for good people to do nothing.*
>
> —Edmund Burke

It wasn't quite 9:30 yet on the morning of this dreadful Tuesday when someone approached me as I was speaking to a few students at a local Islamic school. He asked, "Did you hear about what happened in New York?" As we rushed to the nearest TV, our hearts sank as we saw horrifying scenes of planes crashing into buildings and people running for safety. Everyone in the room became suddenly speechless. Soon our shock turned to sadness, then to anger. Some were sobbing. It was an agonizing and solemn moment.

Soon after the media descended on our Islamic center, and before we realized it, we became part of the news. We expressed our deep sorrow and grief. We condemned this criminal act and supported the government in its call for justice against the perpetrators and their benefactors. We joined our fellow citizens in prayer services in many churches starting on the evening of that dark Tuesday.

On Wednesday—the day after the tragedy—seventy-five members of our mosque donated blood. We felt patriotic, but more importantly, part of a national mobilization for doing good. In addition, over $10,000 was collected for the victims' fund of the Red Cross. On Friday, I gave a sermon in the mosque conveying the Islamic teachings in the Qur'an and from the prophet's life that totally reject the logic of indiscriminate killing and hatred. *"Whoever kills one innocent life is as though he killed the whole humanity, and whoever saves one life is as though he saved the whole of humanity,"* the Qur'an teaches. I further reiterated the Islamic principles of cooperation, unity, and tolerance for all faith communities. Needless to say, in all of our interviews with the media, we expressed our heartfelt grief, sadness, and condemnation.

By the following Sunday our call to an ecumenical service in our mosque the previous day in a full-page advertisement brought over four hundred people—more than half non-Muslims. The service was beautiful. All three Abrahamic faiths were represented. We were united in our grief as well as in our determination to overcome this tragedy. I explained in this almost three-hour service how Islam not only condemned this crime but also called for justice. We said that whoever did this evil act could not invoke religion or use religious texts to justify their twisted logic.

While we were engaging in all of that, our community was suffering from the backlash of misguided people and some media outlets. A gun was fired at a mosque in the area. Several members were harassed with ugly words and acts. Women with their traditional Muslim scarves were especially easy targets for hate-filled comments and gestures. Arab-looking people were taken off airplanes. Others were fired from their jobs. The nonstop talk shows on the radio and television continued to attack the Islamic faith to the point that even some children questioned their parents about why they were Muslim. We had to heighten security at our mosque and school to the tune of $20,000. We felt it was unfair that the Arab and Muslim communities not only had to suffer because of the tragedy at the hands of the terrorists, but they also had to endure the hate, distrust, and threats from their fellow citizens. It must be said on the other hand, however, that we received as a community, as well as personally, many heartfelt expressions of love, support, and embrace. They represented the best of America. We made many new friends.

But the sense of inclusion would soon disappear. On Wednesday, September 26, almost two weeks after the tragedy, I was called by one of the producers of the *O'Reilly Factor* of the Fox News Network. She asked me if I would be a guest on the show and primarily explain the relationship between a think tank I co-founded called World and Islam Studies Enterprise (WISE), established in 1990 and closed in 1995, and the University of South Florida (USF); what the purpose of WISE was; and the controversy that surrounded it six years ago. After much discussion it was agreed that because of the limited time, the show would only address WISE's relationship with USF. I also told her that although I was on the faculty of USF, I wanted to be introduced as chairman of the coalition that was established to defend civil rights and political freedom. Unfortunately, this was never mentioned, because clearly the intent was to put pressure on the university.

Needless to say, the interview was anything but what it was purported to be. The host turned it into a guilt-by-association exercise. You knew A, B, and C. A, B, and C are bad people, therefore you are bad, and must be marked. This was yellow journalism and McCarthyism at its worst. Not only did the producers lie about the purpose of the interview, but also most of what the host said was old news, inaccurate, irrelevant, bigoted, and, most importantly, lacked time-frame and context. On their printed version they called the show "Professor or Terrorist?"

Three individuals were mentioned during this brief "interview." The first topic was a seven-year-old situation that resulted in an extensive investigation by the government, as well as an investigation by USF conducted in 1996 by the former president of the America Bar Association, William Reece Smith, Jr. No wrongdoing was ever found. And certainly no charges were ever filed as a result of these investigations. Mr. O'Reilly never mentioned the time frame of this situation, and that it had absolutely nothing to do with the September 11 tragedy.

Another individual that was mentioned was Dr. Mazen al-Najjar, who is also my brother-in-law. He was never charged or implicated in any wrongdoing. A judge ruled in October 2000 that there was absolutely no evidence that he did anything wrong, and that he was not a threat to national security. Judge R. Kevin McHugh said in his ruling: "Although there were allegations that the ICP [another charity] and WISE were fronts for Palestinian political causes, there is no evidence before the Court that demonstrates that either organization was a front for the P[alestinian] I[slamic] J[ihad]. To the contrary, there is evidence in the record to support the conclusion that WISE was a reputable and scholarly research center and the ICP was highly regarded."

It was simply irresponsible journalism for some media outlets to exploit the current tragedy and deflect the blame, looking for scapegoats so that they might increase ratings or serve their hidden agenda. After the program aired on the Fox news channel, I received death threats as well as numerous hate-filled emails. It was terrorism perpetrated by journalists against innocent civilians and public institutions. Because of these threats against me and the university, USF administrators put me on paid leave because of their "concern" about my safety and the safety of USF. I regretted the decision because over ninety of my students were affected by it. I was also disappointed that the administration did not forcefully defend academic freedom.

After the Fox network interview, many other media outlets started their own onslaught and attacks on me because of anti-Israeli positions or statements I made many years ago. For instance, as I was active during the first Palestinian uprising (intifada) between 1987 and 1993, the words "death to Israel" were uttered in one of the rallies in 1988. The reference to this slogan spoken fourteen years ago was in the context of a speech, given in Arabic, about the brutal and continuing occupation of the Palestinians by Israel. It simply meant death to occupation, to oppression, to the Israeli apartheid system instituted against the Palestinians. It certainly did not mean death to any Jewish person, as it was being portrayed. In this I am reminded of the early American revolutionary patriots such as Patrick Henry, Joseph Warren, and the poet John Trumbull. They called for the "burial of the British Empire," and wished for the "Empire's everlasting grave." I'm sure that these early American patriots did not mean to bury the citizens of the British Empire, but rather to end the brutal British occupation of America. Patrick Henry's "Give me liberty or give me death" speech during the American Revolution is probably one of the most admired speeches of all time. His words describing the American sentiments against the British then prophetically tell of the Palestinians' plight and their predicament today.

Nevertheless, the media attacks as well as an orchestrated campaign that was waged by pro-Zionist groups across the U.S. continued to pressure the university to terminate my employment, although I have been at the university since 1986. On December 19, 2001, the USF Board of Trustees met in an "emergency" meeting and recommended my termination. Later that day, USF president Judy Genshaft sent me a notice of her intention to terminate my employment despite the fact that I have been tenured for ten years.

During all my USF years my record shows that I have always conducted myself professionally. I love the teaching profession and have always enjoyed the challenges of the classroom. I received the best-teacher award as well as the prestigious Teaching Incentive Award in the College of Engineering. I have over forty publications, including a chapter that just appeared in the Mechatronics handbook in early 2002.

The USF president gave three frivolous reasons for terminating my employment at a public institution. First, she maintained that I did not make it clear when I appeared on the Fox news program that I was not speaking on behalf of the university. Secondly, that I appeared on campus once in early October. And finally, she claimed that I caused disruption at the university because of the death threats against me, the hate mail that ensued, and supposedly the decline in financial contributions to the university and its alumni association.

Needless to say, I was invited on that program not because I was a USF faculty member, but because I was considered a leader in the American Muslim community, as well as a civil rights activist. Obviously, I do not speak, nor have I ever spoken, on behalf of the university. I have on many occasions made it clear to journalists and reporters that I speak as a leader of the American Muslim and Arab community and in my capacity as the president of the National Coalition to Protect Political Freedom (NCPPF), a group of over forty organizations coming together to defend civil and constitutional rights. A July 16, 2001, article in *Newsweek* magazine about the participation of Arab-Americans in the 2000 campaign reported: "Al-Arian is one of the country's leading advocates for repeal of secret-evidence laws." I was not identified in that article as a USF professor, but as the country's leading advocate in an important civil rights issue.

Furthermore, I came once to campus on October 5, 2001, to address a campus student organization that I advise. If I had thought that I was "banned" from coming to campus I certainly would not have attended. In fact, the USF provost told me that I could meet with my graduate students on nights and weekends during our conversation on September 27, 2001, when he placed me on paid leave for "safety." When the police asked me if everything was all right on the day I talked to my students, they did not ask me to leave because they did not know that the purported ban was in effect. As for the disruption, it's a classic "blame the victim" argument that defies logic and rationality.

* * * *

I was eighteen when I took my first civics course during my sophomore year, in 1976. On the first day of class, the professor talked about the two Ds of American government, as he called them: due process and dissent. Ironically, a quarter of a century later, these two important concepts are at the center of my professional career. I was neither afforded any due process, nor was my right of political dissent respected or penalty-free as promised by the Constitution. This case is indeed about academic freedom and freedom of speech.

I did not choose to be the poster child for the debate about academic freedom in the post–September 11 world. Now that I am, however, some important questions in this debate must be raised and discussed by all academics:

—Are university administrators justified in terminating the employment of a sixteen-year-tenured faculty member because he did not accompany off-campus remarks with a disclaimer that he wasn't speaking on behalf of the university?

—Should university administrators be able to fire a tenured faculty member because he attended a meeting on campus while on paid leave?

—Should university administrators be allowed to dismiss a tenured faculty member because his public pronouncements conflict with the political views of those in power?

Indeed, if the termination is allowed to stand, then all faculty across the nation will be vulnerable as to their job security and the professional compromises they may be required to make to keep their jobs.

As someone who has lived in the U.S. for over a quarter-century, I value our freedom and openness. I believe the Islamic faith, which has been vilified in post–September 11 America, is not only compatible with democracy, but cannot be fully practiced without it. I believe in the American political system and in the Constitution. If I disagree with a governmental policy, I believe in working within the system to improve it. And this is what I have practiced and taught my children. For over four years, my wife and I have visited over 150 congressional offices in order to ban the use of secret evidence. I believe that we were very effective in bringing to the attention of many members of Congress the due process concerns associated with the use of secret evidence. I believe that our hard work paid off when President Bush and many political leaders spoke against it during the 2000 political campaigns.

Many people have pleaded with me to simply remain silent. This is exactly what my critics want. Some think that there are powerful groups that are out to get me. My answer is simple. I believe in freedom of speech now more than ever. I believe that people have the right to hear what some may consider "unpopular" views as much as I have the obligation to express my beliefs and opinions.

Sami Al-Arian, PhD, P.E., was born to Palestinian parents in Kuwait. He was a Professor of Computer Engineering at the University of South Florida. He is currently the President of the National Coalition to Protect Political Freedom.

THE RETURN OF XENOPHOBIA—AN ASIAN-AMERICAN COMMENTARY
by Helen Zia

"At least it's not Chinese-Americans this time." Those words, spoken by a fellow Chinese-American, greeted me when I finally reached home on September 15, 2001, after five harrowing days spent stranded in Washington, D.C., following the terrible events of September 11. I knew well enough the intended meaning of his remarks and their lame offer of comfort. After years of unrelenting innuendo that cast Chinese-Americans and other Asian-Americans as the evil invaders, "at least this time" some other group would play scapegoat. I suspect that many other Americans felt the same awkward relief that the terrorists were not "their kind." Even so, the words were painful to hear.

I had spent those five days after the attacks in the confusion and rapid militarization of the nation's capital. Much of that time I sat among strangers in the lobby of the charming Tabard Inn, which ordinarily boasts of having no televisions or radios in the guestrooms. So I watched the horrifying news in the lobby, on the only television in the building. With the exception of one other guest who was in town for the same event as I, everyone else watching the news was white and European-American. Some of these lounge-mates were lobbyists from the Corn Belt—young, blond, well-fed, and eager to declare war as they cheered the notion of "ending" other nations. A few of us "left-coast" folks expressed our dismay.

I, too, wept as I watched the dreadful image of the fallen Twin Towers, whose energy and bustle were part of my daily commute from New Jersey to Manhattan for years. Yet in this hotel lobby among these strangers, I felt that familiar stab of self-consciousness. Will the real American please stand up? My Asian face is so unremarkable in the San Francisco Bay area. But elsewhere in America, in D.C. and the mid-Atlantic states where I grew up, or even in much of California, an Asian face still signals "foreigner"—especially at key patriotic moments.

September 11 was unquestionably one of those moments.

Washington in particular was well primed for xenophobia on the heels of the campaign finance probes, the bombing of the Chinese embassy in Belgrade, the persecution of Wen Ho Lee, and the spy-plane showdown. But I also knew that my own sense of racial vulnerability was nothing compared to the fear and distress of Middle Eastern, South Asian, Muslim, and Sikh Americans. Reports of violent assaults were already multiplying. I couldn't wait to leave the uncertainty of this emotionally delicate, partisan environment, to return to the comfort of family and friends.

During the plane ride home I debated whether I should attend a community event that same evening, something I had promised many months ago. All I wanted to do was stay home with Lia, my life partner, to create the illusion of a safe haven from the madness. But with my ethnicity often played as the "perpetual foreigner," I also knew that Asian-Americans could ill afford to retreat and be silent. I willed myself to go. When I arrived at the event, I ran into a Chinese-American colleague from the state capitol who gave me a conspiratorial look. "At least it's not Chinese-Americans this time," he said.

His words made me feel ashamed to be one.

* * * *

As a nation, our collective memory of shared history is so perishable, replaced instead by "instant" news, factoids, and MTV-like graphics that stimulate but fail to educate. This is true for Asian-Americans as well. "The Chinese seem to have a spy problem," was the word in some parts of the Asian-American community during the Wen Ho Lee case. "Campaign finance is not our problem," wrote a columnist in the JACL's *Pacific Citizen*. "What is it with the Koreans?" asked other Asian-Americans during the rash of store boycotts. "It's not my ox that's being gored," an African-American feminist colleague said to me after Jimmy Breslin's racist and sexist tirade against a Korean-American woman journalist. "Me not Japanese" was the sad little window sign scrawled by a Chinese-American shopkeeper during World War II, a sentiment shared at the time by some Korean-Americans who wore buttons declaring, "I hate J-ps more than you do."

There is no escaping the fragility of cross-group unity at times of crisis. Yet there are reasons for optimism as well. While I was stuck in Washington I had the privilege of attending a hastily called meeting of concerned Asian-Americans—most of whom were civil servants at various government agencies and congressional offices, or representatives of the various Asian-American advocacy groups in D.C. The meeting was held at the offices of SEARAC, the Southeast Asian Resource Action Center, and among the organizers were several South Asian–Americans, including Sikh-Americans. Indeed, the meeting's chair was an Indian-American woman.

Only two days after the horrific September 11 events, these organizers pulled together an impressive pan-Asian coalition to plan a press conference and a national candle-light vigil at the Japanese-American National Memorial on the mall. The site memorial was built to commemorate Japanese-American soldiers who fought and died for our country during World War II, as well as the Japanese-American families who were interned in American concentration camps after Pearl Harbor. Their purpose: to draw attention to the need for tolerance and restraint in the face of hate crimes and domestic terrorism against Arab-, Muslim-, and South Asian–Americans. Their truly remarkable efforts succeeded in garnering the attention of the national media, other civil rights groups, members of Congress, and even the White House.

This example stands in sharp contrast to those Asian-Americans who might find solace in the false notion that yellow Americans won't be racially profiled—at least not right away. These folks must not have noticed how the news blared, "SECOND PEARL HARBOR," a comparison that was thin on facts but full of the venom reserved for especially evil enemies. Even as pundits grasped at the Pearl Harbor metaphor, their studied failure to name the architect of the World Trade Center was glaring. The acclaimed Minoru Yamasaki, a second-generation Japanese-American, had designed many American architectural landmarks, and the World Trade Center was his crowning glory, dedicated to peace—as just about every website on the towers prominently recounted. Regarding this omission, I am certain of two things: first, every newsroom covering the continual imagery of the Twin Towers' destruction possessed the knowledge that Yamasaki designed the fallen skyscrapers. Second, I am sure that deliberate decisions were made to withhold this detail, lest the Asianness of the World Trade Center's creator detract from the theme of an America under kamikaze attack.

* * * *

I had arrived in Washington on the evening of September 10 to be part of a panel discussion at the Smithsonian on the occasion of a new exhibit, "On Gold Mountain," tracing the history of Chinese-Americans. The Asian-American exhibit and the panel discussion were the result of historian Franklin Odo's efforts to keep Asian-Americans in American history, to reclaim our "MIH"—Missing In History—past. On September 11, we were to discuss issues facing Chinese-Americans.

There was certainly no shortage of topics—the spy-plane incident over China's Hainan island had occurred only a few months earlier, disgorging a subcortical anti-Chinese, anti-Asian racism that would have made the Exclusionists of the 1800s proud. Talk show hosts called for the internment of Chinese-Americans and made on-air "ching chong" calls to people with Chinese surnames, picked at random from phone books. Members of the American Society of Newspaper Editors, the top editors of the nation's newspapers who are supposedly dedicated to "objectivity" in the news, hooted and howled at a performance featuring white actors in yellow-face pretending to be Chinese as they bowed and scraped. They refused to acknowledge their biases even after one of their employees, a Chinese-American student intern, called them on their racism.

But even before the spy-plane incident, the Committee of 100 had conducted its landmark survey on American attitudes toward Chinese- and Asian-Americans. The results included these points:

> —34 percent of those polled believe Chinese-Americans are more loyal to the People's Republic of China than to their country, the United States of America;
>
> —32 percent believe that Chinese-Americans have too much influence on high technology;
>
> —42 percent believe that Chinese-Americans are likely to pass U.S. secrets to China; and
>
> —68 percent feel negative about Chinese-Americans and Asian-Americans.

The poll had some other "surprises." Pollsters Yankelovich and Co. asked two separate samples of Americans the same questions—one group was asked about *Chinese-Americans* and the other about *Asian-Americans*. There was no statistical difference in responses by the two samples. So here was hard evidence of the "racial lumping" that is so well-known to every Asian-American kid who was ever called the slur of another Asian ethnicity.

Then there was the racial profiling of former Los Alamos nuclear scientist Wen Ho Lee. Dr. Lee was born and raised in Taiwan with no known family in China, but his ethnicity was enough to single him out as a suspected spy, even though there were dozens of other European-Americans at Los Alamos who had the same access to nuclear information and to PRC scientists. The book I co-authored with Dr. Lee, *My Country Versus Me*, details how he was racially profiled by the U.S. government in the name of national security. When the FBI couldn't find any evidence of spying, they charged him instead with fifty-nine counts of "mishandling of classified information," including thirty life sentences, even though no one had ever been similarly charged for mishandling classified information. John Deutch, the former CIA director, had downloaded details of the CIA's international intelligence network onto diskettes and his home computer, which was linked to the Internet. He could not account for what happened to those diskettes. Deutch, a white male, received a mere slap on the wrist, and then a Clinton presidential pardon; he is now teaching at MIT. In contrast, Wen Ho Lee spent nine months in solitary confinement, where he was held in chains and manacles under "pre-trial detention." He was only released after he pled guilty to one of the counts against him; the government dropped the other fifty-eight charges. Unfortunately, there are many reports from other Asian-American scientists and technical workers who have also been racially profiled.

Looking forward, it seems clear that the chill over Asian-Americans during the campaign finance headlines of 1996–99 and the spy-mongering years of 1999–2000 were only the "tip of the egg roll," as Senator Robert Brownback (R-Kansas) quipped. Those disturbing and harmful episodes have set the stage for something worse yet to come. Historically, xenophobia and racism heighten during times of economic depression. Yet the 1990s were marked by unprecedented prosperity, a high-tech boom driven by the intellectual and entrepreneurial creativity of Asian-Americans, especially immigrants from China, India, and Pakistan. Would the economic tailspin of 2001 bring more racial scapegoating in America?

These were some of the issues to discuss on September 11, 2001, for the panel at the Smithsonian. The event, of course, never happened. But the racial profiling against "Middle Eastern–appearing people" followed with a vengeance—more than seven hundred reported hate incidents in only a few weeks, with several deaths. Among them were South Asian–Americans, particularly those of the Sikh faith. To the list of those killed by international terrorists, we now have a growing list of those killed in hate crimes by domestic terrorists.

* * * *

Each day after September 11 has brought on some new uncertainty—and some new erosion of the principles that have made our country great. It was the recent argument of Peggy Noonan, a *Wall Street Journal* columnist who claimed that we must all "accept the necessity of racial profiling." She said that all Americans have to sacrifice some of our liberties in this post–September 11 world. If it turned out that blond women in blue jeans like her were profiled as terrorists, she said, she wouldn't like it but she would "suck it up" and accept it. I said to myself, yes, so generously said by someone who doesn't truly expect such a request to be asked of her.

I wondered how she would respond if the blond teenage son she mentioned in her column were subjected to profiling at high school because law enforcement finally noticed the profile of teenage mass killers in our high schools. I wondered how she would respond if her sons were subjected to the same police scrutiny that young men of color experience each day. I wondered if she would just "suck it up" if every blond family were rounded up and imprisoned indefinitely, living in horse stalls for the next several years. That was in yesterday's news.

The next day I read that the government is considering using torture to obtain information from some of the estimated one thousand prisoners who are currently being held in indefinite detention for unnamed charges. It may be necessary to drug them or to use force or other torture to get these prisoners to talk. If the American people can't bring ourselves to accept the use of torture by our government, then the suggestion of one official was to ship the prisoners to another allied country, like Israel, where torture is used in interrogations.

Then more news: The White House and National Security Advisor Condoleeza Rice warned the nation's news executives against publishing or broadcasting "propaganda" from the enemy, including possible "coded messages" from Osama Bin Laden. The implication was that the news media is playing into the enemy's hands. Within hours, network executives promised more judicious "editing" [read: self-censorship] in the future.

This bit about "coded messages" from Osama Bin Laden reminded me of the accusations made against Wen Ho Lee. Until September 11, Lee was the poster child for excessive government law enforcement powers and racial profiling. FBI agents had to persuade a federal judge to imprison Dr. Lee because he was so dangerous, so inscrutable, such a threat to national security, he should be locked up pre-trial. Their arguments were so chilling that Dr. Lee was indeed held in solitary confinement and maximum security, complete with shackles and chains. The FBI argued that Dr. Lee's mere "hello" might contain a secret message for agents from China—a message that could result in the production of an advanced nuclear warhead. The FBI warned that Ninja warriors from China might arrive in black helicopters at the mountaintop laboratories of Los Alamos to spirit Wen Ho Lee away. Never mind that Ninjas are Japanese warriors, not Chinese, nor that it would be very tough for enemy aircraft of any kind to go unnoticed in the secluded and heavily guarded laboratory town perched atop thin finger mesas.

This was the same FBI whose intelligence failed to detect any clues of the events of September 11, and which now has unbridled policing powers, thanks to the new anti-terrorism law. Among the many additional powers granted to the FBI and law enforcement, the Patriot Act allows those under suspicion to be imprisoned indefinitely. It allows the government to detain individuals without charging any crime or immigration violation. It also provides no meaningful opportunity for a hearing to determine the reason for an individual's detention. All details of arrests and detention are secret, sealed under court order. All in the name of national security. Of course, "threat to national security" was the same justification used to incarcerate 120,000 Japanese-Americans during World War II, and to keep Wen Ho Lee in shackles and chains.

* * * *

During World War II, politicians and the media had a special beat for the patriotic drum. Newspapers ran headlines about Japanese-American farmers who could grow tomatoes that would point to U.S. airbases, guiding enemy pilots to their targets. The esteemed Edward R. Murrow, patron saint of American journalism, announced on his radio broadcasts that any Japanese fighter pilots who made it to Seattle would surely be wearing University of Washington sweaters.

And the news media is no different today.

There is great danger in the calls from the White House and Condoleeza Rice to news executives, seeking to restrict information to the public and to increase the self-censorship that already takes place inside the newsroom. Some seventy-eight percent of the American public relies only upon the television news or the Sunday paper for information about the world beyond their homes. An entire worldview is shaped from newspaper factoid journalism and the eight minutes of evening news—the actual news time that gets crammed between commercials and infotainment. While the dumbing down of news has led to the dumbing down of the public, it also places tremendous power on the factoids and those eight minutes. So the media is losing whatever arguable independence it had before September 11; some twenty national journalism organizations have signed letters criticizing the government's overt efforts to limit what the media makes available to the public.

Sir Edmund Burke of England had it right when he first coined the phrase "the Fourth Estate" in the 1700s. The first three estates were the Church of England, the House of Lords, and the House of Commons—all the basic institutions of England. The Fourth Estate was the reporters' gallery, and there was clear recognition of the media's institutional power, even then.

All Americans should be concerned about and actively watchful over the media's power. Asian-Americans know this lesson well. Those rare moments in our history when we arose from media "invisibling" and obscurity we were used as a hammer—a wedge—toward someone else's divisive agenda. We've been the "heathen Chinee," the "hordes of hungry Hindoos," and the countless string of other hateful names that raised the ire of white workers; we've also been labeled the "model minority" to divert the civil rights movement and bring down affirmative action. Asian-Americans have been played both as the bystander and the weapon. Indeed, the miracle of modern media was the overnight conversion of Asian-Americans from the Fifth Column and the Evil Enemy Within to the Modern American Success Story.

Today, we find news stories of yellow Asian-Americans attacking brown Asian-Americans—sick players in this patriotic zealotry, weird mutants of equal-opportunity hate. This is not the time for any Asian-Americans to breathe easy and sigh, "At least it's not us this time." It is us, every one of us. If Americans of every color and religion aren't speaking out against these travesties, then we are part of the problem, collaborators in our own oppressions.

* * * *

Not long after September 11, I drove down to San Diego from San Francisco with Lia. We didn't want to fly—not because we were fearful, but to avoid the camouflage uniforms, the automatic weapons, the searches, and the reminders of the military state we are rapidly becoming. Near San Diego, I pulled into a gas station. The entire shift was immigrant labor—Latinos, Arabs, East Asian. The young Latino cashier shoved a plastic license-plate flag into my face. It was decorated with a painted American flag. "You should buy this, only $3.95." I muttered a "No, thank you," and he tried again: "Don't you love the flag?" This time I said, "I wear the flag in my heart, not on my car." He tried again: "You can show you are American." I thought of my immigrant parents and felt sad for all the immigrants who are now so compelled to have the most prominent American flags. I took my change and said, "I am American. You are too. Even without a flag."

I actually do have an American flag, made of heavy canvas. It's folded in a neat triangle. The last time it was unfurled, it decorated the coffin of a laundry worker and a World War II veteran, David Bing Hing Chin—the father of Vincent Chin. He died six months before Vincent was beaten to death by two white auto-workers in 1982. His mother, Lily Chin, gave the flag to me when she moved to China, after spending forty of her sixty years in the U.S., as a naturalized American. She left her home here because it was too painful to be reminded that her son was killed out of hate, struck down like an animal and then discarded by a justice system that didn't believe an Asian-American could be the target of racism. She gave the flag to me because she didn't want it anymore.

For almost fifteen years now I have kept this flag in a safe place. I took it out a few weeks after September 11. Not out of sentimentality, I confess, but because a professor asked me to find a document related to Vincent Chin's case. When I searched through my files, there was the flag. Its colors were as vibrant and strong as ever. The indigo blue. The deep blood red. As I held the canvas triangle of red, white, and blue, I gave silent remembrance to Vincent and David Bing Hing Chin. Other names came upon me as well, those of the new victims of domestic terrorism—Balbir Singh Sodhi, a South Asian–American; Adel Karas, an Arab-American; Surjit Samra, a Sikh-American; and so many others. I remembered those who died in the World Trade Center, the Pentagon, and the hijacked planes, as well as those killed by the Taliban—for example, the count-less women stoned and executed over recent years. The U.S. and member nations of the International Coalition against Terrorism had ignored the demands of women around the globe to stop the Taliban's femicide. I hugged the flag and remembered that this country was founded in defense of liberty, against tyranny. This is also what it means to be American.

As I finish writing this, the book on what happened to Wen Ho Lee will soon be published. I hope it will dampen some of the exuberant demands for racial profiling, some even made by those who have been racially profiled themselves. I hope Asian-Americans will use our special experiences in this nation's history to speak up, as Americans, to offer some light on these dark topics. We have much experience to share that will strengthen this nation. I hope all Americans will remember the words of the Reverend Dr. Martin Luther King: "Darkness cannot put out darkness. Only light can do that."

Helen Zia is the author of Asian-American Dreams: The Emergence of an American People *(Farrar Straus & Giroux, 2001), and co-author of* My Country Versus Me: The Story of Dr. Wen Ho Lee *(Hyperion, 2002). This article is adapted from an essay that first appeared in* AmerAsia Journal, *Spring 2002, pub-lished by the UCLA Asian-American Studies Center.*

HOW MUSLIMS HAVE BEEN HURT BY GOVERNMENTAL ACTION SINCE 9/11
by Mohammed Sohail

We, as Americans, live with certain core, traditional values. Chief among those values are our deep commitment and respect for individual liberties, civil rights, and human rights. We teach our children to judge individuals by their actions, not by who they are. However, the horrific tragedy of September 11 has put America and its values to the test of a lifetime, a test of constitutional magnitude. We are still undergoing this test, and we wait for the results to see how we fared with our reputation around the world as a beacon of democracy and hope. As an American Muslim, one thing remains clear to me: No matter what the final result is, my life and the life of many Americans has changed forever. Our government's immediate and continued response to the September 11 tragedy has made many Muslim-Americans and Arab-Americans feel that American values are eroding, and a majority of Americans do not seem to care. In his address to the nation soon after 9/11, President Bush stated that this war is going to be a long war, that this war is a war on terror. While we are fighting this war on terror, we should not and cannot afford to turn this into a war of terror concerning our civil rights and civil liberties.

In light of the September 11 tragedy, there have been many victims; besides those who lost their lives, there are many others who did not die but are suffering some of the harsh after-shocks. Chief among them are many Muslims.

What I have also observed post–9/11 as an attorney, an individual, and an American Muslim who has a deep interest in the civil rights issue, is the degradation and attack on our American civil liberties and civil rights. I understand that raising these issues is not very popular in the public opinion; I realize public opinion is not in favor of the argument that I will be making. One thing we have to realize is that however unpopular my views may be, however unpopular the civil rights issues may be, the bottom line is that we are in a democracy; and no one said a democracy is a popularity contest.

Individuals who do not agree with my view may point out that civil liberties ought to take a backseat during times of turmoil, times of national security, and times of heightened security such as we are now faced with since 9/11. I think the best response that I could give to those individuals is what Benjamin Franklin once said: "Those who would like to sacrifice individual civil liberties to obtain a sense of temporary security deserve neither security nor freedom."

As an immigration attorney, it is a stark reality that I am facing during these troubled times. In the past seven months since this tragedy, I have witnessed the fact—and civil rights advocates agree—that the United States Department of Justice has been engaged in a disturbing trend. In its war against terrorism it seems to be focusing on a certain segment of our community, mainly the Muslim and Arab-American communities.

The Muslims in America constitute a small minority of those individuals who are here illegally or who are out of status. Estimates are that Muslims constitute five to ten percent of the illegal population. Yet, more than ninety-five percent of the individuals that were detained after 9/11 were individuals of that small five-percent group. When one begins to examine the cases of individuals who are detained, interrogated, arrested, and deported, it becomes clear that one thing these individuals share is their faith. That faith is Islam.

What is ironic about how these people were detained can be learned from the answer to a simple question: Why were these individuals brought into the system to begin with? The answer is: Most were in the wrong place at the wrong time.

I have represented about a dozen individuals who were picked up in the New Jersey/New York area on minor immigration violations. It's interesting to note that out of the thousands of detainees that were being held in detention on INS violations—up to 27,000 or so interviews that were conducted in New Jersey alone after the 9/11 investigation—not a single individual has been charged with direct involvement or direct criminal involvement with the 9/11 tragedy.

Yes, there has been one individual who has been charged and indicted — Zacarias Moussaoui, but he was detained and arrested prior to 9/11.

So, to use profiling to focus on a certain segment of our population is not only undemocratic, it's not only unjustifiable, it's not only unfair, it not only runs counter to our democratic values, it not only forms the tactics that repressive governments use around the world—it has been scientifically proven not to be an effective, investigative law enforcement tool. From the very beginning after 9/11, I have been consistently on national television, in newspapers, as well as on national radio; I have been stating that this type of practice will not result in any usefulness to law enforcement. And I am right. Six months, seven months later, FBI Director Robert Mueller acknowledged that their investigation revealed, basically, that there was no involvement of U.S. individuals or individuals who reside in the U.S. with the nineteen individuals that have been pointed out as the people who caused the tragedy.

My frustration has been that the American media—the print media, the television media, and the radio media—were basically silent, at least during the first four weeks after the 9/11 tragedy when individuals were being detained and interrogated.

One must examine the price these individuals had to pay. Individuals who had absolutely no connection with, and have not been charged with, any criminal wrongdoing related to 9/11. Some have spent close to six months in jail not knowing when they will be freed, not knowing what, if any, charges will be brought up against them, and not knowing what their fate will be. One must also realize that many of these individuals came from countries where their experience had been that once an individual has been picked up by law enforcement authorities, they know for sure that person will not return. Some of the individuals that I have represented had absolutely no family members here; their spouses and children were overseas. Some of my clients lost loved ones. I had one individual whose wife had a miscarriage as a direct result of his detention in the United States; this was to be his first child. While this individual recently left after spending close to five months in jail, I can assure you he will never forget the time he spent and the price he paid for being a member of a religious faith that the government perceived to have been the faith of those who perpetrated the tragedy.

It is also interesting to observe that close to ninety percent of those detained belong to two countries: Egypt and Pakistan. Those individuals that I represent could not understand why they are citizens of a country that has been an ally in this war on terror, and not only an ally in the war on terror, but also an ally for decades. They could not understand why this country's own citizens were being treated as if they were nationals of an enemy country. The excuse that these individuals were picked up because of their INS violations is ludicrous, at best.

The onslaught on individual liberties is continuing and will continue at least in the foreseeable future unless America and its leaders take on the responsibility of eradicating profiling in all of its forms. The world has seen an individual whose job it is to protect and guard the president of the United States kicked off an airplane and barred for life from ever boarding that airline. The Secret Service agent's own attorney's statement was that he was kicked off the airplane because he was considered to be a security risk. This individual happens to be an Arab-American.

Within our Department of Justice there is a distinct division, the Division of Civil Rights, charged with enforcing the laws against discrimination, profiling, and violations of civil rights. For Muslim-Americans, that division has lost its credibility because it is under the control and guidance of the Department of Justice, presently headed by Attorney General John Ashcroft. The directives that are coming out (one after the other) after 9/11 are all focused on a segment of the population and are clearly directed against Muslim-Americans and Arab-Americans. When the Division of Civil Rights investigates how the law enforcement agencies throughout the United States are practicing non-discrimination, what response will they have when, for instance, the New Jersey State Troopers ask the Department of Justice a simple question like, "While you are monitoring our behavior to make sure we do not engage in profiling or bias, who is monitoring you?" It's a tough nut to crack and only time will tell the damage that has already been done when America recuperates from the onslaught of infringement of individual liberties and civil rights during the post–9/11 era.

Those individuals who have been detained, interrogated, and finally brought before a judge have been under a veil of secrecy surrounding the entire proceedings. For instance, attorneys like me have not had access—at least automated access—because these cases are considered to be special national-security-risk cases and the INS chief judge issued a directive in light of 9/11 that all cases deemed to be special cases ought to be held in secret proceedings. This means that besides the judge, the trial attorney, the attorney for the detainee, the translator (if needed), and the court staff, no one is permitted to be in the courtroom. While we see that there might be incidences where secrecy may be required, particularly in national security issues, none of the proceedings that I have been involved in had any rationale for blanket secret directives, especially in light of the fact that no one has been charged with any criminal wrongdoing,

It is interesting that rather than giving the discretion to the judge as to whether a proceeding should or should not be held in secret, it is a blanket provision that takes any discretion away. It runs counter to our democratic system of justice in which we have an open court system. The New Jersey Superior Court recently agreed with the American Civil Liberties Union's lawsuit in which they were trying to seek the names and other information about those individuals who were being detained. There has been a similar ruling in Detroit, in a lawsuit filed by the ACLU to have these hearings open to the media and to the public.

The reason to keep these hearings open is accountability. The important principle that is served by keeping these hearings open is that our government does not engage in the practice of arresting people, charging people, holding people, prosecuting people, and incarcerating people in secrecy. While we all understand the heightened security issues we are faced with post–9/11, we cannot and should not, as a democratic society, provide a veil of secrecy under the cloak of national security. If we try to carve out an exception for one segment of the population, if we carve out an exception for one particular type of tragedy, we might as well close our books and not exercise our civil liberties, the fabric that makes America what America is.

I must also point out that there are enough provisions in our justice system, such as protective orders, sequestering of witnesses, and other means that have proven to be quite effective in other cases. We have tried Mafia cases, we have tried the first World Trade Center bombing case, and we have successfully prosecuted people. So there is protection built into our system. The strategy of using national security as the reason to conduct our activities in secrecy is counterproductive; we might as well give our police officers and law enforcement agencies a gavel and a robe so they can arrest, sentence, and incarcerate individuals indiscriminately. But that is not America. We are at a crossroads in this great country.

According to the Immigration and Naturalization Service, there are approximately 300,000 undocumented or deportable immigrants residing in the United States. Of those, only two percent, or roughly six thousand, are Muslims; but we have seen that more than ninety-five percent of those individuals detained and imprisoned are Muslims. What is troubling me is that as a Muslim-American, an American citizen, and an accomplished attorney, I positively contribute to our society, but I cannot help the feeling that I, or any other Muslim-American, am in danger in these times.

Prior to 9/11, people would retain an immigration attorney like me to prolong their stay in the United States, obviously within legal means. But things have changed so much now that I, as well as other attorneys, am being retained so that the individuals can leave the United States as expeditiously as possible.

For those individuals who were finally deported, they received the ultimate punishment in the immigration law—banishment from this country—but their problems are not over. Their lives have changed forever. They will live for the rest of their lives being treated unfairly by individuals in their own countries because there is a stigma, a scar, attached to them. As one of my clients stated, "No one in my country will believe that I am innocent." He added, "No one will believe that America could do what it did to me."

In talking to these detainees about their experience in America and about what dreams they had of America when they came to the United States, the response I received was rather troubling. When I asked one of my clients if he would ever consider coming back to America once he is deported to Egypt, he responded as follows: "If I was stranded and found myself in a shark-infested ocean and there was an island with individuals calling out to assist me and the island was within my reach, if that island happened to be America, I would rather be eaten by the sharks than reach out to America." When I asked him what his view of America was before he was arrested, he took a deep breath, smiled, and said that he thought America and Americans were law-abiding individuals who had the utmost respect for the law and respect for individual human rights and human liberties, and that those were the values that brought him to America.

There was another individual I represented who shared the same sentiment. This individual was a fifty-year-old Egyptian physician who admitted that it was his lifelong dream since he was seven or eight years old to come to America; to see for himself what America was like; not only the landmarks, but to live and have a taste of the American way of democracy. He, too, after spending five months in jail awaiting deportation, confessed that his dream of America was shattered by his prolonged detention absent the charge of any criminal wrong-doing. He told me that prior to his arrest and detention he had thought about returning to his home country of Egypt where his wife and children live and letting them see America through his eyes, i.e., numerous pictures that he has taken of America. Unfortunately, when he was arrested, all of his pictures were taken away from him.

I represented one client who eventually ended up in detention not because law enforcement went looking for him, not because there was an anonymous tip, not because he was involved in some criminal activity, but because he relied on a police officer in Newark, New Jersey when he was lost. He needed directions and asked someone who he thought was the best person who could help him under those circumstances. Rather than give him directions, the officer inquired about his status; when he learned that the individual was out of status, he offered him a ride. The Joint Terrorism Task Force detectives were called in and he was interviewed; after many hours, he was determined not to be a suspect or an individual that law enforcement would have an interest in for an ongoing investigation. He was referred to the Immigration and Naturalization Service and waited over five months to be deported to his home country of Egypt.

Similarly, another individual was picked up after he had stopped on the side of the road in New York City to look at a map because he was lost. A New York City police officer pulled over and questioned him. What followed had become more or less of a routine two months after 9/11—Middle Eastern and Muslim-looking individuals were questioned and taken into custody by authorities. What was interesting about this individual case was that at the time he was actually arrested, this individual had filed for a six-month extension of his visitor visa a month before its expiration. Prior to 9/11, the INS office would have taken that into consideration and not even arrested him or put him into a deportation proceeding. When this individual told the INS that his application was pending, it did not have any affect. However, when he went before an immigration judge, that immigration judge was sympathetic and did not see any reason why he was brought in before her. The judge was glad to adjourn the case to allow him to retain an attorney to argue his case. Unfortunately, my client, who was not represented by me at that time, inquired how long it would take and whether he would be able to get out of jail during that time. When the judge told him it would take two to four weeks to get the case adjourned, this individual opted to take a deportation order because he did not want to remain that long in detention. What he thought was going to be a week or two weeks of detention lasted five months.

Another post–9/11 issue we, as attorneys, have gotten through is the idea that there are normally bonds provided for release of individuals from detention who are charged with minor violations. Prior to 9/11, individuals who were detained on minor INS violations and who had no criminal charges pending were routinely granted modest bonds. However, immediately after 9/11, we could not get any individuals released on bond. In those few instances when individuals were able to have the government consider releasing them on bond, the bonds were set very high. For a lot of immigrants who were working at low-paying jobs, posting a $15,000 bond was impossible. Once when I asked my client if he was able to post a $15,000 bond, his response was, "If I had $15,000, I would not even be in the United States in the first instance." In any event, after 9/11, individuals are considered lucky to get released on bonds, even high bonds. This is another area in which we see a ratcheting up of enforcement toward Muslims detained by the INS.

The selective enforcement of our laws is inherently detrimental to the very fabric of our democracy, and as in the past with Japanese internment, I am quite certain that fifty years from now, America will apologize to Muslim-Americans. But that's not what Muslim-Americans like me are waiting for. We do not want to hear an apology, since we will never be able to give back those precious lives that were lost or the dreams that were shattered or the days and months that the detainees lost. No one can be certain if our apology fifty years later will reach everyone whose rights we infringed upon. Furthermore, a "sorry" fifty years later will be too little, too late. Instead, we should stop being a society that makes mistakes and does not learn from them.

In conclusion, I want to ask my fellow Americans, isn't the bedrock principle of our democracy that we as individuals are not free and that our country is not free unless the freedom of every individual is secure? This is a challenge for America, a challenge we can only achieve if we pay attention. If we ignore it, it will only be a cancer to our democratic form of government.

Mohammed Sohail is a prominent New Jersey attorney.

RACIAL PROFILING IN THE PURSUIT OF ARABS AND MUSLIMS IN THE U.S.
by Mervat F. Hatem

It is possible to denounce the events of September 11 as horrific attacks against largely innocent Americans and also be profoundly critical of the U.S. government discourse that facilitated the large-scale racial profiling of Arab- and Muslim-Americans as the primary suspects of terrorism. This public discourse split the world into "good Americans" vs. "evil Muslim/Arab" perpetrators of terrorism. It left no room for one to be positively and securely Arab/Muslim *and* American. Worse, this discourse has presented members of these communities and the larger American public with mixed messages about how to think about and deal with Arab- and Muslim-Americans.

Consider for a moment the following confusing public statements and policies made by the Bush administration about Muslims, Arabs, and the war on terrorism. In his first address to the nation from the National Cathedral, three days after September 11, President Bush represented the Arab and Muslim terrorists who launched these attacks as "evil." Next, he told a joint session of Congress on September 20, 2001, that the terrorists "practice a fringe form of Islamic extremism"—they supported the Taliban regime in Afghanistan that oppressed women and men and hated our democratically elected government and our freedoms. President Bush also argued that the terrorists did not represent Islam, which is a peaceful religion, or Arabs. Many Arabs, Muslims, and their many governments were friendly to the U.S.

* * * *

Paradoxically, U.S. law enforcement agencies immediately began the large-scale arrest and detention of Arab- and Muslim-Americans as the primary suspects of terrorism. The commendable instructions by both President Bush and Attorney

General John Ashcroft for Americans to not engage in violent acts against other Americans of Arab, Middle Eastern, and Muslim descent was coupled with the call for Americans to be alert and to inform on suspicious individuals and behaviors, which in this context was a euphemism for reporting on Arabs and Muslims in their midst. As a result, the war on terrorism, which was described as a war to defend freedom at home and overseas, led to the curtailment of the civil rights of those Arab- and Muslim-Americans, specifically the right to due process, the right to legal counsel, and the right to be treated humanely while in custody.

Increased suspicion of Arab- and Muslim-Americans led to the outbreak of anti-Arab and anti-Muslim violence. The earliest victims of this violence were Arab- and Muslim-American women, who wore the Islamic mode of dress in the streets. It led many of them to stay at home in fear. This occurred at a time when the Bush administration began to describe the war against the Taliban regime in Afghanistan as a war to liberate Afghan women from fear.

Finally, the media's extensive reporting on American Muslims during this period focused on the religious segment of the community and highlighted their "difference" from other Americans, leaving out the large segment of secular Americans who blended seamlessly into the American social fabric. The result was to reinforce the view of American Muslims as "different" and separate from other Americans.

* * * *

To demonstrate the differences that separate these communities that were lumped into one by law enforcement agencies, let me offer the following brief descriptions of their defining characteristics. American Muslims are divided into three major groups: thirty percent are African-American, another thirty percent are from South Asia (largely from India, Pakistan, and Bangladesh), and twenty percent are from the Middle East. The rest are Muslims from the African continent (both from East and West Africa), Latino, and white American converts. Exact figures regarding the size of the American Muslim community are not available. The estimates vary from 2.5 to 7 million. There is consensus, however, on the fact that Islam is the fastest growing religion in the U.S. What the above highlights is that American Muslims are an ethnically and racially diverse group. Religiously, American Muslims are also a diverse group. The majority might be

Sunni, but there are many Shiites, Druze, and those who belong to other minor sects. There are also Muslims who belong to the Nation of Islam, with its distinct African-American history.

Arab-Americans hail from the twenty-one Arab countries that include Mauritania, Morocco, Algeria, Tunisia, Libya, Egypt, the Sudan, Somalia, Eritrea, Yemen, Saudi Arabia, Oman, UAE, Qatar, Kuwait, Bahrain, Iraq, Syria, the West Bank, Lebanon, and Jordan. Americans may think that all Arabs are Muslim, but some Arabs are Christian and Jewish. The Arab world has many Jewish and Christian minorities. The Christian minorities include Roman Catholics, Maronites, Protestants, Greek Orthodox, Armenians, Copts, Caldeans, and Assyrians. Jewish minorities also exist in Lebanon, Syria, Yemen, and Morocco.

Finally, Middle Eastern Americans do not only include Arabs, but also people from Turkey, Iran, Afghanistan, and Pakistan, who did not speak Arabic but other languages: Turkish, Farsi, and Urdu. While those from Turkey, Afghanistan, and Pakistan are Sunni Muslims, Iranians are largely Shiite Muslims. There are Shiite minorities in many Gulf states. In Iraq, the Shiites represent the majority of the population, and in Lebanon, they represent the largest religious group among the Muslims and Christians.

* * * *

The racial profiling of people of Muslim, Arab, and Middle Eastern descent led to the detention of large numbers of people whose religious, regional, and linguistic identities went far beyond the profile of those who were said to be responsible for the September 11 attacks. It was fair at the time to assume that law enforcement agencies did not appreciate and/or have knowledge of the complex religious and ethnic character of Arab, Muslim, and Middle Eastern Americans. Anti-Muslim violence in the U.S. in the wake of the attacks made no distinction between Arab Muslims and Arab Christians, and confused Muslims with members of other unrelated Asian religions. The first fatality of this violence was an Indian Sikh who, because he wore a turban, was mistaken for a Muslim.

* * * *

For the longest time, the law enforcement agencies refused to release figures of how many people they had detained after September 11, 2001, but it was safe to assume that the numbers were large. In response to continued pressure from civil rights groups, the FBI finally released information regarding those who were still in detention and their national origin/nationalities in January 2002. It showed that racial profiling had clearly become both national and global. Resident and non-resident Arabs, Muslims, and Middle Easterners, as well others from all over the world, were detained as part of the effort to enforce homeland security. Arabs in the U.S., who traced their places of birth to any of the twenty-one states that belonged to the Arab League, were on the top of the list of those who were still detained as suspects of terrorism. They included ninety-eight Egyptians, thirty-nine Yemenis, thirty Jordanians, twenty-eight Saudi Arabians, twenty-one Moroccans, twenty Palestinians from Israel, four-teen Tunisians, thirteen Lebanese, twelve Syrians, seven Algerians, six Mauritanians, three Eritreans, three Kuwaitis, three Iraqis, two Palestinians from the occupied territories, and one each from the UAE, the Sudan, and Libya. The total was 302 out of 722, which represented forty-one percent of those detained. The only Arab states that did not have some of its citizens detained were tiny Bahrain and Qatar, as well as Oman. Next, the list of detainees included people from the larger Middle East: 242 Pakistanis, fifty-one Turks, nine Iranians, six from Afghanistan, and six from Bangladesh. The total was 314, which represented forty-three percent of the detainees. Finally, there were Muslims and non-Muslims from everywhere: six from Mexico, four from France and Sri Lanka, three from Germany, Russia, and Spain, three from Tanzania and the United Kingdom, two from Albania, El Salvador, Kenya, Senegal, Trinidad, and Zaire. One from Australia, Canada, Cyprus, the Czech republic, Honduras, Indonesia, the Ivory Coast (Catholic), Nepal, Singapore, South Africa, Venezuela, and even an unknown country. The war on terrorism, which had been described as a war without borders, reflected this fact in the U.S. detention of suspects from everywhere on the globe.

Law enforcement agencies clearly targeted Arab, Muslim, and Middle Eastern communities, treating them as one. The targeting of more than one group as suspects of terrorism indicated that racial profiling had gone national. Worse, other ethnic groups whose members looked like Muslims, Arabs, and Middle Easterners were also victimized and detained. Latinos and light-skinned African-Americans, the earlier victims of the practice of racial profiling, were fre-quently confused for Arabs, Middle Easterners, and Muslims, the new victims of that practice. What the past and present history of racial profiling in the U.S. showed was that law enforcement agencies only used this tactic against people of color.

Despite the extensive detention of so many suspects, no useful information was generated about terrorist cells or future plots. Homeland security was not enhanced, as the anthrax attacks demonstrated. The most that these aggressive tactics contributed was to give law enforcement agencies a chance to somewhat mend their tarnished image which had suffered from their failure to apprehend and to stop the perpetrators of the September 11 attacks.

* * * *

Most of those detained have described extensive violations of their civil rights. They were secretly held. Their names were not released. Many were not charged and were denied the right to counsel. When they were allowed legal representation, only few and very brief meetings with their lawyers were permitted. They were denied contact with their families. They faced harsh prison conditions. Many were put in solitary confinement for long periods. They suffered verbal and physical abuse from their jailers. They were not allowed to exercise or to take showers.

In addition to the detention of people, law enforcement agencies have targeted the institutions of these communities as possible channels of funds that finance terrorism. Under the Patriot Act, federal agents used secret evidence to dismantle different charities as part of the so-called effort to undermine the infrastructure of terrorism. This infringed on another civil right of these communities, i.e., the freedom of association. It left these communities without institutions that served the needs of their members. Next, the community's schools were put under a microscope by media reports that claimed that they were not producing loyal Americans.

Finally, the polarized public discourse reflected in the adage that "you are either with us or against us" restricted the scope of public debate for all Americans. Only apologetic views of government policies and its war on terrorism were tolerated in the print and other media. In a war with targets that continued to shift and expand, American public intellectuals from within and outside the academy, who criticized aspects of the official discourse on September 11 and the war on terrorism, were given a cold reception. Those intellectuals, who traced their national origins to the Middle East and who tried to discuss and explain the failures of U.S. policy in the Middle East as a background for understanding September 11, were accused of serving as mouthpieces for the terrorists. They were expected to simply condemn the terrorists and to voice support for government policy as proof of their loyalty. It was as though the attempt to reflect on these developments and to share with the larger public aspects that were missing from public debate were equal to condoning terrorism.

* * * *

Other Americans who questioned the civil rights implications of the government's response to terrorism found an equally hostile public reception. For example, the commencement speaker at California State in Sacramento who warned against the abuse of power of sweeping anti-terrorism legislation was heckled, booed, and forced off the stage by the graduating class before she finished her speech.

The only hopeful signs in this very conservative and restrictive public arena came from the private acts of individual Americans who extended support to Muslim- and Arab-Americans in their communities. Some sent cards or flowers to those who were the victims of anti-Muslim and anti-Arab violence. Many local women offered to do the shopping for Muslim women who were too afraid to leave their houses. Peace activist women in Michigan put on the Islamic head dress to confuse those who were targeting Muslim women for attack. Finally, American men and women participated in candlelight vigils around mosques designed to represent community support for the rights of Muslims to worship in safety.

* * * *

September 11 proved that we live in a global world where the grievances generated by American policies in different parts of the world can directly affect us as citizens. Response to September 11 showed two possible reactions to feeling vulnerable and wanting to attain security. One proposed to meet the dangers inherent in a world made smaller by global forces through the vilification of the enemy, the attempt to punish it and those in our midst who may have any national or cultural connections to it. The Bush administration's public discourse and the actions of its law enforcement agencies represent this particular response. It is clear that this discourse and its policy of racial profiling have not improved the security of our homeland. The second response to September 11, which was represented by the private actions of average Americans, sought to reinforce our freedom and security by making sure that it continues to be available for all. In the long run, this is a better way of expanding freedom and ensuring our own security.

Mervat Hatem is Professor of Political Science at Howard University. She has published work on Arab-American feminism.

PSYCHOLOGICAL LOSS OF FREEDOM SINCE THE ATTACKS
by John Tateishi

The horrors of the terrorist attacks on September 11 and its aftermath brought about an interesting consequence for most Americans. For the first time, mainstream Americans felt what people of color in America have lived with for generations: a sense that their lives were controlled by inexorable forces outside of their own personal control. Not the foreboding Orwellian nightmare vision of Big Brother, but being at the mercy and the whims of those who would harm any of us.

For the first time, mainstream Americans lost their sense of freedom, the kind of freedom one can only know and experience in this country: to be completely free of intimidation by any force or group, to be able to go wherever we want by whatever means we want, to enjoy the luxury of being so free that we are unaware of those around us as a threat to our safety and well-being, and to feel it is our *right* to be who we are and do what we want, so long as it doesn't harm or infringe on the rights of others. In many ways, the consequence of September 11 has been manifested in its worst ways by the psychological intimidation it has imposed upon us. It is that gnawing sense that the terrorists might be in our midst and that we need to exercise caution walking down the street, crossing bridges, sitting in public places, getting on airplanes, being at very crowded events.

Now, six months later, Americans seem to have gotten past the immediate fears of further terrorist attacks and go about their daily lives as before, but in those weeks following September 11 we experienced a kind of fear the likes of which we have never had to live with as a nation. It was the sense that one could never know where the next attack might be because the reality was (and continues to be) that it could happen anywhere, and rather than risk being in the wrong place at the wrong time, one diminished the risks by not going *there*, wherever *there* might be.

As a friend of mine, a person of color, mused out loud one day, "Welcome to my world."

Being a Japanese-American, I understood that statement only too well, for I have personally experienced the limitations of freedom in my lifetime in many ways. As a very young boy, I was herded along with my family and other Japanese-Americans from our homes into America's concentration camps following the bombing of Pearl Harbor on December 7, 1941. Without regard to the fact that we were American citizens, we were denied our basic constitutional rights and became the victims of a policy of social and institutional racism. I grew up behind barbed-wire fences, looking up at American soldiers in guard towers armed with rifles and machine guns. This was the America I came to know in my earliest years.

If being imprisoned taught me lessons about freedom by the absence of it, I learned perhaps even greater lessons in the years following the war as we struggled to rebuild our lives and once again become part of American society. In a climate sometimes harsh with discrimination and hostility, I grew to understand that life was not always fair and equality had limited application when it came to my Japanese-American friends and me. In the process, I learned that we had our place in the world and that certain social lines were just never crossed. Those were boundaries imposed upon us, and they were as much psychological boundaries as they were social.

Ultimately, I've come to learn that freedom is very psychological. It is often as much a state of mind as it is a fact. You are only as free as you feel, and as those who limit your freedom allow you to feel. In the presence of hostile whites, for example, a person of color *knows* his or her limits, just as a white person understands his or her limits in the presences of a hostile group of non-whites. The difference, I would argue, is that people of color grow up with that knowledge and learn from an early age that being "different" automatically places limits on your sense of being free. Frequently, it is not that anyone intentionally imposes such limits on you, but you understand that it is there simply as a fact of life. It is there as a discomfort of not belonging. At its extreme, it is there as a sense of fear.

In the world after September 11, that's what Americans experienced, this sense of fear and discomfort knowing that their lives were vulnerable to the whims of some insane terrorist. In some ways, this is not so different from an African-American man who knows that running down the street at night in a white neighborhood makes him particularly vulnerable and at risk. As an Asian-

American, I don't experience this same kind of fear on a daily basis, but I *know* what that is like because in my past, I have personally experienced such things. And I know what it is like to feel limits put on me simply because of who I am and the color of my skin.

America has changed since September 11; we will never be the same, as a nation or as a people, because we know now that we are vulnerable. We know that at any given moment, life can turn to disaster because of some unleashed anger and hatred against us. But at the same time, we are strong as a nation and will not let this deter us, because if we do, we have truly allowed democracy and freedom in America to be damaged. And so we continue our lives, strong and true to the ideals of America democracy. But we live with that edge of knowing what may lie around the corner.

John Tateishi is the Executive Director of the Japanese-American Citizens League.

BRAVING THE STORM: AMERICAN MUSLIMS AND 9/11
by Hodan Hassan

Shock, disbelief, horror, and confusion were just a small fraction of the emotions that I felt on that fateful Tuesday morning in September. I was in my hometown of Oakland, California visiting my family for the first time after moving to the East Coast. Like most Americans, and indeed much of the world, I was glued to the television, my eyes transfixed on images of death and destruction. While I was able to locate relatives who worked in Manhattan, my heart ached for the thousands of others who were not as fortunate. As the day progressed, theories surfaced on television about who was behind the attacks, and invariably the name that was on the tip of every commentator's tongue was Osama Bin Laden. Soon after, CNN and other news outlets began to report on acts of violence against Muslims, Arabs, or those appearing to be Middle Eastern, throughout the country. America had never suffered such an attack on her soil and I wondered how my fellow countrymen would respond if those responsible were indeed Muslims. I had every reason to be concerned, for I am an American and a Muslim.

A week after the terrorist attacks, I returned to Washington, D.C. and began working with the Council on American-Islamic Relations (CAIR), one of the largest grassroots advocacy and civil rights organizations for Muslims in the United States. I knew they were under incredible stress with the increasing numbers of backlash cases reported to them. I was dispatched to the civil rights department and immediately put on the phone to begin taking in cases from around the country. Every time the phone rang my heart would leap, out of fear that the worst was yet to come. Of the hundreds of people I spoke with on the phone, there are a few that I will never forget. There was the mother in New York whose teenage son was beaten so badly that he lost an eye. Or the paraplegic man who was tossed out of two planes because his Arabic name made the stewardesses nervous. Within the first month, CAIR received over seven hundred reported cases of discrimination, compared to six hundred for all of 2000. Many of the incidents involved public harassment, property damage, physical assault, airport profiling, employment discrimination, and in a few instances, murder.

The very public announcements by local and national leaders, including President Bush, urging Americans not to lash out against their Muslim, Arab, and South Asian neighbors helped reduce the number of hate crimes. There were also many instances of Americans reaching out to their Muslim neighbors or colleagues in a sign of support and solidarity. CAIR received numerous cards and letters from all over the country expressing sympathy for victims of hate crimes. My roommate, who wears a headscarf, was told by her supervisor to park at work for free until she felt safe enough to take public transportation.

With the subsequent passage of the U.S.A.-Patriot Act and the increasingly aggressive tactics by the Justice Department in its investigation into the 9/11 attacks, we noticed a dramatic increase in cases of discrimination and profiling by law enforcement officials. On a daily basis, CAIR received reports from people who were questioned by the FBI, and family members whose relatives were detained by the FBI or INS. The dragnet approach by the Justice Department, with the detentions of over 1200 people (almost exclusively Muslim), was resulting in serious civil rights violations. Any non-citizen from a country deemed to be an al-Qaida recruiting ground was considered a potential terrorist and was subject to questioning, indefinite detention, or immediate deportation without a hearing. Racial and religious profiling had become the official policy of my government, and from radio talk shows and opinion polls, it appeared that most Americans approved the practice.

With most backlash cases, we were able to advise people on laws which could protect them if their rights were violated. However, what can I tell a wife whose husband is being held on secret evidence not made available to his lawyer? There is little recourse when the law sanctions such violations of our basic constitutional rights. Time and time again, I heard the refrain from those who sought our assistance that this was not the America they had imagined. What happened to due process and the right to a speedy and public trial? The challenge for CAIR and other civil rights organizations was and is to convince Americans that we don't need to sacrifice our fundamental constitutional rights for safety and security. Today the enemy is the swarthy Middle Eastern Muslim man, tomorrow who is next?

Hodan Hassan is the Communications Coordinator with the Council on American-Islamic Relations (CAIR). Previously, she worked on international development projects in East Africa with the International Rescue Committee, and was a contributing writer to Africanwatch *magazine. Ms. Hassan received a B.A. in Political Science and an M.A. in African Studies from the University of California, Los Angeles. Although born in California, her parents originally hail from Somalia.*

A FEAR OF FLYING
by Asma Gull Hasan

I had never been nervous about flying. As a little girl, several times a year, I would fly between Denver and Boston, where I attended boarding school. For holiday weekends, vacations, and breaks, I flew on airplanes the way other people drove their cars. At fourteen, I was hardly even old enough to read most of the magazines sold at airport newsstands, yet I had accumulated more frequent flier miles than the average American adult. I have flown in bad snowstorms, in turbulence, and for up to thirteen hours at a time. I have been on stand-by, cancelled flights, holding patterns, and sitting on the tarmac for more hours than I can remember. My sister, who attended boarding school with me, even faked an illness in the family to secure seats for us on an over-booked flight.

Until I went to college, I never knew that there were people who were afraid to fly. In college, I met some of these people. I pitied them. I thought their fears were childish and silly. In contrast to them, I was like a superheroine—I could be in any city in America within a few hours. I was at home on planes, while they were relegated to staying home. I did not understand how anyone could be paranoid enough to be scared of flying.

The only times I bristled at flying were when I traveled on Pakistan International Airlines (PIA). My parents are immigrants from Pakistan, so we return every few years to visit family. Besides generally being vexed about being away from American food, television, and clothing, I am a less-than-ardent fan of flying there because of PIA security. Each passenger's carry-on is searched several times at several different points in the boarding and check-in process, each time receiving a stamp on the "hand baggage" tag looped onto the bag from that particular checker. My family and I would always joke about how strange PIA's security was. I found especially odd the body searches. Each passenger was felt up quite thoroughly by a member of the same sex in a curtained-off, dressing-room-type area. Private parts were focused on—my sister and I laughed about how we received more action at PIA security than we ever had before. PIA and its seemingly innocuous and arbitrary security were the source of many laughs. A common joke among Pakistanis is that PIA really stands for "Perhaps I'll arrive," acknowledging the airline's frequent delays and unscheduled stops.

But that was all before September 11, 2001. I was scheduled to speak at the Queens Library in New York City at the end of September, an event that had been booked months in advance. I used to be the person who flew at the drop of a hat, who boarded a plane the way others changed their socks. Now, the last thing I wanted to do was board a plane, and especially to New York City. Besides the importance of sticking to one's word and pre-scheduled events, I knew I had to address this new fear of flying. Because I knew very well that I could have been sitting on one of the planes that the September 11 hijackers crashed.

Even with this resolve, I doubted taking that flight at almost every step. I kept waiting for my mom to say, "Maybe you shouldn't go," the way we all use our mothers as barometers of doing the right thing, I expected her to intervene and facilitate my succumbing to my fears. All that talk of letting the terrorists win if I didn't travel would disappear like soap bubbles in the same way that Mom can give you permission not to brush your teeth if you're really tired that night. But she never did. In fact, what she did say, when I expressed reluctance, was that she was not worried about my flying. Not because, as I tried to reason logically, airplane travel was safe because terrorists would not attack by airplane again. To the contrary, she said that she was not worried because she had decided that I did not really "look" Muslim or Arab and, for that reason, I would not be the victim of bias or hate crimes while traveling.

So while I was worrying about terrorists, my mom was worried about backlash. I was so consumed with fear of another terrorist attack that I didn't even consider what would happen to me if other passengers thought I looked a little too dark, or if the security people decided to take me aside for interrogation. We American Muslims, especially those who share that shell of Islamicity—brown skin—live in this purgatory. We are scared of being targeted by terrorists almost as much as we are scared of being targeted by non-terrorists, particularly law enforcement. Many American Muslims have been stopped and questioned or specially interviewed by the FBI, even multiple times. Email memos of FAA fact sheets on what to do if you're asked off an airplane fly around the Internet between various American Muslim listserves. In the American Muslim community, emails like this are just as newsworthy as terror alerts issued by the national government are for the rest of America.

I'm sure those who profit off of sensationalizing Islam (and Islam in America) would take my fear of flying as proof of American Muslim insensitivity to the attacks of September 11. Nothing could be further from the truth. I carry a double weight that adds to the sadness I feel as an American. I am afraid to fly for two reasons: I don't want to be the victim of another terrorist attack, and I don't want to become the next detainee in the "ask questions later" War on Terror. Of the five thousand-plus citizens and legal residents who have been detained since September 11, I don't know if one serious and important lead has developed out of the detainment. What's preventing me from becoming one of the next detainees? With the new Patriot Act, the legal definition of a suspected terrorist is so broad that any person having a bad day could be held indefinitely under suspicion of terrorism. What if I make a funny look at a national guardsman at airport security? What if I express indignation at being randomly stopped? I hope that I am wrong and that law enforcement will exercise responsibly the powers they have been given to curb terrorism. The use of "secret evidence" indicates otherwise. Prosecutors detain legal residents and possibly even citizens on charges and evidence they will not disclose to the defendant. Disclosure could harm national security, so the defendant must make a case without knowing what he or she is being held on.

The use of secret evidence existed before September 11, but the acts of that gang of young men who learned to fight in their neighborhood gyms have given secret evidence new life.

I did fly though—the once-valiant flyer I had been was now reduced to a nervous, vigilant mess. I was exhausted with the strain by the time we reached New York. The return flight was slightly less stressful for me. Several flights later, I'm still anxious. If I'm trying to figure out how to avoid being stopped by airport security, then surely the terrorists are too. Because I am my grandmother's granddaughter, I take more than I need in my carry-on, which usually bursts like a young woman carrying quintuplet babies in her eighth month. So of course my bag is always stopped. The contents often come out as a black abyss on the screen that anywhere from one to three security guards stare at in rapt attention, almost in the same way that a sleepy driver would stare at the road ahead on a dark night. On one occasion, a security guard, who prodded the rims of my bag with the black wand and cloth combination that apparently can detect bomb residue, quietly told me to take my shoes off. I passively asked if I could sit on the counter that bags were being examined on, and then hopped up on to it, relieved that I would not be standing around in the security area in my socks alone.

So there I sat, at Denver International Airport (DIA), dangling my legs over the side of the waist-high carpeted security counter where my bags have been checked before many times, mostly on those trips to boarding school. Being stopped at security or subjected to "random" searches was not new for me, even before September 11. Actually, despite the increased awareness of the racial profiling of Arabs and other brown-skinned people since September 11, I feel I was the victim of profiling more often *before* September 11 than after. What was new this time was that I was actually taking an important article of clothing off. Removing my shoes in such a public setting made me feel as though I was actually taking off something more intimate than just shoes. I felt defenseless against the bacteria and germs of the floor and slightly humiliated at the idea of being in stockinged feet in front of people I did not know. Lately, many Muslim women who wear a khimar or similar cover have also been stopped and asked to remove their head scarves. If I felt ashamed of taking my shoes off, I cannot imagine what a woman who has worn a scarf most of her life must feel.

I thought that I might have imagined being asked to take my shoes off. I asked the security person if she had asked me to do so. She replied yes all three times I asked her. So I just untied my sneakers and handed them to her, one at a time, thoughtlessly, for, if I had thought about what I was doing, I would have felt even odder than I already did. The white businessman who stood at the table I was sitting on, re-packing his now-searched bag, returned my dazed, indirect glance and said, "I had to take mine off too." The camaraderie of those who live in times of war was shared between us: shoes off, dirty socks, and the fingerprints of security all over your bag and its contents. Someday, hopefully, when we have won the War on Terror, I will tell my grandchildren, who will sit at the feet of my wooden rocking chair, with my gray hair in a bun, glasses perched on my nose and a knit blanket over my frail legs, in sincerity: "It was a different time then, when people had to take their shoes off to board a plane."

Thinking that the worst was behind me, I lined up to board my plane, innocently cutting in front of a number who were forming a loose constellation outside a roped-off area by the jetway door. When I was stopped by another security person as I approached the flight attendant who was taking our tickets at the door, I'm sure the constellation was quite pleased. Along with the first person in line—another white businessman—I was directed to a small area, partitioned off by chest-high, thick blue plastic "United Airlines" screens. I was suddenly in an assembly line of checking. My bags, which I had been directed to place on a fold-out table, were now being thoroughly searched, including the stuffed one that had already been searched once at the main security desk. I was pulled to the side and told to hold my arms out so I could be checked with the metal detector.

When the detector beeped over my waistline I lifted my sweater to show her that my pants had a metal hook, inadvertently giving everyone in line to board the plane and the security guards examining bags a free show featuring my midriff. Good thing I never had a gigantic tattoo of my name or Tinkerbell grafted onto my stomach. I was dazed by the surreality and ignorant to the fact that the security persons checking my bags were flitting through my things like they were worthless: my driver's license, my boarding pass, my toiletries, my walkman, my laptop computer, and more were all spread out on this folding table, mingling with the contents of the bags of others being searched. With his gloved hand, the security guard dipped his fingers through the contents of my jewelry box, pulling up with his finger a mosaic of junk pieces all knotted together.

I was going through PIA security but it was now at DIA! The difference was that Pakistani airports had sufficient space for such checks, while DIA was bogged down in bottlenecks and general malaise. To be treated with less dignity at DIA than I received at PIA was so sobering that I felt as though I must have been imagining it. Meanwhile, while I was subjected to such inaccurate searches, most passengers boarded the plane unsearched. What was the point of humiliating me twice when most other people, possibly terrorists included, breezed on by?

I stuffed my feet back into my shoes, which I had to take off again, and quickly tied them. I wanted to gather my things together, as they were strewn all about like a flea market explosion. I wanted to make sure nothing was missing. The security guards were supposedly "re-packing" my bags, but I looked inside one bag to find the remaining contents so disheveled that I wondered how I would ever zip it up again. As I re-packed my things, the security people, one by one, told me to move my bags off the table in that neutral but annoying tone: "This table needs to be cleared, miss." I told them that I was being very cooperative considering their disrespect toward my personal property and that I would need time to re-pack my things properly. Thank goodness the security did not detain me for being difficult. They surely could have, and I would have become one of the detained, an immediate suspect. Some of my rights as an American were infringed upon, and, in a war, I expect that to happen. Yet I doubt that this curtailment of my rights—these PIA security measures, good as they may make some feel—brings us any closer to catching terrorists. I want them caught just as badly as everyone else does. But as an honest person, I have to point out that making me anxious to fly is not the way to do it.

I've been American my whole life, and I've been Muslim my whole life. What makes America great is what makes Islam great. George Washington could have easily declared himself king of the small British colony that had successfully fought the world's greatest superpower at the time for independence. Instead, he presented a revolutionary idea: Why not have a leader who is chosen from among the people, a democratically elected leader? Such an idea in those days would today be the equivalent of Congress' declaring the U.S. presidency a monarchy. But Washington did it anyway, and he was right. He and the other Founding Fathers wrote the U.S. Constitution, a living document that could be reinterpreted as the country and the people in it changed. The Constitution set out rights of equality for all Americans of all backgrounds.

Centuries before Washington was even born, another man also proposed that the leader of his community be chosen by the community, selected in a democratic fashion as opposed to appointed by the previous leader. This man's message was as revolutionary at that time as Washington's was in his time, particularly since the people clamored for the naming of a successor. This man also left behind a great document that set out a way of life with respect for all, for all time, and to be reinterpreted as times changed and as the people who followed it spread out all over the world. This document held that all humans must pursue justice in order to gain entry into Paradise.

That document was the Qur'an, and the man who called for democracy 1400 years ago was the Prophet Muhammad (peace be upon him). The Qur'an proposed, like the Constitution, that all people were equal, regardless of color or gender. Some scholars say that Thomas Jefferson and Washington, among other Founding Fathers, had copies of the Qur'an in their libraries. The ideas of democracy and equality presented in the Qur'an are believed by these scholars to have inspired them in writing some parts of the U.S. Constitution. These same ideas inspired some of Muhammad's (peace be upon him) contemporaries to convert, especially women and poor people. Islam told these people what nothing else did: that they had rights, and that those who wronged them were, in fact, wrong. Islam meant to undo the injustices present in Arabia and to bring about justice under one God.

Unlike the Qur'an, the Constitution required years of interpretation to fulfill the promise of equality. In Islamic societies too, people are often not treated in accordance with the Qur'an, despite Prophet Muhammad's (peace be upon him) example. Both documents set out similar ideals for people to strive toward. To the credit of the profound message that both expound, they live on long after the founders have died. Sadly, just as Islam has been manipulated by terrorists, the Constitution has been ignored by many of our governmental and elected officials. Terrorism represents a major threat to America, but so does the continuing use of enforcement devices like racial profiling, secret evidence, and overly broad language in our security legislation. Like I said before, I've been Muslim my whole life, and I've been American my whole life. I know enough about both to say that terrorism does not represent Islam, and a minimizing of civil liberties does not represent America.

Asma Gull Hasan, author of American Muslims: The New Generation *(Continuum, 2000), wants everybody to know that she is not a terrorist, even though she may be detained for an arbitrary reason. Visit her website at www.asmahasan.com to read excerpts from her book.*

THE JAPANESE INTERNMENT EXPERIENCE
by Lillian Nakano

Who can forget the horrendous tragedy of September 11? We all mourned for the thousands who died and felt deep sorrow for the surviving families. The devastation was forever seared into the minds of all Americans, and though we felt vulnerable, we were not daunted. American flags waved and a sense of patriotism heightened. At the same time a tragedy of another kind—that of guilt-by-association—once again reared its ugly head as people of Middle Eastern descent—Muslims, Arab-Americans, and others—became targets of hate crimes, violence, vandalism, racial profiling, and terror, in the name of patriotism and national security. It was, for me, a flashback to sixty years ago—reliving the fear and trepidation Japanese-Americans experienced in the aftermath of the Pearl Harbor attack in December of 1941. It brought out my empathy for the Arab-Americans who are now ostracized and terrorized on the basis of their ethnicity . . . Can this be happening again?

I take this opportunity to share some of the Japanese-American experience, not in a vacuum, but in the hopes that such a travesty will not be repeated again in these times of crises, for the parallels of then and now are too disturbing. Sixty years ago, in the aftermath of the attack on Pearl Harbor by Japanese Imperial forces, Americans of Japanese descent, for no other reason than our ethnic heritage, were rounded up and placed into internment camps for the remainder of the war. Within weeks after the attack, about two thousand first-generation Japanese were arrested and separated from their families to be shipped out to Justice Department detention centers for an indefinite period. In a similar fashion, we are seeing the arrests and detention of Muslims and Arab-Americans without trial or due process based on evidences slim to none in connection to the events of 9/11.

Back in 1942, following the Pearl Harbor attack, in an atmosphere of anger, jingoism, inflamed patriotism, and talk of war not unlike today, the momentum behind anti-Japanese sentiment translated only too quickly into Executive Order 9066 and the wholesale incarceration of an entire ethnic group based solely on race. One hundred and twenty thousand of us from the West Coast and Hawaii were shipped to the most desolate God-forsaken high deserts of California, Arizona, Idaho, Utah, Wyoming, and the swamplands of Arkansas. Our living quarters became tar-papered barracks with community mess halls, community baths, and community bathrooms. Even so, this was a step above the horrible horse-stalls in racetracks and fairgrounds which served as temporary assembly centers for tens of thousands until the permanent camp construction was completed. There were tearful farewells as families and friends were separated and assigned to one of ten designated camps, leaving behind all precious lifetime belongings, selling possessions for almost nothing, abandoning businesses, homes, and properties.

When put in a historical context, we can see that the incarceration of the Japanese-Americans did not happen in isolation. Before the war, already hundreds of anti-Asian laws and Asian Exclusion Acts had been enacted. The wholesale roundup of Japanese-Americans in the aftermath of the Pearl Harbor attack was but a continuation of that glaring racism and discrimination, orchestrated by politicians and special interest groups, and then implemented by our government. Prior to 9/11, Arab- and Muslim-Americans had already been vilified and stereotyped for years—from the oil crises to the Gulf War—making them targets for mistreatment connected to the 9/11 event.

I was fourteen on a bleak wintry day of December 1942. Unlike the trains in the movies, ours had the shades pulled down and MPs (military police) stood guard at the doorways between each car. The noise of clickety-clack in the background for five days (from California to a camp in Arkansas) provided a monotonous backdrop to the sounds of crying babies, mothers nursing their young, children's laughter, teenagers' chats and giggles, men hunched with blank stares or deep thoughts, and, from afar, the strumming of guitar and singing . . . how melancholy . . . Was this a dream? How I wished it were, as my brother, three younger sisters, and I sat huddled in grim silence and bewilderment, with little consolation from our parents, who had no answers either. Those teenage years in camp were a jumble of images—some still clear and others not so clear. Among the vivid images was the terrifying day when my father was taken by the FBI for questioning immediately after the attack. We thought he'd left for good since he was gone for so long. A year later, he joined us on the trip to our first camp in Jerome, Arkansas.

The following year, we were transferred to Heart Mountain, Wyoming. In the summer months, the miserable dust storms came whirling swiftly in blinding fury, and when it was over, there was nothing but dirt and dust everywhere— you tasted it, you felt it, and it settled all around you. Camp life was a caricature of the outside with all the mindless teenage activities. There was one glaring exception, however—the guard towers and barbed-wire fence that surrounded us and reminded us of why we were here, instead of there on the outside.

An incident which stands out in my mind was a day-trip to the town of Cody, when we were overcome with excitement at the thought of a rare—though brief—encounter with the outside world. No sooner did we sit ourselves down in a drugstore booth than we picked up the menu and saw in bold letters—"WE DO NOT SERVE JAPS." So much for that . . . Our bus ride back was in glum silence broken only by sporadic bursts of laughter to fight back the tears.

In the summer of 1945, camps were beginning to close down. We left one day that summer by bus, and toward evening, the radio announced that the atomic bomb had been dropped on Hiroshima, and Japan had surrendered. Suddenly, everyone stood up in euphoric pandemonium and wild celebration. The next thing you knew, all eyes were upon us and I felt dizzy as my heart pounded in fear. They stood all around us yelling something about "them Japs . . ." How fortunate it was for us that a clear-thinking, sympathetic bus driver yelled for order and control and somehow got everyone to sit down. We had arrived at a town in Montana where a Japanese-American tavern-owner came with blankets and sheets to cover us and quickly whisked us through an alleyway into a back room of the tavern. The din of celebration continued all night in the next room and outside in the streets. We took the train the next morning.

Soon, parents and adults began picking up the pieces of their wrecked lives— in the face of continuing racism and discrimination, no less. Not uncommon were feelings of anger and bitterness in the process. For years, former internees found it almost impossible to talk about the camps with non-Asians, let alone family members—sons and daughters. How does one go about explaining the "imprisonment without due process or due cause" to a general public that knew little or nothing about the camps? There was the stigma of shame and guilt too, for after all, we were locked up behind a barbed-wire fence for three to four years. Also, many internees cringed at the thought of bringing up the past again for fear of renewed hostilities and other backlash. It took some thirty to forty years after the camps before we were able to assert ourselves in pursuit of justice and vindication, finally winning redress from the U.S. government fifty years after the internment.

This time around, we can't let fifty years go by before wrongs are corrected. Already, the momentum of racism and racial profiling directed at Arab- and Muslim-Americans is frightening, and there is a major initiative by the Bush administration to institutionalize this in the form of legislation, as Executive Order 9066 did sixty years ago. It goes without saying that hearing the voices of concerned individuals and civil liberties groups raising questions about the protection of civil and constitutional rights of Muslim- and Arab-Americans is most reassuring. I am also heartened by the voices of some who have the courage to question the government's response to the crisis, and our government's foreign policy and role in the Middle East. But, like sixty years ago, there are many, both in government and outside, who work to suppress these voices of dissent in the name of patriotism. Our country's trademarks of democracy and justice are all brought into question by the current atmosphere. Examples such as the graduation ceremony at Cal State University, Sacramento, reflect how fragile such principles are. A speaker at the event was booed, heckled, and finally made to sit down all because, while lauding the renewed sense of patriotism nationwide, she criticized practices of racial profiling and secret military tribunals, and she encouraged students to question government policies and our willingness to compromise our civil liberties.

Sixty years ago, there was hardly a voice of dissent heard on our behalf. Japanese-Americans were left totally isolated and alone in an atmosphere rife with rabid jingoism. Under such duress, many in our own communities were reluctant to protest and some felt we should willingly be led into camps, in order to "prove" our loyalty to the country. Today, while we all condemn the tragedy of 9/11, there is no excuse for any suppression of dissent in the name of patriotism. Voices of dissent must be encouraged for our government to be made accountable—moreso in these times of crises. Only such voices can stop the tragedy of sixty years ago from playing out again today, and in these voices is the essence of the free, democratic society that we must protect.

Lillian Nakano is a Japanese activist whose experience in the internment camps of World War II has made her a champion of civil rights.